# Motorcycle Journeys Through the Appalachians

Third Edition

Dale Coyner

Whitehorse Press
Center Conway, New Hampshire

All photographs were taken by the author unless otherwise noted.



Whitehorse Press books are also available at discounts in bulk quantity for sales and promotional use. For details about special sales or for a catalog of motorcycling books, videos, and gear write to the publisher:

Whitehorse Press
107 East Conway Road
Center Conway, New Hampshire 03813
Phone: 603-356-6556 or 800-531-1133
E-mail: CustomerService@WhitehorsePress.com
Internet: www.WhitehorsePress.com

ISBN 978-1-884313-91-2

5 4 3 2 1

Printed in China

# Acknowledgements

When I first wrote the Appalachian installment of the Journeys series, I had little idea it would have such a long run. Many people have contributed to the lasting success this title has enjoyed, but two people stand above all others. Dan and Judy Kennedy at Whitehorse Press deserve a lot of credit for serving the motorcycling public. They've worked hard to make books like this prosper, and they've rediscovered and republished classics that otherwise would have been forgotten. The opportunity they've given me to write about a pastime I love has changed my life. Literally. Dan and Judy, I thank you.

I'd also like to thank everyone who has contacted me over the years with stories of their own journeys, pictures, new places to visit, and more. It means a lot. Many people responded to my request for photos for this edition. Thank you for having the interest and taking the time to send me your pictures. I wish I could have used them all.

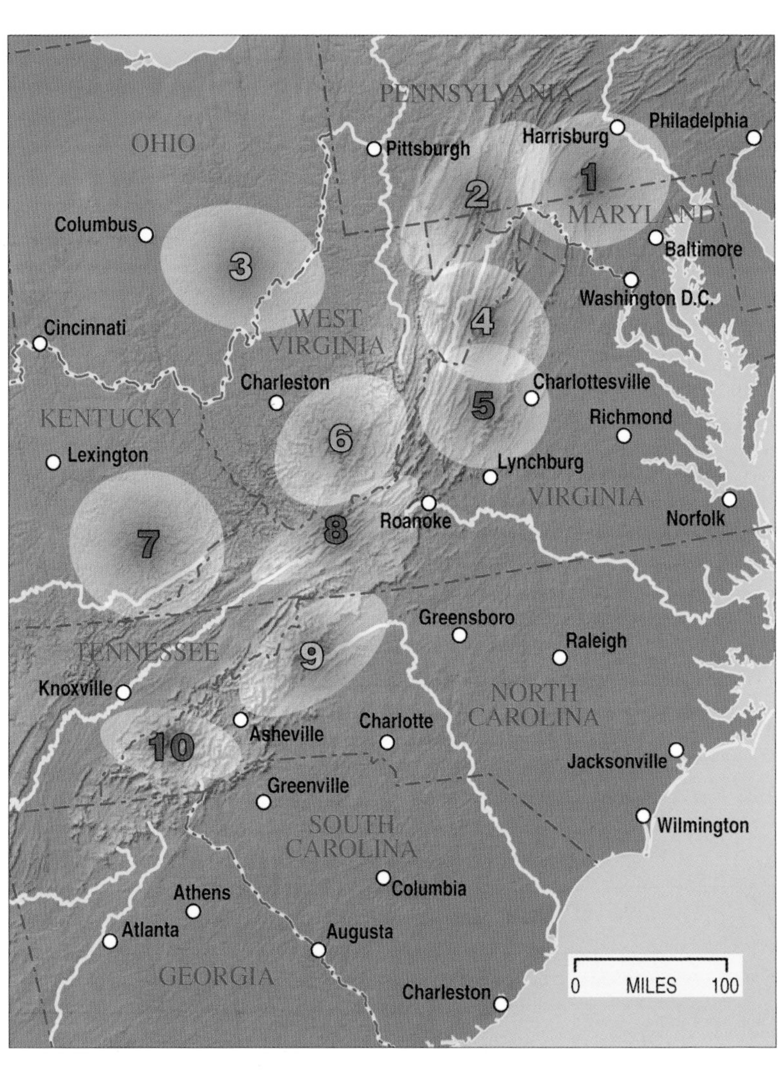
PENNSYLVANIA
OHIO
Pittsburgh
Harrisburg
Philadelphia
1
2
MARYLAND
Columbus
3
Baltimore
Washington D.C.
WEST VIRGINIA
4
Cincinnati
Charleston
Charlottesville
5
KENTUCKY
6
Richmond
Lexington
Lynchburg
VIRGINIA
Roanoke
Norfolk
8
7
Greensboro
Raleigh
TENNESSEE
9
Knoxville
NORTH CAROLINA
Asheville
Charlotte
10
Jacksonville
Greenville
Wilmington
SOUTH CAROLINA
Columbia
Athens
Atlanta
Augusta
GEORGIA
Charleston
0 MILES 100

# Contents

# Introduction

## FIRST, A LITTLE STORY

Somewhere along the line, perhaps in a passing conversation, reading an article, or gazing over a map filled with squiggly lines, you've gotten the idea that there might be some good riding to be found in the Appalachians. I won't argue with you. In fact, I've spent the last 20 years reveling in it. If you have a few minutes, let me tell you about it.

Back in the 1990s, I had this bright idea to put together a collection of rides—cookbook style—in the Blue Ridge Mountain area of the Mid-Atlantic. I felt the need to explore the area around me and the thought of doing that on a motorcycle added to the appeal. The idea that others might enjoy the same was what brought me to the conclusion to put it together in book form.

This was before the popular acceptance of e-mail and the Web, mind you, so I collected all the addresses of motorcycle clubs I could find and wrote them letters, soliciting their input for routes they enjoyed that they might like to share with others. I mailed over 200 inquiries to such groups, hoping to get enough responses to put together 20 or 30 good routes. After three months of waiting, I had three responses.

*Route 16 in West Virginia is just one of the many Appalachian roads waiting for you to explore.*

One of them suggested following the Blue Ridge Parkway. I knew about that one, thank you. Another included a stretch of fifty or so miles on Interstate 95 between Richmond and Fredericksburg. I-95? I didn't think that was anyone's idea of fun. The third suggested a stretch of road outside of Front Royal, Virginia, that passes through a narrow river gap in the Massanutten Mountains called Fort Valley Road. Never heard of it, but at least that suggestion held some promise.

Well, I could tell from the response to the survey that my idea would never come to fruition by relying on mass mailings for input, so I decided a more direct approach would be in order. Until that time, my motorcycling comfort zone had been well within the Washington, D.C. suburbs. The idea of riding thirty miles into West Virginia was mildly crazy, so the further idea of covering hundreds of miles to put together a list of routes was deliciously insane. (I hadn't yet been introduced to the touring-bike concept.)

Still, something told me my effort would be rewarded. I had this romantic notion of riding along a blue highway at dusk, my silhouette cast against the setting sun. So with a little digging, I found Fort Valley Road on a map and set out one bright Saturday morning to see what promise this notion might hold. That's the day I got hooked on touring the Appalachians.

I grew up in the country. My people are from the country. I know and love the country. But I had never experienced the country as I did that day on the bike. It is not the same as riding along a backroad in the bed of a pickup truck. Traversing those narrow country lanes in the open air on a powerful little two-wheeled machine obeying my every whim—that was a transforming experience for me.

That brief trip confirmed my hunch and erased all doubts. This was something I needed to pursue. Coincidentally, I ran across a press release in *Rider* magazine for a newly published book called *Motorcycle Journeys Through New England*. It was billed as a collection of trips for that region and it sounded intriguingly like what I was thinking. I ordered a copy and found it was exactly what I had in mind. I wondered if the publisher might like an installment covering the mountains of the Mid-Atlantic? And as they say, the rest is history.

So you have this book in your hands, and I'm hoping it will help you make a wise investment of your precious leisure time. With the updates and additions I've made in early 2011, I have every intention of seeing that it does exactly that.

*Old fences and high meadows enhance the beauty of Appalachian highways.*

## WHY THE APPALACHIANS?

Like me, you've probably heard tales told about the people and places of the Appalachians. Many of them paint pictures of isolation, ignorance, and violence. I knew a lot of those stories weren't true, but still, they raised questions.

What was it really like to wander through the hills and hollows of these seemingly endless ridges? Was it still possible to experience the Appalachians as my ancestors did? Did anyone remember and value the "old ways?" Was there still beauty and mystery and wildness to be found? Or had all of that been lost to strip mines, satellite dishes, and fast-food restaurants?

My trip down Fort Valley Road began to answer those questions. So, too, did standing alone at a stop on the Cherohala Skyway in western North Carolina, a spot so remote that no matter how hard I listened, no sound of human activity could be heard; savoring peanut soup at the Southern

*You can enjoy perfect pavement, sunny weather, and views of manicured estates near Middleburg, Virginia.*

Kitchen Restaurant; starting at the crack of muzzle-loaded rifles at Gettysburg; reliving the story of the Trail of Tears in Cherokee, North Carolina, and tracing the Trail of the Lonesome Pine in eastern Kentucky; smelling wet leaves along a winding forest road after a sudden, drenching rain; riding along the Blue Ridge Parkway with riders met at a rest stop; reveling in the sound of 160,000 race fans and the roar of 800 hp engines at Thunder Valley in Bristol.

Yes, these and many other delightfully unique experiences have convinced me that the Appalachians are a great place to invest my time on two wheels. The returns, counted in wonderful memories, are immeasurable.

Remember, too, that this is not a comprehensive guide to the region. It's a starting point to aid you in avoiding the overcrowded, urbanized areas of the East, and finding those better suited to two-wheeled wanderers such as yourself. Popular attractions and destinations are often treated lightly, while the not-so-obvious towns and points of interest are given much more coverage. Buy yourself a good map, cultivate some ideas, and grow your own personal journeys. Consider these suggestions merely the seeds.

## HOW THIS BOOK IS ORGANIZED

*Motorcycle Journeys Through the Appalachians* is a collection of tours ranging from the patchwork farmlands of Amish country in Pennsylvania to the deep recesses of western North Carolina, from the genteel and rolling foothills of the Virginia Piedmont to the hardscrabble hills and hollers of eastern Kentucky. As a matter of convenience, comfort, and peace of mind, the tours have been arranged around a series of base camps, with four or five rides plotted from the same spot. Unless you're traveling across a region, it's unnecessary to break camp every day, pack the bike, and haul everything with you everywhere you go.

The range of most tours makes them a comfortable day's ride at a leisurely pace with plenty of opportunity to visit, explore, hike, and eat. Some of the longer trips can be broken into two days or more if you prefer. You could easily spend a week in each region, riding in a different direction each day without retracing a single path.

In the years since the first edition of this book was published, many riders have contacted me for suggestions on riding the region from north to south or vice versa. I've been asked repeatedly "Honestly now, what was your favorite road?" or "Which hotel was really the most rider friendly?" So to respond to your requests, I've added a section to this edition called Through-Routes and Favorites, which contains a list of memorable trans-regional routes as well as a long list of features I found most enjoyable about the region (and a few that were decidedly not).

I still enjoy motorcycle camping, but as I've grown older, so my affection has grown for the comfort of a roof that doesn't leak, a mattress that isn't flat in the morning, and food that I didn't have to cook. So I've tried to locate these routes in areas with travel accommodations that serve both riders who prefer to rough it and those who don't.

One of the goals of this book is that it should pay for itself—that is, it should suggest ways to increase your travel experiences without lightening your wallet. If I didn't feel like I got my money's worth out of an attraction or restaurant, I didn't list it here. The same is true of lodging. And while these are not exhaustive lists of travel services, I did try to include a range that would suit a variety of budgets. Heck, you can always find ways to spend more money for something if you want to, right?

## ADDITIONAL TRAVEL RESOURCES

If you really want to get off the beaten path and explore for a lifetime without the fear of getting lost, invest in a set of DeLorme maps. Most of the good roads I found weren't shown on the complimentary state maps offered by departments of tourism, but rather in the DeLorme Atlas and Gazetteer series. DeLorme's topographical maps of each state include all the backroads, paved and otherwise. Detailed maps are available for all the states in the region. DeLorme also offers Street Atlas, a CD-ROM mapping program that contains every road in every state. Street Altas is especially useful for mapping out roads to get a reading on the length of the route.

A lot of folks are now using GPS devices to help them keep their bearings. I know I've gotten a lot of use out of mine. Rather than create a pre-programmed route, I set the GPS for my destination, then wander off on any road that strikes my fancy. With the GPS tied to my ultimate pit stop, I can follow any trail I please with the comfort of knowing I'll get there. I could have used that assurance a few times on some of my backroad excursions.

The Mid-Atlantic area is fortunate to have an excellent bi-monthly publication for motorcyclists, *Motorcycle Times* magazine (motorcycletimes.com). Each issue contains an exhaustive listing of events for the area, including poker runs, open houses, dirt-track races, and anything else related to motorcycling. It's a great way to find out about things happening in the area that aren't nationally promoted.

Throughout this book, I'll alert you to attractions of the National Park Service. If you plan to visit several of these parks, you may find that a National Park Pass will help you reduce your travel costs. An annual pass for adults to all the National Parks is currently $80. If you are a citizen or permanent resident of the United States and age 62 or more, you can purchase a *lifetime* pass to all the National Parks for a mere $10. Visit www.nps.gov for more details about passes. In addition, many people like to record their visits to the National Parks by collecting stamps in their booklet *Passport to Your National Parks.* It serves as your guide to national park sites and provides a space in each region to collect a rubber stamp cancellation, similar to those you receive in your international passport. Visit www.eparks.com for more information about the National Parks Passport.

Finally, you can't overstate the wealth of resources now available on the Internet. Search engines, mapping programs, forums and mailing lists are all invaluable planning tools. I use Google for finding information on historical places and points of interest. Throughout the book, I've made a note of websites that can provide more detailed information about people and places. I've tried to include sites maintained by reputable sources that are likely to be around for a while.

Many towns and tourist bureaus offer websites that give you a sense of what an area is like and you don't need to sift through a mountain of bro-

*Phil Johnson and his son Jay welcome you to Blue Ridge Motorcycle Campground, a popular moto-only campground in Cruso, North Carolina.*

chures to find what you're looking for. For example, the state of West Virginia maintains an excellent site (www.wildandwonderful.com or www.westvirginia.com) where you can find information, directions, and rates for any of the state parks.In the last few years, Google Maps has become my favorite overall mapping tool. Built into Google Maps is a feature called Street View that is nothing short of revolutionary. Using Street View, I can virtually ride just about every road in this book and get a 360-degree view anywhere along the road. Throughout the book, I have included links to specific Google Map locations that will put you in some of the exact spots I've enjoyed. There is an index of these locations at the back of the book for easier reference.

Looking at a map can give you some good ideas, but if you want to get first-hand information about a particular road, the best source is other riders. Dozens of motorcycle-related forums are available on the Internet and many of them are catalogued by Carl Paukistis at micapeak.com.

I run a forum to discuss rides in the Appalachian region and provide updated information for this book at appalachianhighways.com. I hope you'll drop by the site and join in the conversation.

*In season, roadside stands offer the freshest produce you'll find. Great for a biker's stew! Photo by Dan Bard*

## WEATHER NOTES

The Appalachians experience all four seasons in equal measure and though you can travel the region most any time of the year, some are preferable to others. My favorite months for long tours are March through June and September through November. In the early spring months, the higher elevations are chilly, but the cold air brings expansive views. The spring thaw has begun in earnest by the end of March. Early spring flowers are beginning to poke through the damp soil and tree buds are nearly ready to burst. At the higher elevations, winter still lingers but roads are easily passable. Spring arrives on the mountain tops some time in May while the valleys below are vibrant shades of green. Temperature ranges are usually in the seventies and eighties, perfect for a leisurely tour.

Some time in June, the weather patterns change and the valleys are shrouded with the haze of moisture-laden air from the Gulf. The heat and humidity make it feel like Florida, except in the mountains. If you come in late June, July, or August, camp at higher elevations. Temperature differences of ten degrees or more are common between the valleys and summits.

What is a miserable day below is a pleasant one on yonder ridge. If you plan to change altitudes, take along layers of clothing so you can add or subtract as the change in temperature dictates.

By September, most of the Florida snowbirds who came in June to escape the heat of the lowlands are packing up and heading south for the winter. The days become cool and the nights downright chilly. This sets off a domino effect in the hardwoods, which begin to tinge with color. The change begins at the top of the mountains and descends to the bottom, quite the opposite of the arrival of spring. By early to mid-October, most of the foliage in the region is blazing.

Bring a rainsuit and keep it handy: there's a reason why "Allegheny" rhymes with "always rainy." Zip up your tent before you leave camp for the day, even if it dawns bright and sunny. It's uncanny how those stray thunderstorms will make a beeline for your bag if you leave the tent open to air out. If you are camping, move between regions on any day other than Saturday and you'll usually find your destination campgrounds nearly empty. Ride Skyline Drive or the Blue Ridge Parkway during the week and the road will be yours alone, even during the peak of fall foliage.

Average temperatures are roughly the same throughout the region, though my personal experience has been that the Cumberland area is typically cooler than the rest.

| **Average Temperature** | **Jan.** | **April** | **July** | **Oct.** |
|---|---|---|---|---|
| *Summersville, West Virginia* | *33* | *55* | *74* | *56* |
| *Brevard, North Carolina* | *37* | *56* | *73* | *56* |
| *Cumberland, Maryland* | *27* | *50* | *72* | *53* |
| *Front Royal, Virginia* | *34* | *53* | *74* | *53* |

## LAST WORDS

I'd love to hear about your experiences touring the Appalachians—what you found interesting, the good roads and fun places you found that I haven't yet, or the places you wouldn't recommend. Your suggestions and comments will be incorporated to make future editions of this book even more useful. Visit me at appalachianhighways.com. There you can subscribe to a free newsletter to receive regular updates as well as new route and destination ideas.

I hope you enjoy riding in my home country as much as I do. Have a safe, enjoyable journey, and don't forget to write!

1

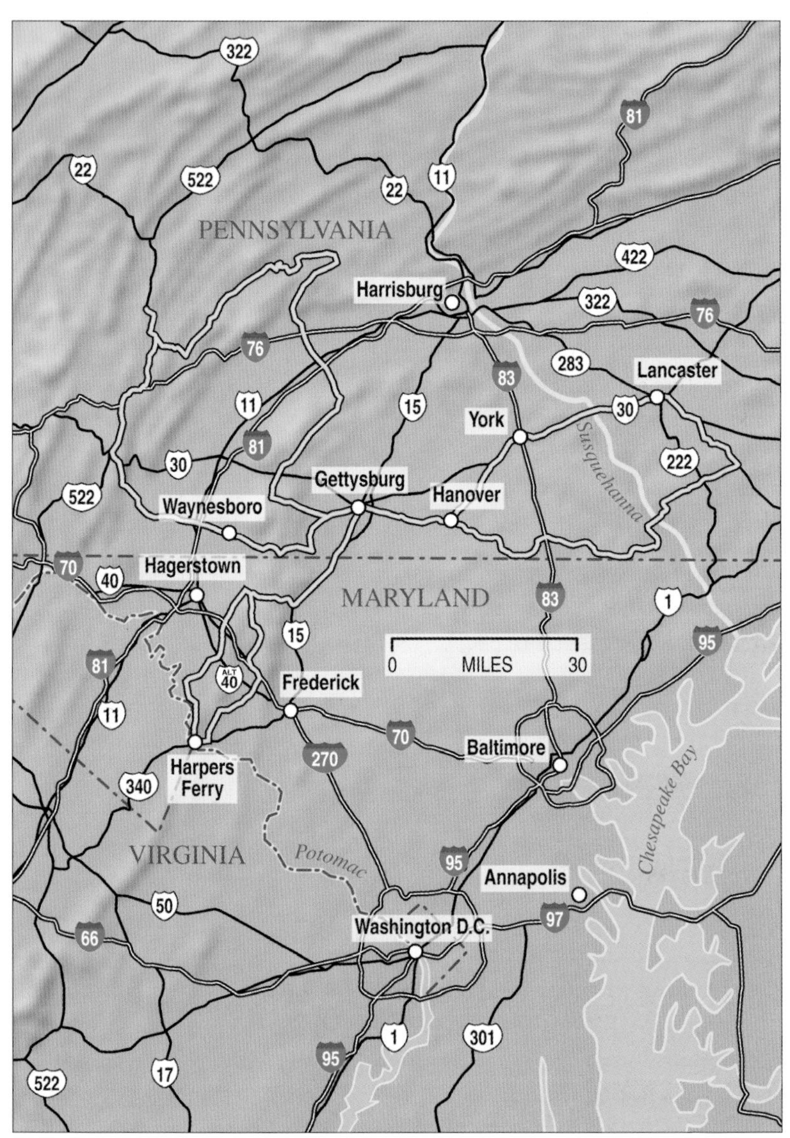
PENNSYLVANIA
Harrisburg
Lancaster
York
Gettysburg
Hanover
Waynesboro
Hagerstown
MARYLAND
Frederick
Baltimore
Harpers Ferry
VIRGINIA
Annapolis
Washington D.C.
Susquehanna
Potomac
Chesapeake Bay
0 MILES 30
322
81
22
522
22
11
422
322
76
76
283
83
11
15
30
81
30
222
522
70
40
83
1
15
95
81
ALT 40
11
70
270
340
95
50
97
66
1
301
95
522
17

# The High Water Mark

## *Gettysburg, Pennsylvania*

Before the War between the States, Gettysburg was a sleepy little town in the rolling Piedmont of southern Pennsylvania. Three days in early July of 1863 ensured that it would never sleep again. The worst battle since the war's inception two years earlier left Gettysburg littered with the devastating legacy of bloodshed.

In the end, the Battle of Gettysburg claimed 51,000 casualties. Five thousand horses, broken cannons, shelled and burned homes, trees felled by heavy fire, and soldiers, some still barely alive, were scattered across the fields. The wise and considered words of Abraham Lincoln's Gettysburg Address (loc.gov/exhibits/gadd) some months later helped people understand what had happened there.

Little by little, as the nation pieced itself together after the end of the war, monuments were erected to commemorate the dead. Together with cannon placements, they total more than 1,000 (www.npca.org/gettysburg). The

*Downtown Gettysburg is great for strolling and browsing.*

battlefield has been preserved in its original state. But most of all, the shadows and spirits of those who were here still roam the fields and woods, at times so tangible you can feel them walk through you as you look across the battlefield. Place your hand on a cannon and it still feels warm. If you don't believe in ghosts or spirits when you come here, you will when you leave.

Today the town rests a bit easier, though it still does not sleep. People from around the world are drawn to this town, some for the glory, some to learn, others to remember. Fortunately for the motorcyclist, there is ample opportunity to experience all three from the seat of your bike. There are 40 miles of scenic tours marked in the immediate area, and the tours in this section of the book venture well beyond those limits. If you aren't tied to a particular schedule and don't plan to attend a battle reenactment (details follow), the best time of year to visit Gettysburg is either side of the summer vacation season. April, May, September, and October offer fine riding weather with less competition from the masses for travel resources.

In town, you'll want to visit several places associated with Gettysburg

*Two Harleys pose in Gettysburg Square.*

*Pennsylvania maintains and celebrates its history.*

National Military Park (www.nps.gov/gett). The first is the visitor center which houses the museum. The brand-new facility features a collection of artifacts displayed and interpreted in typically excellent National Park form. Get your National Parks Passport stamped here. Nearby is the Gettysburg National Cemetery where Lincoln made his Gettysburg Address on November 19, 1863. At certain times of the day, a park ranger will guide you on a walk through the cemetery and offer some commentary on the things that happened in this area.After the walk, you might want to follow the marked tour route of the battlefield. The observation tower on Culp's Hill gives you a good view of the town below and Little Round Top to the south. These two points held the greatest concentration of Union strength and saw the most action in the first two days of the battle.

If your bike is equipped with a CD player, you can pick up an inexpensive narrative tour of the Gettysburg Campaign at the visitor center. The tour starts at the park and follows a well-marked route. You'll get the same tour and information as with a bus tour, but you have the added freedom to explore each stop at your own pace.

Almost overshadowed by the military park is the farm and home of Dwight D. Eisenhower at the Eisenhower National Historic Site (nps.gov/eise). Ike purchased the farm in 1950 and retired there with his wife Mamie after serving as commander of NATO forces in Europe and thirty-fourth

*The Gettysburg Hotel offers accommodation for the discriminating rider.*

President of the United States. They intended to remodel and live in the farmhouse already on the property, but found that it was nearly ready to collapse. Instead, the Eisenhowers built a new home on the site, salvaging as much of the original structure as possible.

Gettysburg is also home to a plethora of private museums, gift shops, and diversions to entertain you during your evenings. The Farnsworth House Inn (farnsworthhouseinn.com) features an attraction perfectly suited to the Gettysburg area—ghost stories. After descending a narrow set of stairs into the basement, guests are seated on benches. It takes a few minutes for your eyes to adjust to the candlelight, but you can feel the cool damp walls and sense the low overhead beams before you can see them. In the front of the room, a black mound of cloth rises to reveal a seated woman. She puts on a spine-tingling performance, telling grisly stories about the things that took place around the time of the Battle of Gettysburg. The show will have you seeing more than shadows on your way back home.

Gettysburg offers an annual reenactment of the famous three-day battle (gettysburgreenactment.com). Sure, there are other reenactments to be found throughout the Civil War's theater, but few are held on a consistent basis and fewer still on the grand scale of this one. In 2003, the 140th such restaging, more than 13,000 reenactors participated. With that number of period actors and 1860s-era equipment and provisioning, you get a much greater sense of what the era was like and what the real soldiers experienced.

Lodging and food in every price range are easy to find. On the south end of town, right on the battlefield, you will pay an average of 50 dollars per night for a room. I hung out at the Colton Motel (232 Steinwehr Avenue; 717-334-5514). It is within walking distance of the major National Park facilities, and is clean and comfortable. Gettysburg Motor Lodge (gettysburgqualityinn.com) is also close by and offers a good value.

If you prefer the added luxury of a bed and breakfast, the Old Appleford Inn (218 Carlisle Street; 717-337-1711) on the north end of town has a dozen nicely decorated rooms. And if the coin is really weighing down your pocket, unload some at the restored James Gettys Hotel (jamesgettyshotel.com). Once again appearing as it did in the 1920s, the James Gettys offers suites, so you can really stretch out and relax. The hotel is just west of the town square, making it the perfect spot from which to launch a reconnaissance mission for hand-scooped ice cream on a balmy evening. Personally, I just like sitting on one of the benches around the square to watch cars negotiate the busy traffic circle.

Many local restaurants are in the immediate vicinity of the battlefield. My favorite is the Avenue Restaurant (avenuerestaurant.net), located at the corner of Baltimore and Steinwehr Avenues. Inside, the '50s-era Formica and chrome decor is sparkling. If you're in the mood for pizza, Tommy's Pizza (tommyspizzainc.com) is the answer. On the other end of town, the Lincoln Diner (32 Carlisle Street; 717-334-3900) offers standard American diner fare. If you want to really do it up in style, the Farnsworth House Inn offers fine dining, featuring dishes from the Civil War era, including game pie, peanut soup, spoon bread, and pumpkin fritters. Reservations are a must.

# Trip 1 Pennsylvania Heartland

**Distance** *191 miles*
**Terrain** *Narrow, twisty backroads through orchards and farms, several passes over mountain ridges, short stretches of gravel on bridge detours*
**Highlights** *Scenic overlooks, covered bridge hunt, East Broad Top Railroad, fall foliage, Appalachian Trail, gossiping at Path Valley Restaurant*

If time is short and you have the chance to try just one route through Pennsylvania, make it this one. This route features more varied terrain, sights, smells, and sounds than any other I've found yet. Go in early October when the trees are heavy with apples and the leaves are at their peak. It will be chilly when you begin, but you'll soon forget about that, I assure you. The route begins by following Route 116 west out of Gettysburg, the Confederate Army's trail of retreat from the Battle of Gettysburg. The retreating train

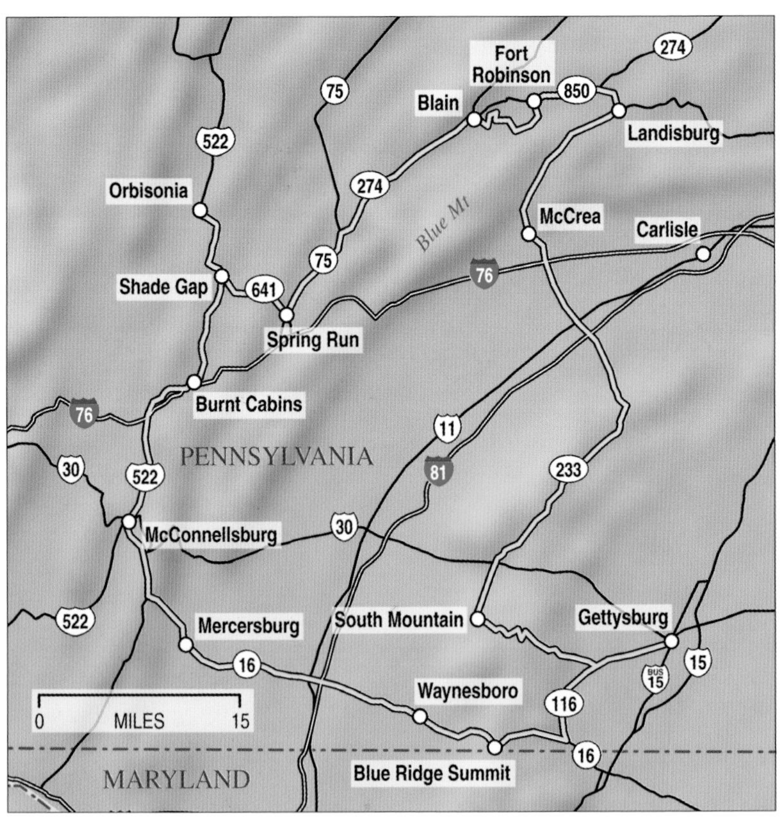

**THE ROUTE FROM GETTYSBURG**

| | |
|---|---|
| 0 | Begin at intersection of PA 116 and US 15 Business in downtown Gettysburg |
| 5.9 | Right on Cold Springs Road |
| 14.7 | Cold Springs becomes South Mountain Road |
| 17.0 | Right on SR 233 |
| 62.9 | Right on Carlisle Street in Landisburg |
| 63.0 | Right onto Kennedy Valley Road |
| 63.4 | Arrive at Rice Bridge, turn around |
| 63.9 | Left onto Carlisle Street |
| 64.0 | Straight on SR 233/SR 850 |
| 66.9 | SR 274 joins SR 850 |
| 75.3 | Left onto Couchtown Road (SR 3008) |
| 79.3 | Right onto SR 3005 |
| 80.2 | Left onto Red Rock Road |
| 81.7 | Left onto Adams Grove Road |
| 82.5 | Right onto T311 |
| 82.6 | Right onto SR 3006 |
| 83.5 | Left onto PA 274 |
| 98.5 | Left onto SR 75 (Path Valley Road) |
| 105.5 | Right onto PA 641 (Spring Run Road) |
| 114.0 | Right onto US 522 |
| 119.4 | Left onto PA 994 (Meadow Street) |
| 119.8 | Arrive Shade Gap Railroad |
| 120.2 | Right onto US 522 |
| 147.3 | Left onto PA 16 (Lincoln Way) in McConnellsburg |
| 179.3 | Left onto PA 116 |
| 191.3 | Arrive Gettysburg via PA 116 |

stretched out seventeen miles along this road. At the time it was so bumpy that many of the wounded who were able, walked the route rather than endure the hardship of riding in wagons without springs. About five miles outside town, look for Cold Springs Road on your right.

Cold Springs Road is a direct route to nowhere, but runs through some beautiful orchard country. When the trees are loaded with fruit, the air is fragrant with the smell of ripening apples. It isn't the smoothest road; an easy pace will be comfortable. You're not in a hurry anyway, right? Just keep plugging away until you reach Route 233 north.

A good portion of time spent on Route 233 will be through state forest land, first Michaux State Forest and then Tuscarora (www.dcnr.state.pa.us/stateparks). Along the way, our path crosses that of the Appalachian Trail (nps.gov/appa) for the first of many times throughout our travels. The trail, which stretches 2,144 miles along Appalachian ridges from northern Maine to Georgia, is managed and maintained by a coalition of public and private interests and has often been called "a gift of nature Americans give themselves." By early October, the foliage in central Pennsylvania will have turned and your route will be lined with a fantastic assortment of fall colors. Your encounters with several major thoroughfares that cross your path will be blessedly uneventful. As you ride under Interstate 81 and hear the traffic thunder overhead, you'll wonder where all those people are going. They seem to be in such a hurry to get there, and it makes your 40 mph pace feel even more comfortable (tinyurl.com/motojourneys04).

As Route 233 passes through McCrea, the front of Blue Mountain looms in front of you. It doesn't look like there is much place for a road to go unless it tunnels under the mountain, but it craftily follows a narrow valley through Doubling Gap and into another small valley. Just ahead at Landisburg, you can take a brief detour to Rice's Bridge—a long, covered bridge still in use over Sherman Creek. At the intersection with Route 850, make a right. Turn right on Kennedy Valley Road and follow it for a few tenths of a mile.

There are more covered bridges in the United States than anywhere else in the world, and more in Pennsylvania than any other state. At one time, there were more than 1,500, but that number has now dropped to 221. (Next in line is Ohio, 140; Vermont, 99; and Indiana, 93. Iowa, the setting for the best-seller *The Bridges of Madison County,* has 12.)

Wooden bridges became popular in the mid-1800s with the development of a support system called the triangular truss. This allowed bridges of substantial length to be built at a lower cost than ones using stone or iron. They were covered to shelter them from the elements and preserve their longevity. Many of the spans in Pennsylvania were built in the 19th century, with those built near the end of the era still in use today, like the bridge here at Landisburg.

If you are interested in finding more bridges, they are near the main route and easy to find. Follow Route 850 west out of Landisburg until it joins Route 274 near Fort Robinson, then follow Route 274 to the left when it splits from Route 850. All of these roads are wide open with gentle

*Enslow Bridge is a nice spot to stop for a picnic.*

sweeping curves and made for power road-sofas like my Honda Gold Wing. However, any bike will enjoy tracing a smooth line through the curves, taking in rural Pennsylvania framed on either side by gentle ridges of the Alleghenies.

Just past Centre, make a left turn on Couchtown Road/SR 3008. The bridge along this route is to your left off the main traffic route. Make a right on SR 3005 and follow it over the covered bridge, then turn left on Red Rock Road, and make a left on Adams Road to the Enslow Bridge. This is a particularly pretty bridge, framed by trees. To the right of the bridge down the creek is a bench perfect for a brief stop to soak in the atmosphere of the countryside. Follow SR 3005 until it ends on SR 3006. Turn right on SR 3006 and follow it through Blain, returning to Route 274 where you resume your westward trek. Two other bridges are close to the road along your

*Don't let the talk about ex-husbands scare you. It's a great place to eat. Photo by Dan Bard*

way, though neither was open to traffic when I passed by. Along 274, look for bridges down Mount Pleasant Road and New Germantown Road, both on your left (tinyurl.com/motojourneys05).

Backroads like these offer a lesson in never knowing what to expect around the next bend. Just after entering Red Rock Road I rounded a corner to find a young Amish boy aboard an old scooter trundling rapidly downhill toward me. Surprised by the encounter, both of us shifted paths to avoid a collision, but he still managed to give me a friendly wave as we passed. Not half a mile later, I rounded a bend to find a pickup truck parked dead smack in the middle of the road. More unusual was the sight of a pair of legs sticking out from under the truck across the road. No reason to call a tow truck when you can fix your vehicle on the spot.

After New Germantown, the route enters the Tuscarora State Forest again and Big Spring State Park. There are some quick switchbacks in this section, so don't let the relatively easy ascent fool you. Descending rapidly, you'll meet wide-open Route 75. Turn left and follow it south to Path Valley.

There isn't much in the way of food service along the route, but if your timing puts you in the area of Spring Run, Pennsylvania, near mealtime, make a point to stop by the Path Valley Family Restaurant (717-349-2900). Last time through the area, I dropped in on a Sunday afternoon well past the usual dinner hour. I squeezed the bike into the last remaining spot of available pavement near the edge of the lot. Inside, the place was packed and my only option was the seat at the counter nearest the cash register. It turns out that was just the place to be.

When I visit places like Path Valley, my favorite pastime is enjoying the conversations around me about local people and events. Oh sure, some might call that eavesdropping. I tend to think of it more as cultural study. At the end of the counter, the waitresses assembled their orders, and it was the perfect spot to engage in a little of that study. Most of the banter was the usual friendly chit-chat that helps pass time at the workplace.

At some point I happened to hear one girl ask, "Honey, did you see your ex at the dance Friday night?"

"Yeah, I sure did," replied the other. "I was so surprised. I turned around and walked right smack into him. And I said to myself 'Lord have mercy, I didn't know he was out of jail yet!'"

Check, please.

When you've, er, done your time at the Path Valley, hop back on the bike for the rest of this run. The restaurant is right at the intersection where you'll want to turn. Head west on Route 641. This is a fun road that jumps over Tuscarora Mountain with pretty vistas along the upper ridges. To the west, you can see the Shade Mountain Gap. That's where we're headed. Route 641 meets US Route 522 at Shade Gap. Follow Route 522 north to Orbisonia and the East Broad Top Railroad (EBT) (ebtrr.com).

The EBT began operating in 1872 to connect the isolated southwestern coal and iron fields of the state with iron furnaces and the Pennsylvania Railroad. In the fall, the railroad hosts a weekend special when they draw

*Future apples in progress along Cold Springs Road near Gettysburg.*

out nearly their whole line of rolling stock. If you're anywhere near the railroad, you'll hear another tradition: the annual whistle salute. Not only does each train have a distinctive whistle, each conductor has his own unique way of using it. This is perhaps the one safe time you can pass through town and rev your straight pipes for all they're worth without disturbing anyone. The EBT offers rides to passengers from June to October. If you're interested in a ride, call ahead for an exact schedule.

Another attraction located near the EBT is the Rockhill Trolley Museum (rockhilltrolley.org). This working museum has a collection of 18 trolley cars and operates on a schedule in conjunction with the EBT. One car in particular is made of Brazilian hardwoods that look as rich and beautiful as the day the trolley started service.

As I stood in front of the railroad taking pictures, a few folks stopped to take a look at the Gold Wing and comment on its enormous size and array of gadgetry. One older gent and his wife stopped for a look. "Nice bike," he said. "What is that, an Indian?" I guess it had been a while since he was part of the motorcycling scene. A few minutes later, an Amish family strolled by, mother and father and two young children in tow. Mother and the children passed by with a polite nod, but the father paused just a moment and glanced at the bike. "Nice Wing," he said and shot me a grin. Now do you suppose he is a closet . . . ? Naah.

The return route passes by another covered bridge near Saint Mary's Catholic Church near Shade Gap and then enters open farmland, much of which is maintained by Amish farmers. You will often see them working the land with a harnessed mule team, or traversing the highway in their familiar black buggies. This setting, quiet and isolated, seems more suited to the Amish than the much-hyped Pennsylvania Dutch country. In Penn Dutch country, the Amish are like a novelty attraction that you pay to view; here they blend into the countryside. But I'll bet that if one particular Amish farmer had his way, his buggy would have a flat-six, reverse gear, and two wheels. Ahead of you is a long stretch of US 522 heading south toward McConnellsburg. Like PA 274, your bike seems to find a naturally soothing touring pace on this road. Perhaps it's because you don't pass through many small towns on this stretch. One in particular though rates a mention.

Today when a developer builds a town, the marketing department will twist itself into knots trying to find a name that strikes just the right chord. Reston, Virginia, and Celebration, Florida, come to mind. But out here in the backwoods of Colonial Pennsylvania, marketing types were hard to find, so folks just called things as they saw them. And that's how Burnt Cabins, Pennsylvania (historicmillandcamping.com), came to be.

*Your chance to "catch the first thing smokin'" at East Broad Top Railroad. 'Course it only goes about a mile.*

What happened was simple. Settlers moving west in the 1740s had invaded land that was occupied by the Native Americans in that region. When the settlers scared off the game, the chief complained to the governor who had the illegal squatters packed up and their cabins torched. That's the kind of direct action you could count on from a governor back in those days.

US 522 intersects PA 16 in McConnellsburg, and at this point, it's time to head east for the return trip. On your way back via PA 16, you'll pass through several towns that, like Gettysburg, feature a large town square. Each square is filled with unique shops that you won't find in any strip mall. These squares (sometimes referred to as "diamonds") are actually the result of the influence of Scots-Irish settlers who patterned them after the cities and towns of Ulster.

After passing through Waynesboro, you'll soon run upon PA 116, the route that began our journey. You'll pass Ski Liberty (skiliberty.com) on your right as you make the return trip. The hills around Ski Liberty won't impress hard-core winter-sports enthusiasts. If you're like me and you just want to slide downhill on a tube and enjoy the benefit of riding a ski lift back uphill, it's a great cold season venue.

Before you know it, you've passed Cold Springs Road and are within striking distance of Gettysburg. You've had a good day's ride, so park the bike and take one last stretch on Gettysburg's town square before rustling up some grub. Just be careful who you run into. You never know who's just finished doing their time.

# Trip 2 Harley Country

**Distance** *162 miles*
**Terrain** *Predominantly rolling hills and farm country. All roads are paved, but some sections are a little rougher than others. Light traffic except for stretch between York and Lancaster.*
**Highlights** *Harley-Davidson manufacturing facility, Pennsylvania Dutch country, Strasburg Railroad, Railroad Museum of Pennsylvania, National Toy Train Museum*

No self-respecting tourbook of this region would be complete without including the mecca of motorcycling, the Harley-Davidson Motor Company assembly plant in York, and the famed Pennsylvania Dutch country.

I like to ride in this area on the weekend, especially in the fall. By that time, the general tourist season has run its course. More importantly, late September is the time for the Harley-Davidson Open House in York (harley-davidson.com). Riders of all faiths are invited to attend the pilgrimage. The event usually draws a few thousand of the Harley faithful, stylers, and posers, and is worth visiting just to stroll through the parking area and browse the incredible array of bikes, many of them heavily modified. As added incentive, you can take a free demo ride on a new Harley, an opportunity you won't have at your local dealer. The open house also features tours of the plant and free food. Who can resist?

Our tour begins by picking up Route 116 on the northern end of Gettysburg and following it through Hanover to Route 30 just outside York. This

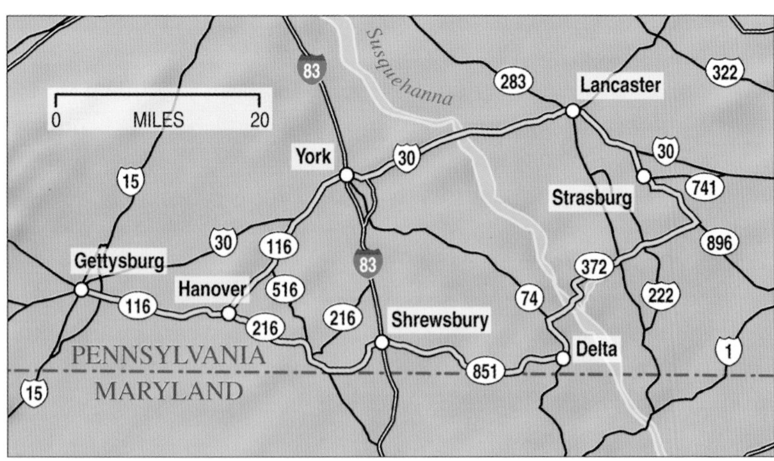

**THE ROUTE FROM GETTYSBURG**

| | |
|---|---|
| 0 | Begin at intersection of US 30 and PA 116. Follow PA 116 |
| 27.2 | Turn right onto US 30 at York |
| 34.7 | Turn left onto Eden Road |
| 34.9 | Arrive Harley-Davidson plant |
| 35.1 | Left onto US 30 Freeway |
| 68.1 | Right onto US 30/Lincoln Highway (Freeway ends) |
| 70.6 | Right onto PA 896 |
| 73.6 | Right onto PA 741 |
| 74.6 | Arrive Strasburg Railroad |
| 75.6 | Left onto PA 896 |
| 81.6 | Right onto PA 372 (Valley Road) |
| 100.2 | Left onto PA 74 (Delta Road) |
| 104.5 | Right onto PA 851 |
| 136.9 | Right onto PA 516 |
| 137.0 | Left onto PA 216 |
| 148.8 | Left onto PA 116 |
| 162.7 | Arrive Gettysburg via PA 116 |

route is a little less traveled than following Route 30 straight from Gettysburg. Following Route 30 east through York, start looking for the left turn after you pass under the Interstate 83 overpass. The Harley plant is marked by a big sign at Eden Road. This won't be necessary if you're in the area during the open house. The swarms of bikes and the echoes of rolling thunder will tell you where to turn.

Route 30 from York to Lancaster used to be a dismal ride and I didn't care to include it as part of the route, except there's no better way to get there from here. However, now that the heavy construction is done, Route 30 is a full-blown freeway from outside York city limits to Lancaster. It's not as scenic as the roads yet to come, but it's a better experience than before. If you're riding on the weekend, you'll find traffic to be tolerably light.

Though the immediate area is disguised with a heavy layer of industrial development, 51 percent of the land in York County is still agricultural, and historical notes abound. York bills itself as the first capital of the United States (yorkcity.org) because it was here, in November 1777, that the Continental Congress adopted the Articles of Confederation, the first document outlining federal powers over the colonies. York's industrial heritage includes the first iron steamboat and first coal locomotive to be built in the U.S., as well as an early cottage industry in horseless carriages.

Following Route 30 east will take you through Lancaster. The freeway ends and this will deposit you onto old Route 30 in the heart of Pennsylvania Dutch country (800padutch.com). It's surprising how much commercial development has sprung up along the corridor, but I found that you need only to slip off onto any side road to return to a gentle pace and find countryside that better represents the true character of the area. After a brief map consultation, I turned off Route 30 onto Route 896 and traced a southeasterly route through the region. This offers a good combination of scenery and passes through some of the out-of-the-way attractions in the area.

As you follow Route 896 through Strasburg, watch for Route 741 on your left. Follow it to the Strasburg Rail Road (strasburgrailroad.com) and the Railroad Museum of Pennsylvania (rrmuseumpa.org) just a few tenths of a mile down the road. If you are a railroad buff, or just a fan of things mechanical, this is a must-stop. Established in 1963 to collect and preserve the elements of Pennsylvania's railroading heritage, the museum has a great variety of locomotives, from some of the earliest to a few of recent diesel-electric origin. When you first walk into the museum, you suddenly feel as if you have shrunk to two inches tall and are walking amid a huge toy train collection.

*A buggy in any color you want—as long as it's black.*

*The Railroad Museum of Pennsylvania boasts an impressive collection of locomotives. Photo by Robert Van Allen*

Don't miss the trains outside in the rolling stock yard (tinyurl.com/motojourneys06). You may find members of local railroad interest groups on hand conducting tours of the stock yards inside and out, and working to preserve and restore some of the locomotives and cars to their original condition. There are several engines you can climb aboard if you want to feel what it was like to command one of these giant iron monsters. As you look ahead out the side window and take in the length, breadth, and weight, imagine how much easier commuting would be in one of these babies during rush hour . . . no one would make the mistake of turning left in front of you!

As much fun as the big engines are, you can go to the other extreme as well. A few tenths beyond the railroad, turn left on Paradise Lane and just up the road you'll find the headquarters of the Train Collectors Association at the National Toy Train Museum (traincollectors.org). The museum features five continuously operating layouts including several different sizes of trains. Even if you're not a huge train buff, you will admire the care, precision, and time invested in making each layout a visual feast.

While you're right here, you should just as well stroll over to the Red Caboose Motel and Restaurant. If you've ever had the hankering to spend the night or take a meal in a caboose, here's your chance. While I can't vouch for the accommodations, I can tell you that the meal at the restaurant was decent enough. The restaurant is also surrounded by a general merchandise gift shop where you can conveniently while away your time whilst waiting for a table.

After you've explored Strasburg to your satisfaction, return to Route 896 to continue the route. The route now becomes Georgetown Road and gently winds through farm country, eventually intersecting with Route 372 at Green Tree. From this point, turning right will start the return trek to Gettysburg. There is plenty of interesting riding left though. Route 372 is wide open and fast, but lightly traveled and soon ends on Route 74, another wide-open road. Follow Route 74 south to Delta, where you'll find another satisfactory dinner option. It will take a couple of hours from here to negotiate the twists and turns before you return home, so if you didn't partake in Strasburg, you'll probably want to grab a bite at the Delta Family Restaurant (717-456-5233). The Delta is conveniently located at the very intersection where you need to make your right turn onto Route 851. The menu is standard fare, but better than fast food and just a couple of dollars more.

Now you're ready to tackle Route 851. It's a challenge to follow, not because it is particularly twisty—though it has its moments—but because of the extraordinary variety of roads it follows to get from one place to another. It has to be a route designed by committee and drawn by connecting the dots on the map. It must touch every single hamlet, burg, and 'ville along

*The Red Caboose Motel. Disney World it ain't, but it's near all the "action" in Strasburg.*

*"That joke just kills me every time you tell it, Fred."*

the way. You'll have some scouting to do, but this is a fun route to travel. It follows creeks, fence rows, and railroad beds. It gets narrow and bumpy, then turns wide and smooth. It passes through towns like New Freedom, Constitution, and then there's Sticks. If you've ever wondered where "the sticks" are, now you know.

Eventually you end up in the general vicinity of nowhere. After a brief stint on Route 516, follow Route 216 west. Just outside of Hanover, you will ride through Codorus State Park and over Lake Marburg. The lake doesn't look like much from this view, but this is only a small portion; the rest is hidden away in the forest. From here it is three miles into Hanover and a simple matter to follow Route 116 to Gettysburg.

# Trip 3 Monument Valley

**Distance** *128 miles*
**Terrain** *Twisty roads over and around small hills*
**Highlights** *Cunningham Falls, The Cozy, Catoctin Mountain Park, Washington Monument State Park, Antietam National Battlefield, Harpers Ferry National Historic Park*

I call this loop "Monument Valley" in honor of the real Monument Valley on the Arizona-Utah border. In this case, the monuments aren't towering rock formations, but rather the memorials raised to those who served in the Civil War. This loop is relatively short in mileage because you'll want an op-

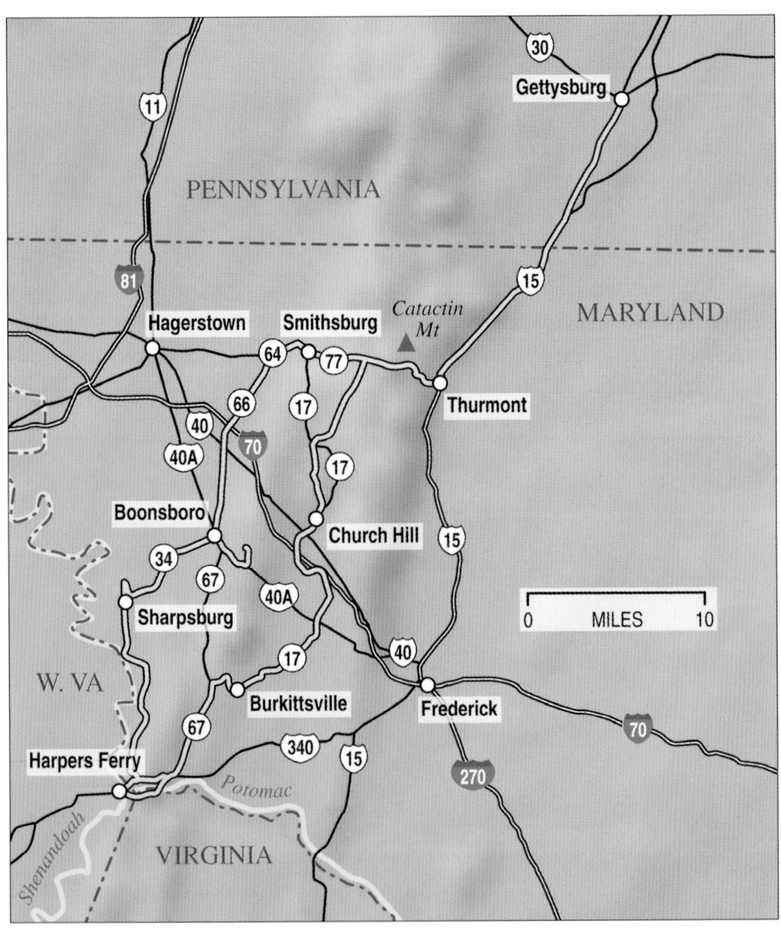

## THE ROUTE FROM GETTYSBURG

| | |
|---|---|
| 0 | Begin at town square in Gettysburg, US 15 Business south |
| 7.0 | Join US 15 south toward Emmitsburg |
| 18.0 | Right onto MD 77 West at Thurmont |
| 28.0 | Left onto MD 64 at Smithsburg |
| 29.1 | Left onto MD 66 |
| 39.4 | Left onto US 40 Alt in Boonsboro |
| 42.3 | Left onto Washington Monument Road |
| 43.5 | Arrive Washington Monument State Park, then turn around |
| 44.7 | Right onto US 40 Alt toward Boonsboro |
| 47.0 | Left onto MD 34 (Potomac Street) |
| 53.3 | Right onto MD 65 |
| 54.2 | Arrive Antietam National Battlefield, then turn around |
| 55.2 | Left onto Mechanic Street (becomes Harpers Ferry Road) |
| 67.7 | Left onto Keep Tryst Road |
| 68.1 | Left onto US 340 south |
| 71.6 | Arrive Harpers Ferry Battlefield Visitors Center, then turn around |
| 75.4 | Right onto ramp for MD 67 north |
| 80.9 | Right onto Gapland Road |
| 82.4 | Arrive Gathland State Park, then continue on Gapland Road |
| 82.9 | Left on MD 17 in Burkittsville |
| 96.3 | Left onto Harp Hill Road |
| 99.7 | Right on Stottlemeyer Road in Wolfsville |
| 105.2 | Right onto MD 77 |
| 110.2 | Right onto US 15 north toward Gettysburg |
| 120.5 | Follow US 15 Business north, first Gettysburg exit |
| 128.5 | Return town square in Gettysburg |

portunity to get off the bike and browse the museums, walk the trails, or meander the battlefields at a leisurely pace.

A good way to start is by following West Confederate Avenue out of town. You are behind Confederate lines, looking over the meadow that separated the western ridge from the town of Gettysburg. On the third day of the Battle of Gettysburg, in a last-ditch attempt to take the town and shift the momentum of the war to the South, General Lee hesitantly approved a bold plan to allow George Pickett, one of his field generals, to lead the Army of Northern Virginia across the wide open expanse directly into the strongest point of the Union line. Pickett's Charge, as it came to be known, was a disaster. As the Rebels marched toward the entrenched Union position on the other side of the field, a barrage of Union musket and artillery fire raked the Confederate lines. In a matter of minutes, the Rebel advance was shattered. The Union Army held off the strongest offensive the Confederate states could mount. This would be the last significant invasion the Rebel army would make into Union territory, prompting historians in later years to label this battle "the high water mark of the Confederacy."

West Confederate Avenue intersects with Route 15. Take Route 15 south and stop in Thurmont, Maryland, for breakfast at the Cozy Restaurant (cozyvillage.com). The Cozy is a favorite of local motorcyclists. You'll often find a group of bikes in the parking lot, especially on the weekends. On Sundays the Cozy puts out a tremendous brunch buffet that stretches 20 or 30 feet. Not only is it a huge spread, everything is freshly prepared and tastes great.

After tanking yourself and your bike up, the journey begins straight out of Thurmont into the Catoctin Mountains. Follow Route 806 north into town, make a left on Water Street, then turn left on Main Street, MD 77 west. Close at hand are Catoctin Mountain Park (nps.gov/cato) on the right side of the road and Cunningham Falls State Park (dnr.maryland.gov/publiclands/western/cunninghamfalls.html) on the left. Route 77 threads through the middle, an inviting strip of pavement that will whet your appetite for the curves that follow. The short hiking path to Cunningham Falls is perfectly suited to working off a dozen or so of those 10,000 calories you

*You never know what you'll find just lying around in Appalachian hill country.*

*Stars, birds, and other good luck "hex" signs adorn buildings in the region.*

just ate for breakfast. Don't forget to stop by the visitor center at Catoctin Mountain to get your National Parks Passport stamp.

Once Route 77 reaches the summit of Catoctin Mountain, the pace picks up as the road straightens out. It ends on the outskirts of Smithsburg. Make a left on MD 64 for a couple of miles, then another left on MD 66, then slip under the roar of Interstate 70 and pass into the rolling rural countryside of western Maryland. At Boonsboro, make the left turn onto Alternate 40 and follow the signs for Washington Monument State Park (dnr.maryland.gov/publiclands/western/washington.html). Just outside of town you'll begin climbing again, this time ascending South Mountain. There are countless monuments to George Washington scattered all over the country, but the large stone tower erected on this site by local patriots in 1827 was probably the first. Enter at the base of the tower and ascend the narrow circular stairs to reach the platform at the top. From here you can see well into West Virginia across the upper Shenandoah Valley, known here as the Great Valley. Members of local conservation groups are often present, observing the movements of migrating hawks that follow the thermals created by the mountains. You can also impress your friends by telling them that while you were at it, you hiked a portion of the Appalachian Trail on your vacation.

*The first monument to George Washington near Boonsboro, Maryland. What it lacks in design aesthetics it makes up for in security.*

You don't need to tell them it was only from the parking lot to the monument and back.

Return to Boonsboro on Alt 40 and make the left turn onto MD 34 toward Sharpsburg and the Antietam National Battlefield (nps.gov/anti). The Battle of Antietam marked an earlier attempt by General Lee to take the offensive in the Civil War. His goal was to capture the Union capital, Washington, D.C., which, if attained, might generate European support for and recognition of the Confederate States. Fighting between the opposing forces was ferocious. A field of corn which stood between the two armies was cut to the ground by the exchange of fire. So many soldiers from both armies fell at Antietam Creek that for a while during and after the battle, the creek ran red with blood.

The battlefield is preserved in a state much as it was when the war raged, and a series of drives allows you to tour the battlefield on your bike to see

*You could spend all day meandering the backroads of New Germany Valley.*

how the engagement was played out. A reenactor buddy of mine says that to this day it isn't unusual to find artifacts lying around. Once during a reenactment of the battle in the cornfield, he said that as the soldiers advanced, they could be seen stooping over. They weren't pretending they'd just been shot. They were picking up spent miniballs lying all over the ground. Of course, pocketing any artifact is a violation of federal law, so if you do see anything, I'm sure you'll just leave it alone. Before you leave, stop by the visitor center and add another stamp to your Parks Passport.

In the town of Sharpsburg, follow MD 34 into town and turn left on Mechanic Street. This becomes Harpers Ferry Road. If you've been looking for a little more riding excitement to go with your scenery, this road delivers. It's a favorite route of area riders and you're apt to meet up with a few along the way (tinyurl.com/motojourneys07). The ride gets even twistier as you near the Potomac River at Harpers Ferry and parallel the C&O Canal Park Towpath (nps.gov/choh) for a mile or two. The towpath is great for a leisurely stroll alongside the river. Just ahead, the Potomac and Shenandoah Rivers meet before turning southeast toward Washington, D.C.

A bike can always find a parking spot along the narrow strip of road that parallels the towpath. You can stop here, hike the towpath along the Potomac for a stretch, then cross the bridge at the confluence of the Potomac and Shenandoah Rivers to arrive in Harpers Ferry National Historic Park (nps.gov/hafe). You can get yet another Parks Passport stamp here. If you'd prefer not to walk, it's also just a short ride from this point on the route.

Follow Harpers Ferry Road underneath the railroad bridge and make the left turn onto Keep Tryst Road. Before Harpers Ferry, first a lunch note: Cindy Dee's Restaurant (301-695-8181) is at the intersection of Keep Tryst and US 340. It's a good stop for lunch if you've been holding out.

At US 340, turn left to head south across the Potomac River crossing and into Harpers Ferry. On a nice weekend, this brief stretch will be crowded. Once over the Shenandoah bridge you have a couple of options. For the official Harpers Ferry tour, head south on US 340 to the visitor center on the left. Plenty of parking can be had there and a shuttle bus will escort you to the historic district. Your other option is to turn right on Shenandoah Street and drive down into the historic district yourself. Parking is always an issue here, but riders enjoy a distinct advantage since you can often find a place to stash a bike.

Make the return trip by following US 340 north across the Shenandoah and Potomac River bridges into Maryland. Make the turn onto MD 67 north toward Boonsboro. Just a few miles up the road, hang a right onto Gapland Road. The ride up the mountain will bring you to Gathland State Park and a wealth of stories. Pull into the parking lot and hop off for a tour.

The first thing you will notice is the large stone monument. This arch, know as the War Correspondents Memorial (dnr.maryland.gov/publiclands/gathlandhistory.asp), was built in 1896 by George Alfred Townsend to honor journalists of that conflict. Townsend himself was the youngest correspondent of the Civil War and later he was considered an important writer of the Reconstruction era. Townsend designed and constructed many buildings at this retreat. Some have fallen into ruin while a few structures, including the memorial arch, are maintained by the state.

The arch is unusual, but there's something even stranger about this area I'll bet you didn't know. Head down the hill on Gapland Road and you're entering Blair Witch country (blairwitch.com). If you're not familiar with the film, the premise is that in 1994, three students went into the woods to shoot a documentary near Burkittsville, Maryland. Their film was found one year later. The characters and events depicted in the movie are entirely fictional but the village is real.

Pity then, the residents of Burkittsville, especially on Halloween. So many people have made the pilgrimage to Burkittsville in search of the fictional places depicted in the movie that both village officials and residents continually attempt to explain it wasn't real (burkittsville.com). But read some of the letters they've received and you'll soon agree with P. T. Barnum that there really are suckers born every minute.

At Burkittsville, turn left onto MD 17 to make the return trip to Gettysburg. Route 17 is wide and smooth, a great touring road. As it makes its way

*War Correspondents Memorial Arch near Burkittsville, Maryland. "Eclectic" is one word that comes to mind.*

north, the ride entertains you with several series of tight curves that will have you swaying your bike from side to side to stay with it.

A nice diversion is to follow Harp Hill Road north over higher ground. You'll have to drop down a gear or two as some portions of the road rise and fall like the streets of San Francisco. Harp Hill Road rejoins MD 17 at Wolfsville. In Wolfsville, a right turn on Stottlemeyer Road will bring you back to MD 77 just outside Catoctin Mountain Park. Follow MD 77 east to Thurmont, then US 15 north to retrace your path to Gettysburg.

But please, do check your saddlebags for stowaway witches on your return. The good folks in Gettysburg have all the supernatural manifestations they care to handle, thank you.

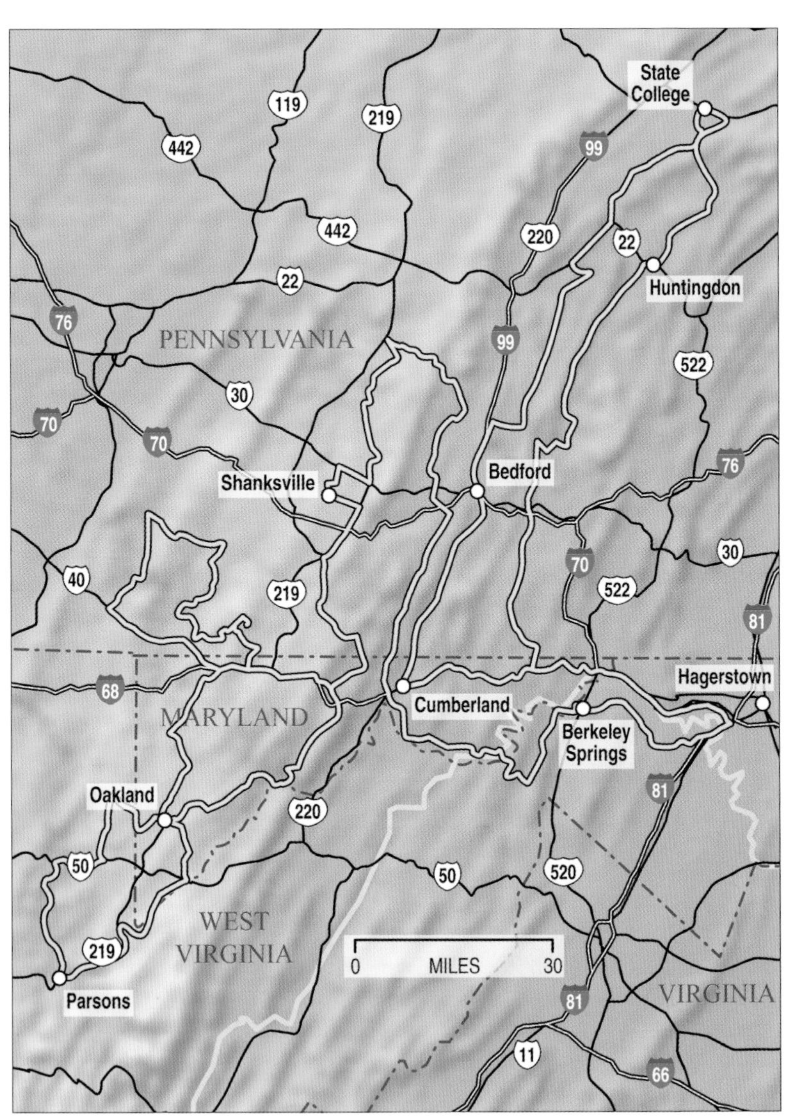
State College
119
219
442
99
442
220
22
22
Huntingdon
76
PENNSYLVANIA
99
522
30
70
70
76
Bedford
Shanksville
30
70
40
219
522
81
68
Hagerstown
Cumberland
MARYLAND
Berkeley Springs
81
Oakland
220
50
50
520
WEST VIRGINIA
219
0
MILES
30
Parsons
VIRGINIA
81
11
66

# The Trail West

## *Cumberland, Maryland*

Cumberland, Maryland, for many years a destination of travelers heading to points west, is known as the Queen City of the Alleghenies. It is plainly obvious for all to see that the queen has lost some of her royal beauty, but carries herself with dignity nonetheless.

The town sprang up around a large gap in the Allegheny Mountains called The Narrows. This corridor, first discovered by Native Americans, marked the route for the National Road, the first federally funded highway.

During the 1800s, thousands of settlers poured through The Narrows on their way to claim homesteads in the territories of the Great Plains. Situated at the end of a day's journey along the route, Cumberland was a popular stopover on railroad and stagecoach routes and it was this fact that fueled much of its early growth. The advent of automobile travel changed all that, and not for the better.

Today, Cumberland (ci.cumberland.md.us) can be reached in two hours from metropolitan areas of the Mid-Atlantic, making it little more than a convenient rest stop on the way west. Having lost much of its strategic

*Cumberland, Queen City of the Alleghenies, is situated near a strategic gap called The Narrows.*

transportation value, the city began a long, slow slide into economic depression, from which it still seeks to recover today.

For us, Cumberland remains the perfect strategic position from which to discover the byways that wind through the surrounding mountains.

From Cumberland you can launch a day trip into southern Pennsylvania to discover the hundreds of tiny farming valleys that lie between the ridges. You'll meander through towns that have successfully resisted the urge to keep pace with modern America. No pay-at-the-pump gas stations, automated teller machines or fast-food restaurants in this region. You can also venture west into Maryland's Deep Creek Lake area (dnr.maryland.gov/publiclands/western/deepcreeklake.html). West Virginia is just over the Potomac River, and some of that state's greatest beauty can be found along its northern border.

Cumberland itself is like a large patchwork quilt spread out over uneven ground. Its streets are a tangled web of intersections, underpasses, and access roads. The only way to figure out how to get around town is to navigate by points of the compass rather than by street directions. "I think the restaurant is south of town. Let's see, the sun is setting over there so that must be west . . . let's go down this street."

While you are in town, there are a few places you will want to check out. The History House at 218 Washington Street is a restored 1867 town house that is now a museum of Allegany County history. While you are on Washington Street, check out the other large homes that line the street. These were all built around the same time, during Cumberland's economic peak during the mid-1800s. To get a better idea of the forces that shaped this region, visit the Transportation and Industrial Museum at the Western Maryland Station Center (13 Canal Street). While you are there, you can book a ride on the Western Maryland Scenic Railroad (wmsr.com). The 16-mile trip from Cumberland to Frostburg passes through The Narrows and through a tunnel. You are conveniently dropped off at the Old Depot Center and Restaurant in Frostburg for a 90-minute layover before returning. Gee, what should you do with that hour and a half? Eat? Shop? The folks in Frostburg sure hope so.

Speaking of Frostburg, some of the departure points for routes in this section leave from the Frostburg area. Where you start a route is, of course, up to you, but recently I have stayed in this western suburb of Cumberland. Like many of our other base camps, Frostburg is a college town, home to Frostburg State University.

Frostburg is a bit easier to navigate and offers all the travel services you might need within a couple of miles. Downtown features the Gunter Hotel

*Engine 475 prepares to tour the Amish tobacco fields.*

(failingershotelgunter.com). Originally built in 1896, today's version of the hotel has the modern conveniences you'd expect, along with a hotel prison and cockfighting ring in the basement. Those features aren't employed as often as they once were, but it's nice to know they're there. Directly across the street, the Princess Restaurant (princessrestaurant.com) serves up a good meal most any time of the day.

One of my favorite places to camp is just outside Cumberland at Rocky Gap State Park. This is one of the newest and largest state parks in Maryland, with almost 300 sites. Few of them have hookups, though, so this park isn't as popular with the home-away-from-home, RV set. Rocky Gap borders a large lake with three beaches and rowboats and canoes available for rent. At night, the conversation of nearby campers filters through the heavily wooded site, but the sounds are dampened by the heavy undergrowth. During the summer season, make reservations at Rocky Gap early to avoid disappointment.

# Trip 4 Pioneer Loop

**Distance** *82 miles*
**Terrain** *Wide, well-paved roads through mountains and valleys. Big sweepers and a few tighter ones*
**Highlights** *Casselman River Bridge, Penn Alps, Deep Creek Lake, Westernport*

The Pioneer Loop begins on Alt US 40 west at Frostburg. US 40, also known as the National Road (route40.net), has had a long history. It began as an Indian trace, then became a pioneer road, and is now a major gateway to the west. It wasn't always as smooth as it is now. Thomas Jefferson signed the enabling legislation that created the National Road in 1806 and construction began in 1811 near Cumberland.

By the time the road reached its terminus in Vandalia, Illinois, nearly forty years later, it was obsolete—train travel was all the rage. The road fell into a five-decade decline, with some sections becoming virtually impassable. It wasn't until the introduction of the automobile in the early 20th

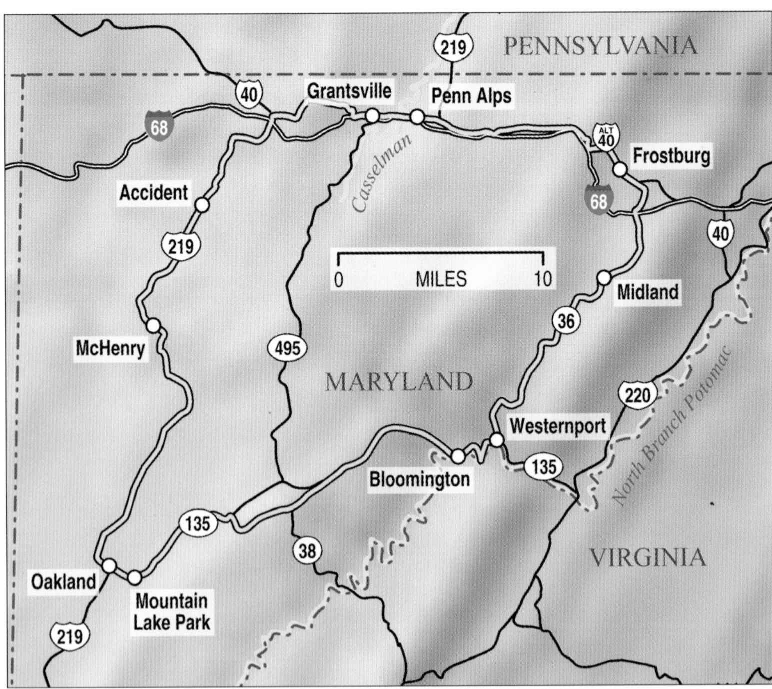

*No weather radar needed for this forecast: I'm gonna get wet.*

century that these sections of the National Road were improved and resurfaced. In the early part of this decade, the first American highway was officially added to the Interstate Highway System.

Twenty miles west of Frostburg and just east of Grantsville is a wide spot in the road called Penn Alps. The tug of the highway would ordinarily pull you past Penn Alps without a second thought, but a visit to the Spruce Forest Artisan Village (spruceforest.org) there is worth the time. The village is a group of restored log cabins occupied by Appalachian artisans who demonstrate their crafts and sell their wares. These are not weekend woodworkers either. Many of the artists-in-residence have won international recognition for their work. I was particularly impressed with Gary Yoder's bird carvings. Even up close the detailings of each carving are so realistic, you expect his works to scatter in all directions as you lean over to inspect them.

Other buildings have been restored just to display frontier life. One is a restored log schoolhouse which is authentic right down to the books on the desk and the boots arranged neatly in the rear of the building. On the day we visited, a schoolmarm was there to tell us about how school was con-

**THE ROUTE FROM FROSTBURG**

| | |
|---|---|
| 0 | Begin at US 40 Alt (West Main Street) in Frostburg at Gunter Hotel |
| 19.5 | Left onto US 219 at Keyser's Ridge |
| 45.5 | Left onto MD 135 in Oakland |
| 68.8 | Left onto MD 36 in Westernport |
| 82.2 | Arrive Frostburg via MD 36 |

*A few miles west of Cumberland, Frostburg combines small town charm and travelers' amenities.*

ducted. From her description, it was clear that she had firm control over her classroom. On the way out the door, she even reminded me to mind my manners and to "say please and thank you!" Also in the village, The Penn Alps Restaurant (pennalps.com) is a good bet for lunch. On the way out, you can pick up locally made breads, cakes, and other treats.

Immediately adjacent to the village is the Casselman River Bridge, (dnr.maryland.gov/publiclands/western/casselman.html) built in 1813 as part of the National Road project and in use until 1933. The night before it was to be officially dedicated, the builder came to take away the construction scaffolding to see if the bridge would fall down—he was convinced it wouldn't stand on its own and would collapse in front of everyone at the ceremony! The bridge didn't fall, and the workmen were directed to put the scaffolding back into place that evening so it could be dramatically removed at the official dedication ceremony the next day.

The bridge was originally built much larger than was required as a political ploy to attract the C&O Canal project through the area. Local government officials thought that by building a large bridge over the Casselman River, they would provide a route for the engineers that wouldn't require any further bridge construction. Good idea, but the Ohio end of the canal never got past Cumberland. However, when you consider the bridge was in use for 120 years, they probably got their money's worth out of it anyway. Today the state has set aside the bridge area as a state park with tables and grills.

Continue west to US 219 south. A scenic overlook to the right gives you a superb view of the valley below as pretty as any you'll ever see. For the most part, the pace is relaxed on 219, there isn't a great deal of traffic, and the view is nice. Shortly thereafter 219 winds through the town of Accident, Maryland. I've been through some places with funny names—Mouthcard, Kentucky; Bat Cave, North Carolina; and Loafer's Glory, North Carolina—but none of those names had the same effect as Accident.

Later, I came to learn what many believe to be the origin of the name. About 1750, England's King George granted 600 acres to repay a debt. The receiver, George Deakins, commissioned two survey parties to survey land, each without knowledge of the other. It was later discovered that both parties had, coincidentally, chosen the same oak tree to begin their measurements from. As a result of the happy accident, the tract took the name "The Accident Tract."

Outside of Accident, traffic will increase as you approach the Deep

*Despite the builder's concerns about collapse, the Casselman River bridge stands firm.*

Creek Lake State Park and resort area. Deep Creek is popular both as a summer resort and—because the area receives an average of 82 inches of snow each winter—as a popular skiing destination. The result is an abundance of places to stay if you wish to layover, and a good range of places to eat from casual snacks to fine dining. One place I especially enjoyed was Doctor Willy's Seafood. Another fact to file for Really Trivial Pursuit: Deep Creek is 72 feet deep.

Eventually 219 runs into the town of Oakland (oaklandmd.com) From there, hang a left onto Route 135 east. About ten miles out of Oakland, 135 falls off the top of a mountain ridge in one straight, fast, four-mile descent. Signs every 50 feet warn trucks to stay in first gear and not to exceed 10 mph. The road didn't seem that steep to me, but at the bottom of the mountain I found a road crew picking up the remains of a shattered guardrail and a log truck—guess the signs were right after all. Route 135 makes an abrupt right face at the end of the downhill run and then hugs the north bank of the Potomac River for the next 20 miles.

Maryland's entire southern border is etched on the map by the course of the Potomac River from the Fairfax Stone at the far southwestern corner to the Eastern Shore. In the 1700s, when Lord Thomas Fairfax commanded a massive stretch of land known as the Fairfax Proprietary, he was told that the western boundary of his claim would be defined by the headwaters of the Potomac. It was in Fairfax's best interest to see that the headwaters be as generously defined as possible. At the Fairfax Stone, you can literally step across the Potomac (see Trip 9, Romancing the Stone, for more details).

*Sometimes you just don't even want to know how a place got its name.*

*Gary Yoder's bird carvings are fantastically detailed and realistic. How does he do that?*

The area's primary employer is Westvaco, a large paper mill, which supports several towns. On my way through one of them, Westernport, I stopped for a breather at a town park next to the river. There is a bright red caboose on display in the park. I thought that maybe this was just the hull for youngsters to crawl on. Luckily, I was wrong.

Inside, the caboose has been completely refurbished and is crammed full of old photographs, lanterns, and dozens of other mementos of the railroad. I was lucky enough to even get a personal guided tour, front to back, by Ellsworth Kenealy, a 40-year veteran of the rails. Each item or picture he picked up had a story associated with it, and Mr. Kenealy's personalized tour meant a lot more than if I had simply walked through an exhibit in some museum. Thanks, Mr. Kenealy.

From Westernport, turn north on MD 36. This runs back into Frostburg to conclude the Pioneer Loop.

# Trip 5 Lion Country

**Distance** *240 miles*
**Terrain** *Mostly well-paved state roads with long sweepers. Backroads are narrow, with some tight curves and occasional gravel hazards.*
**Highlights** *Miles of beautiful Pennsylvania farm country and small towns framed by low ridges, the mysterious Bedford Springs Resort, Indian Caverns, Pennsylvania State University campus (home of the Nittany Lions), Baby's, Boal Mansion and Museum, Raystown Lake*

This is a long route, one of the longest included in this book. It is here because of the important lesson it teaches to the patient rider: by no other means of transportation (save, perhaps, a bicycle) could you absorb as much of the scenery and atmosphere of a place as by riding a motorcycle. You have

## THE ROUTE FROM CUMBERLAND

| | |
|---|---|
| 0 | Begin at US 220 intersection with I-68 near Rocky Gap. Head north on US 220 |
| 22.2 | At split, follow US 220 Business to the right, follow US 220 Business through Bedford |
| 33.5 | Continue straight. US 220 turns left and rejoins I-99. Straight ahead, road turns to SR 4009 |
| 37.1 | Turn right onto PA 869 |
| 46.0 | Left onto PA 36 |
| 50.5 | Right onto PA 866 |
| 72.8 | Right on US 22 |
| 81.3 | Left onto PA 45 |
| 81.9 | Turn right to follow PA 45 |
| 106.6 | Right on US 322 Business |
| 106.8 | Arrive Boal Mansion and Columbus Chapel, turn around |
| 110.4 | Right onto SR 26 north (one way) |
| 111.0 | Left onto Garner Street (Baby's) |
| 111.1 | Left onto PA 26 south (one way) |
| 214.6 | Right onto US 40 Alt Scenic |
| 239.2 | Follow US 40 (MD 144 in some sections) to Cumberland |

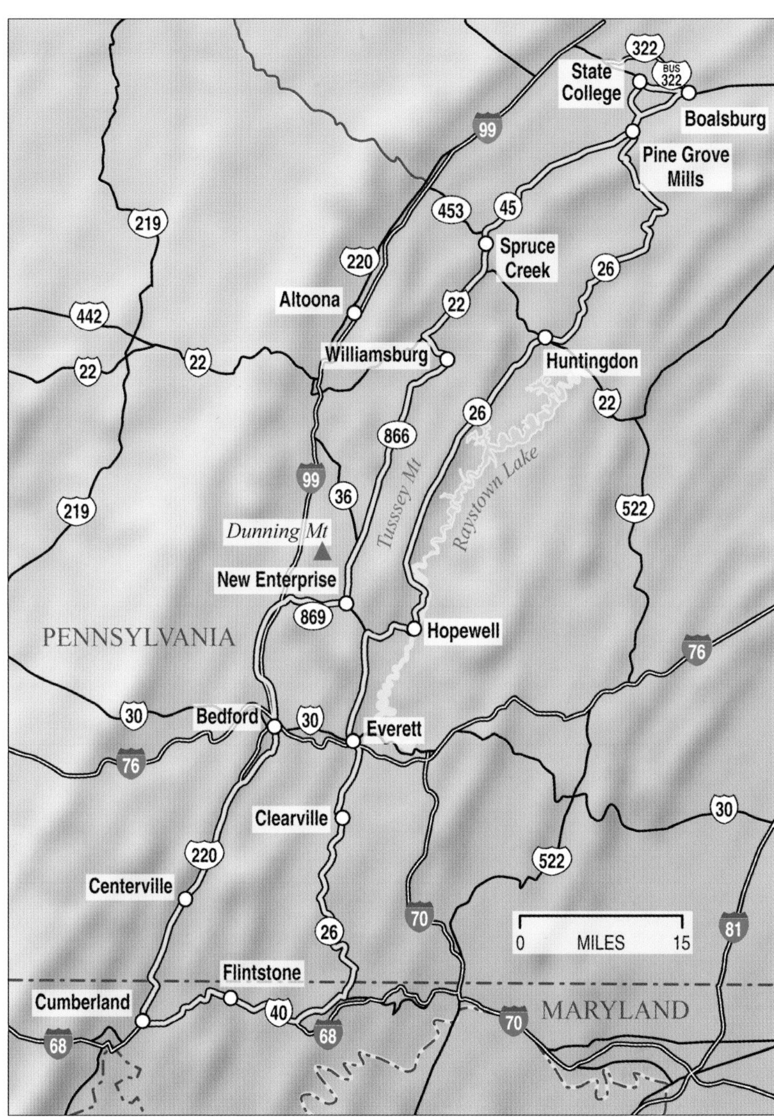


probably often read that travel is its own reward and the fun is not where you are going but in getting there. This route proves it.

We begin our journey to the center of the Keystone State from Rocky Gap State Park, following US 220 north toward the state line. If you happen to travel this route in May, as I did, you can't help but notice how sweet the Commonwealth of Pennsylvania smells. Laugh if you will, but it's true. Lining the creek banks and bottoms along the route were large flowering

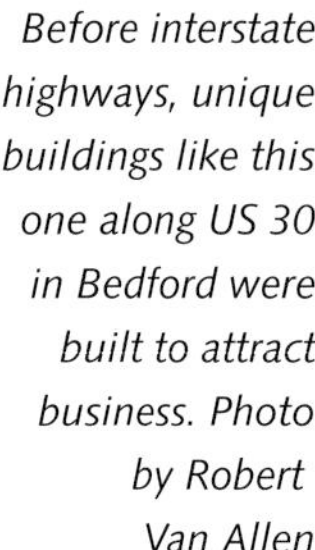
*Before interstate highways, unique buildings like this one along US 30 in Bedford were built to attract business. Photo by Robert Van Allen*

shrubs filled with delicate but intensely fragrant white blossoms. The effect was so pronounced it was almost as if the bike was cutting through a cloud of perfume. I haven't yet learned the name of this plant, but I intend to find out and put one or two of those in the yard at homestead.

As you near Bedford, bear to the right to follow US 220 Business north. This is our preferred entrance into town. Not only is it a quieter route, it's also curvier. As you round the corner into Bedford Springs, you'll be immediately struck by the huge resort complex on the left-hand side of the road.

Building began here in 1804 around a series of springs with reputed restorative powers. Bedford Springs (historichotels.org/hotel/bedford_springs_resort) became a full-fledged resort in the mid-1800s and flourished until after the turn of the century. James Buchanan, our 15th president, made Bedford Springs his summer White House. After World War II, the resort's prospects waxed and waned until it closed in the 1980s.

When I first wrote about Bedford Springs Resort years ago, it was still shuttered. Today, after a $120 million restoration effort, the 2,200-acre property has been restored to its former glory and is now part of the Omni Hotels group. I mean, after spending that kind of coin, you'd certainly expect it to be glorious. If you're a golfer, strap your clubs on the back of the bike, and bring 'em along to Bedford for the weekend.

Downtown Bedford is just ahead. You'll enter at the main intersection of US 220 and US 30. If you took off without breakfast, I can recommend the Landmark Restaurant (814-623-8185). You'll see it at 647 East Pitt Street as you meander through town (That's US 30 east of the intersection with

US 220). If you're really hungry, try the pancakes. They were almost more than I could eat, but I was somehow able to put them away.

You could spend a couple of hours in Bedford just cruising the streets checking out the variety of historic homes and buildings. Two of the most popular are Fort Bedford Museum (fortbedfordmuseum.org) and Old Bedford Village (oldbedfordvillage.com). The fort is built near the site of the original, and features exhibits of frontier life. Of the two, I preferred the fort. Old Bedford Village strikes me as too touristy and though the purpose is to recreate the atmosphere of an old village, there's something about it that doesn't ring true. Maybe it's the endless roar of the Pennsylvania Turnpike which runs along the back boundary of the property.

Follow Business 220 out of Bedford along Black Oak Ridge and exit onto Route 869. As you reach the summit of Dunning Mountain, you can see Morrison Cove spread out below you. Slow down and enjoy the countryside as you pass through. Occasionally you will catch up to an Amish horse and buggy, as I did along the route. Give them a wide berth to prevent spooking the horses.

All the roads through Morrison Cove will lull you into a slow touring rhythm with their gentle sweeping curves and peaceful scenery. I passed through the area just after the harvest and the aroma of sweet rich earth filled the air. Farmers were in their fields tilling under the stubble after the year's harvest to prepare for the next year, returning my wave as I drifted by. Route 869 ends on Route 36 where I turned north. I followed that for a few miles before turning right on Route 866 on a whim. It turned out to be a good one, too. I passed neatly kept farmhouses and small towns so perfect they looked nearly like scale models. Finally winding out of the cove, the route follows US 22 for a short way, left on Route 453 and shortly a right on Route 45. Be sure to follow Route 45 and not the special route for trucks. Somewhere along the route, you will begin to see signs for Indian Caverns (indiancaverns.com). I stopped there. You should stop too, but perhaps not for the obvious reasons.

Indian Caverns is one of those tiny little enterprises that manages to eke out an existence by selling the touring public on a notion based partly on fact and largely on imagination. Traveling along Route 45, you can't miss the place. Holding a brochure of the caverns up against the real thing shows that the place could use a little more upkeep, but then you notice that the cars parked outside the cavern in the brochure can now sport antique license plates. At least one of the cars in the picture hasn't moved since.

To me, the gift shop is the real attraction at Indian Caverns; pure all-American kitsch with genuine rubber tomahawks, plastic Indian dolls, and

*The Columbus Family Chapel is just where you'd expect to find it, near Boalsburg, Pennsylvania.*

a wide assortment of gimmicks and gadgets with the Indian Caverns logo stenciled on them. There is no lack of authentic souvenirs to choose from.

I stood in the gift shop for 15 minutes waiting for a guide to return from the caverns, wondering if I was simply being given ample opportunity to browse the merchandise. Eventually a small group of two adults and two children appeared from the cavern and descended upon the gift shop, snatching up plastic bow-and-arrow sets, cedar boxes of myriad shapes, and an official Indian chief's headdress. The register happily rang up a seventy-five-dollar sale and the proprietor gave them a wide, toothy grin. He could afford to.

The ticket for the cavern tour is nine dollars (a coupon for a ten percent discount is available on their website). Frankly, I suggest you take the tour—not to see the cave, but to listen to the tour guide recite her speech. I was an audience of one, but our relationship was strictly tour guide-tourist. This meant I was the entire audience, and when she dutifully executed each pause in her script, I was clearly expected to respond with some exclamation of wonderment. The tour would simply not continue until I made the appropriate comment. I obliged as best I could, but it was awkward. Occasionally she would ask, "Does anyone have any questions? Anyone??"

As you enter Boalsburg on Route 45, hang a right on US 322 Business. You will soon find signs pointing to the Boal Mansion and Museum (boalmuseum.com) and the Columbus Chapel. This tour is worth seven dollars but only costs a dollar-fifty. It contains some of the oddest and oldest artifacts of our country's European heritage to be found anywhere on the North American continent. It is the most fascinating museum I have ever visited.

The Boal family was highly placed in colonial social circles, influential in trade, politics, law, the military, and so on. As a result their home is a living history of our ties to the European continent. The home had humble beginnings but was gradually expanded and enlarged until it assumed its present grandeur. Members of the Boal family still live in the home. Only a few rooms are open to the public, but they are stuffed with antiquities and oddities.

In one corner stands a piano which once belonged to Dolley Madison. Could this have been an heirloom Dolley sold from Montpelier to pay her son's gambling debts? (See Trip 14, Home Country, for details.) In a picture hanging on the wall, a stern-faced elderly woman stares at you from ages past. The chair she occupied sits in the corner. Bronze busts and statuettes of famous people are scattered throughout. Dueling pistols are displayed in cabinets in the living room, along with locks of Napoleon's hair, given to one of the members of the family who was highly placed in Napoleon's army. Gazing on Napoleon's hair on American soil is a little amazing, but it gets more amazing still.

Theodore Davis Boal was a fifth-generation family member who married a descendant of Christopher Columbus. Through this connection, a good many artifacts from the Columbus family found their way across the same ocean their ancestor had navigated hundreds of years before. Eventually Theodore Davis erected a chapel on the grounds of the Boal Mansion to the exact specifications of the original chapel building in Spain. He then imported all the contents of the original chapel. Inside is a wealth of treasures from the family, including the wooden admiral's desk Columbus used in his voyages as well as a few of the wooden crosses he planted on newly discovered lands. Many of the papers and other items housed in the chapel also date back to the 1400s, including the intricately carved door on the front of the building.

The whole area of Boalsburg and State College (statecollege.com) deserves a full day of your time because the Boal Mansion is just the first point of interest. Just across the street from the mansion is the Pennsylvania Military Museum. It displays a range of weaponry and military gear from colonial times to the present day, but its outstanding feature is a full scale World War I battlefield. To complete your tour of Boalsburg, turn right on Church Street and follow it to the downtown area where you will find quite a few quaint (read: dangerous to the wallet) shops and boutiques.

Just a few miles west of Boalsburg lies the town of State College, home to Pennsylvania State University (psu.edu). When school's in session the town's population swells from 38,000 to nearly triple that. On a warm autumn afternoon, the town is literally buzzing with activity.

Plans for Penn State started in 1850 with the desire of some area residents to begin a farmers' high school. Since those humble beginnings, it has grown into one of the nation's largest universities, complete with a nationally recognized football dynasty. There are five different museums on the main campus ranging from anthropology to the history of cable television, all of them free to the public. If you don't want to deal with the crowd on your visit to State College (though it's kind of fun, actually), go during the summer months when there is less activity at the university.

Asking around for a good place to eat, I kept getting the same answer—"Baby's"— (babysburgers.com) so I decided to check it out. Baby's is a '50s diner on the northern end of town. It's a little hard to find if you don't know where to look, but if you like the '50s era and good burgers, this place is worth the effort to find. When you leave Boalsburg, follow 322 west into downtown until you reach PA 26 northbound. You'll go almost through town, past a number of large residence halls, offices, and campus buildings. On your left, look for a large stand-alone automatic teller. The next street on your left should be Garner Street. Turn left onto Garner and Baby's is just ahead on your right. If you miss it, drive through to PA 26 southbound, go down a couple of blocks and circle around. You'll eventually find it. If you don't, just about anyone on the street should be able to point you in the right direction.

This is a long tour and you might want to stay over the night in the area and make your return the following day. This is an especially good idea if you want to take advantage of any of the recreational opportunities at Raystown Lake (raystownlake.com). There should be no problem finding a room in town unless something special is going on. With the large selection, you can find prices under thirty dollars.

As I worked my way south on Route 26, I passed through a dozen more small townships and countless villages of a few homes backed up to the long Tussey Mountain ridge. It was early evening and the air, no longer warmed

*Jennifer, your waitress at Baby's, says, "Meatloaf anyone?"*

by the sun, was taking on a real spring chill. It was television time and the front windows of many homes had that eerie, faint, phosphorescent glow. While these gentle people watched the evening news and *Jeopardy,* my machine and I glided past, silent and unnoticed, like a ghostly shadow.

A large portion of Route 26 parallels the western shore of Raystown Lake, the largest lake in the state. Want a cabin with a view of the lake on four sides? At Raystown you can rent a houseboat! You can motor one of these beauties away from the dock at Seven Points Marina for a three- or four-day vacation on the water, exploring every cove and island of the lake, starting at $500. If you're shy of making such long-term commitments, you can rent an open utility boat for the day for $65.

The remainder of Route 26 below Earlston finishes in fine Pennsylvania fashion, becoming narrow and crooked and full of fun twists and turns. It ends all too soon, crossing over into Maryland and soon returning to the National Road. Your best bet for a final dose of riding satisfaction is to follow the scenic portion of Scenic Route 40 for as long as it lasts before returning to the wide, sprawling, and blessedly empty superslab.

We've covered a lot of real estate in this tour, but I think you will gain an appreciation, as I did, for the tremendous diversity of things to do, places to go and ways to get there. With a good map, you could explore the backroads for weeks along this route and never travel the same road twice. It's a tough job, but somebody has to do it. It had just as well be you as anyone, right?

# Trip 6 The National Road

**Distance** *130 miles*
**Terrain** *Pennsylvania's "high country"*
**Highlights** *Mount Davis, Frank Lloyd Wright's Fallingwater, Ohiopyle State Park, Springs Farmers' Market, Springs Museum, Addison Toll House*

We tend to think that squabbles about transportation issues and back door politicking are unique to today's social climate, but our forefathers were well versed in the matters themselves.

The National Road, built in response to the pressure of westward expansion, hadn't been around more than 20 years or so before Congressional controversies raged over who would pay for its maintenance and upkeep. Congress decided the best way to resolve the issue was to dump it on the states. Sound like a solution you just heard about yesterday perhaps?

The states promptly established toll houses and began to charge for the use of the road. This road has seen all kinds of traffic: covered wagons, stage coaches, and even flocks of sheep and cattle. Today just two of those original toll houses remain including one that is right along our path of travel in Addison, Pennsylvania.

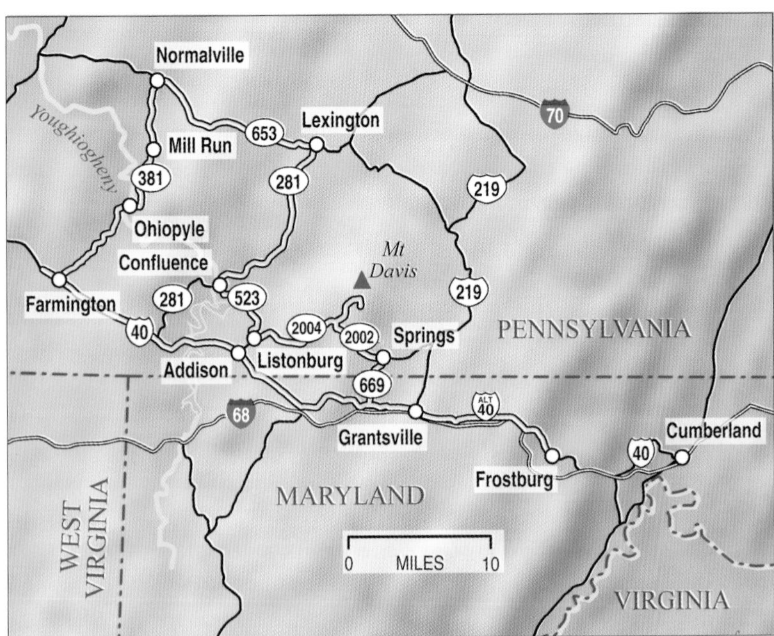

**THE ROUTE FROM FROSTBURG**

| | |
|---|---|
| 0 | Begin US 40 Alt west in downtown Frostburg |
| 25.3 | Left on SR 3002 to Addison Toll House |
| 25.5 | Arrive Addison Toll House. Continue on SR 3002 through Addison |
| 27.4 | Left onto US 40 west |
| 40.8 | Arrive Fort Necessity National Battlefield, turn around |
| 40.8 | Right onto US 40 east |
| 42.2 | Left onto PA 381 |
| 59.2 | Right onto PA 653 (Jim Mountain Road) |
| 72.2 | Right on PA 281 (Kingwood Road) |
| 85.3 | Pick up PA 523 in Confluence |
| 90.9 | Left onto SR 2004 (becomes Mt. Davis Road) |
| 101.4 | Right onto Wolf Rock Road and follow signs for Mt. Davis Summit |
| 102.0 | Arrive Mt. Davis Summit, turn around |
| 102.6 | Left onto SR 2004 (becomes Mt. Davis Road) |
| 105.8 | Left onto SR 2002 |
| 110.6 | Right onto PA 669 (Springs Road) |
| 114.3 | Left onto US 40 Alt east |
| 129.0 | Arrive Frostburg via US 40 Alt east |

You'll see a sign for the Addison Toll House (qcol.net/tollhouse) soon after you cross the state line. Hang a left to follow Main Street up into the hamlet of Addison. The toll house is just ahead on your right. On weekends you can usually find members of the Daughters of the American Revolution giving tours and answering questions about the toll house, and passing out toll house cookies.

Other remnants of the old road remain besides the name—a marker here, a historic home there, an occasional bridge. As you breeze across the Youghiogheny River (pronounced YOK-ah-ganey) on a modern steel and concrete bridge, another old link to the past remains, submerged under 50 feet of water. Lurking somewhere below is an original stone arch bridge similar to the one preserved at Casselman Bridge State Park. This one was the longest bridge on the National Road.

In the winter, if water levels drop far enough, the old bridge emerges from the water like a monster rising from the depths of a Scottish loch.

*On a hot day, folks go tubing in the Youhiogheny at Ohiopyle State Park. Photo by Dan Bard*

Drought conditions in 2002 dropped levels far enough that people could once again walk across the bridge. Despite decades under water, it was reported to be in marvelous condition. One year later, record-setting rainfalls restored water levels and the bridge has once again taken refuge in its underwater lair.

If you're a fan of old forts and battlefields, you'll want to drive past the turnoff for Ohiopyle at Farmington and make the short trip (less than two miles) to the Fort Necessity National Battlefield (nps.gov/fone). This was just one of many wooden stockade forts that once marked the western boundary of settled territory. The conflict at this fort in 1753 marked the opening of the French and Indian War, a tussle between Britain and France for control of North America. Young George Washington commanded the small force here, and ultimately surrendered to a vastly larger contingent of French and Indian forces. It's noted that this was the only time he surrendered to opposing forces.

To continue the tour, turn back on US 40 to Farmington and make a left turn on Route 381. Ohiopyle State Park (fay-west.com/ohiopyle) is situated on the banks of a broad, calm spot in the Youghiogheny River. Tubing, canoeing, and just plain wading are big business here. In Ohiopyle Station, a dozen outfitters will rent you nearly any type of device that floats. But if you prefer to picnic and perhaps just get your feet wet, there is a nice park on the northern end of town with big grassy areas.

Just north of Ohiopyle is Fallingwater (wpconline.org), one of the most acclaimed designs of architect Frank Lloyd Wright. Fallingwater, so named because it was built in conjunction with a waterfall, was designed in 1936 and finished by 1939 for the family of Pittsburgh department store owner Edgar Kaufmann. Wright's particular genius was in creating buildings that worked in harmony with their surroundings rather than competing.

I felt that way about PA 653. It's the right turn just a few miles north of Fallingwater. The route begins with a long view of the road ahead. I'll freely admit that I am often envious of the pictures in John Hermann's volume of journeys through the Alps. Viewing mile after mile of empty switchbacks has to be intoxicating. This view along 653 won't compare to the Alps, but it does give you a good glimpse of what lies ahead, and that is enough to assure you this will be a good touring road.

At New Lexington, turn right on Route 281. A rarity among Pennsylvania roads, this one has a freshly paved, smooth-as-glass surface, combined

*Compton School reminds us that not too long ago, it was a privilege to get an education.*

*If you're good, Louise or Dixie will serve you a toll house cookie.*

with long sweepers (tinyurl.com/motojourneys09). On arriving in Confluence, pick up PA 523 headed south toward Listonburg.

Unless someone told you, you might not notice that this is Pennsylvania's high country. The mountains look more like tall hills out here, but in Pennsylvania, that's about as big as they get. Continue down PA 523 and we'll head toward Pennsylvania's highest point at Mount Davis. On arrival at Listonburg, make the left turn onto SR 2004, also known as Mount Davis Road.

This section of SR 2004 is my favorite little stretch of road in the Keystone State. It's not particularly winding, though there are a few good sweepers. There's a spot along this road just after you pass a church that ascends a short hill, and when you look to the south you see green pastures falling gently off the ridge. Behind that the forested slopes and gentle folds of Winding Ridge stand firm and silent. I just like to get off the bike, turn off the engine, and listen to the silence here. It's good for whatever ails you.

The northern entrance to the summit is just a few miles ahead on the right and is semi-paved. Once you've turned on the road to the summit, you can skip the summit itself and continue for a short distance to a large wooden observation deck. This will give you the best view of the region, known locally as the Laurel Highlands. To continue the tour, retrace your path on SR 2004 to the junction with SR 2002 at Savage. Hang a left on SR 2002.

Much of the country in this area is employed farmland and much of that is worked by the Amish. If you want to see what real work is like, stop by the roadside some time and watch an Amish farmer work the field with a team of horses. I didn't catch any out on this occasion, but I did see fields filled with precision rows of hand-sown grain.

A good place to sample some of the fruits of that harvest is at the farmers' market in Springs. Out here a farmers' market is as much a social occasion as it is an opportunity to buy food. You'll find a wide assortment of vehicles at the market with a horse and buggy tied up next to a tractor, or sometimes, actually to a tractor. You will not find better picnic lunch supplies anywhere in town. Also be sure to stop by the Springs Museum (springspa.org). For only a buck and a half you can wander through a massive collection of household items commonly used by people of the region from a few hundred years ago to the present day. Not only that, you'll learn the origin of the term "stogie," and how the phrase "I'll be there with bells on" came to be. When you're ready to depart the museum, turn back south on Route 669 and you'll soon find yourself back at Route 40 in Grantsville, Maryland. All that remains is to turn left on US 40 to make your trek home, as so many have, along the National Road.

# Trip 7 In Search of Prospect Peak

**Distance** *136 miles*
**Terrain** *Several mountain passes along the National Highway followed by a course tracing the Potomac River and more mountain passes*
**Highlights** *The National Road, Sideling Hill, Park-n-Dine, C&O Canal, Fort Frederick, Berkeley Springs, Prospect Peak, and the Paw Paw Tunnel*

Begin your search for Prospect Peak by following the older alignments of the National Road, out of Cumberland. These alternate routes are either labeled US 40 or MD 144 and are sometimes referred to as National Road, National Pike, or the Baltimore Pike. Whatever. The point is, all these old alignments parallel I-68 between Cumberland and Hancock.

There are some special sections of highway waiting for your personal discovery along Scenic 40, graceful curves that lead you into a turn at a quick pace and set you up perfectly for the next. They beg to be ridden on two wheels. Thank the Interstate Highway System for taking most of the traffic off this road and opening it up for pleasure riding.

Topping out at Town Hill, you can see Sideling Hill in the distance, identified easily by the big notch carved into the mountain, marking the point where I-68 passes through. The Town Hill Hotel (townhillbnb.com)

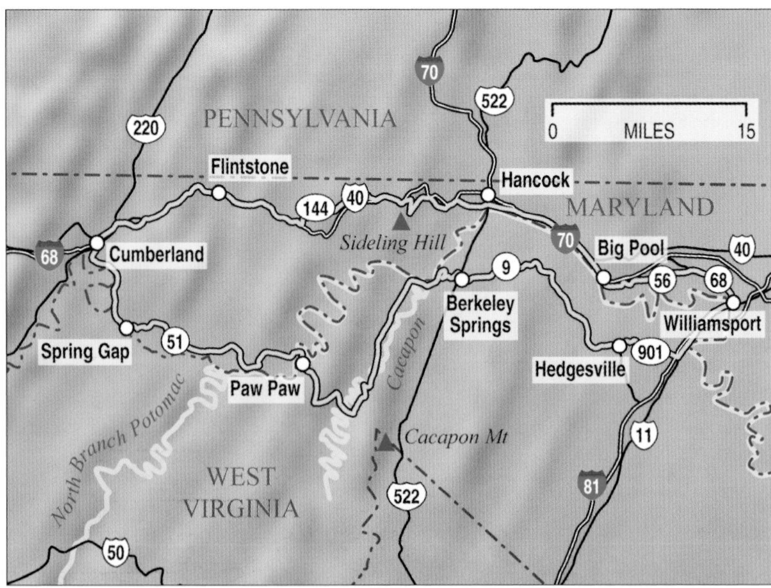

### THE ROUTE FROM CUMBERLAND

| | |
|---|---|
| 0 | Begin MD 144 (Baltimore Pike) at Pleasant Valley Road/Rocky Gap Camp |
| 17.4 | Right onto Orleans Road |
| 17.9 | Left onto I-68 east ramp |
| 23.9 | Arrive Sideling Hill Visitor Center, then continue straight |
| 26.9 | Right onto MD 144 |
| 31.7 | Arrive Park-n-Dine |
| 32.1 | Join I-70 east toward Hagerstown |
| 40.4 | Right on MD 56 at Big Pool |
| 41.7 | Right on Fort Frederick Road |
| 43.2 | Arrive Fort Frederick |
| 44.7 | Right onto MD 144 east |
| 51.4 | Right onto MD 68 south |
| 55.9 | Right onto US 11 west |
| 62.3 | Right onto WV 901 west |
| 67.7 | Right onto WV 9 |
| 110.8 | Arrive Paw Paw, West Virginia, WV 9 becomes MD 51 |
| 136.0 | Arrive Cumberland, Maryland |

is perched atop the ridge, looking neat and trim. This would be a great place to stay on a warm summer evening, enjoying great views and refreshing breezes. A few miles past Town Hill, Scenic 40 intersects with I-68. Jump back on the interstate to catch the Sideling Hill exhibit just ahead (dnr.state.md.us/publiclands/western/sidelinghill.asp).

Sideling Hill is a western Maryland landmark. In order to straighten a challenging section of the roadway, engineers blasted down a few hundred feet through the middle of the mountain to a point where a straight section of road could be made. During construction they found that during the time the Appalachians were being formed the mountain had sagged in the middle like a fallen layer cake. Perhaps it should have been baked another million years or so. The state built a pedestrian bridge across the highway to give you the best opportunity to view this natural wonder without the risk of parking on the side of the road. A visitor center is accessible from the walkway with more information and displays explaining how the mountain was formed, plus general travel information.

The ride into Hancock is short, eight or ten miles. If you wait on break-

*Beautifully situated atop a ridge crest, Town Hill Hotel started life as a fruit stand.*

fast till you get to Hancock, I promise you will not go unrewarded. Hancock is home to the Park-n-Dine (www.hancockmd.com/newparkndine.htm), one of those places where the cooking is good, the plates are loaded, and the price is delightfully low. When you order a three-dollar breakfast, you'd better be ready to let out your suspenders and pop the top button on your trousers. Riders of all brands flock to the Park-n-Dine, especially on the weekends.

Directly behind the restaurant is the Potomac River and the C&O Canal National Park (nps.gov/choh). In the early 1800s, speculators and politicians were all afire about finding new ways to move goods between the East Coast colonies and the newly opened Midwest. The ridges of the Appalachians made that no ordinary task. Some people thought roads were the answer, some gambled on the canal, and others built railroads. Canal construction began in 1828 in Washington, D.C., and crawled into Cumberland some 22 years later, but was made obsolete by speedier railroad service almost as soon as it was opened. The towpath along the canal is now a trail for hiking and biking and is a good place to walk off that third stack of pancakes you polished off. Also in Hancock is the C&O Canal Museum, which features a slide show, artifacts, and photos. Maybe after a short hike to the canal and museum you can swing your leg over the bike again. Then again, maybe you'll need a hoist.

The route out of Hancock follows Interstate 70 for a brief period, making an exit at Big Pool. Turn right and follow Route 56 east. Fort Frederick State Park (dnr.state.md.us/publiclands/western/fortfrederick.html) is just about one mile down the road. Fort Frederick is the only remaining original fort from the French and Indian War (1754–1763, for those who snoozed in history class). You can tour the fort and visit the barracks, which have been restored to show you what a soldier's life was like. Be glad you live in the 21st century, friend. You can have equal fun touring the well-appointed museum or just strolling around the large, open grounds. The quiet, green lawns would make a great place to spread out a blanket for a picnic lunch.

Resume the tour on Route 56 east and take advantage of the whoop de doos—those sections of the road that lift you out of your seat and cause your co-rider to hold on tighter. Route 56 ends on Route 68; turn right. Route 68 starts wide then narrows and remains a straight shot into Williamsport, a small blue-collar city on the West Virginia border that was once considered for the federal capital. Your best bet is to follow Route 68 into town where it intersects with US Route 11 into the Mountain State. Route 11 passes through a small section of suburbia, then Route 901 appears on your right. Follow Route 901 west and get set for some good riding.

It's too bad Route 901 is only a few miles long, because it winds through beautiful countryside. Side roads in this area are bound to reward you with

*The Park-n-Dine is a favorite of riders around the region.*

more good riding. It ends all too quickly on Route 9 at Hedgesville. Turn right on Route 9.

Between Hedgesville and Paw Paw, some forty miles distant, there are far more good riding miles than there are bad. The initial traffic you encounter in Hedgesville quickly fades as you head deeper into the country. Soon the entire roadway is yours. Entering the town of Berkeley Springs and seeing all the traffic is almost a culture shock. Berkeley Springs State Park (berkeleyspringssp.com) is the site of a watering hole that has been popular since colonial times. Imagine soaking your tootsies in the same refreshing waters as our founding fathers did! Okay, maybe that image doesn't capture your imagination, but these springs have long been known for their restorative powers. Berkeley Springs is a popular day ride destination for riders from the Washington metro area, so don't be surprised to find the town full of bikes on a warm weekend. There is plenty of good food to be found at small cafes and restaurants lining the streets. If you're looking for a really good meal, stop by Tari's Cafe (tariscafe.com) for a lunch made from fresh local produce that you won't soon forget. Tari has a couple of rooms over the

*It's labeled "George Washington's Bathtub (1749)." I wanna know how THEY know.*

*The notch through Sideling Hill reveals an interesting geological history.*

restaurant that she'll rent, too. While you're in town, check out the Star Theater, next door to Tari's (tinyurl.com/motojourneys10). This Depression-era movie house still shows first-run movies and serves hand-popped popcorn at the concession stand. If you stop in at Tari's, be sure to tell 'em Dale sent you.

West of Berkeley Springs, the road winds slowly up Cacapon Mountain on a steep incline, testing the bottom end of your bike's power curve. I remember the first time I toured this area a few years ago, my wife clinging to me on the back of a little 600cc sport bike. We were searching for a spot called Prospect Peak. The peak has been named by National Geographic Society as one of the ten prettiest spots in America. (Road trip!) As you reach the summit of Cacapon (KAK-upon or CAKE-upon) Mountain you'll find an overlook for the peak on your right. In the valley below, the Potomac looks like a thin silver ribbon draped over the landscape. Sideling Hill starts here and runs from left to right into Maryland. To the far right lies Pennsylvania and to the left, the small village of Great Cacapon slumbers. These are the Appalachians as few people see them.

When you descend the ridge and ride through the country you've seen from above, it's like stepping through the frame and into the painting.

*Tari's is a great place for lunch or dinner. Rent a room upstairs if your meal slows you down.*

Route 9 follows the contours of the Cacapon River in places accounting for some of the curves. Other times it takes a turn seemingly for the fun of it. Forest lines the road on both sides so thick it looks as though you are flying through a long green waterslide.

Your entry into Paw Paw is likely to go completely unnoticed. The road enters the edge of town and quietly exits on the north side. Just over the line in Maryland, look for the C&O Canal Paw Paw Tunnel sign (berkeleyspring.com/tunnel.htm). The town and the tunnel took their name from the Paw Paw, a fruit-bearing tree that grows wild along the ridges in this area.

Tunnel construction began in 1836 and cut through 3,118 feet of rock to avoid a six-mile stretch of the Potomac River—a major engineering feat in its time. You can walk through the tunnel now, but bring a flashlight. There is also a hiking trail that crosses over the top of the tunnel.

It took 14 years to build the tunnel instead of the two years originally planned and when completed, it was just wide enough for one boat at a time. This usually didn't cause problems, but occasionally two boats entered from opposite ends and met somewhere in the tunnel. I heard that on one occasion, a standoff ensued between a couple of captains, neither of which would agree to back out of the tunnel. After a couple of days, the tunnel superintendent was finished with such nonsense, so he built a smoky bonfire of green cornstalks on the upwind side of the tunnel. It didn't take long for both boats to make their way out of the tunnel. There's no record which boat backed out first, but the ultimate winner of this standoff was the superintendent.

When you cross over the river, Route 9 becomes Route 51 in Maryland. In addition to the tunnel, there are a number of spots along the route marked to indicate the remains of locks along the canal. They represent a good chance to hop off the bike for a quick stroll. Dual sport fans will find a plethora of side roads leading over the ridges and into the arms of the mountains. When you're ready to wrap up the loop, just follow MD 51 west to return to Cumberland.

# Trip 8 Johnstown Loop

**Distance** *139 miles*
**Terrain** *Low hills and ridges, farming country, and state parks*
**Highlights** *Covered bridges, Blue Knob State Park, Johnstown Flood National Memorial, Flight 93 Temporary Memorial Site*

It had rained for weeks on end as I prepared to revisit western Maryland and, for most of my visit, the fog was so heavy, I could barely make out buildings across the street from my hotel room. So it seemed fully appropri-

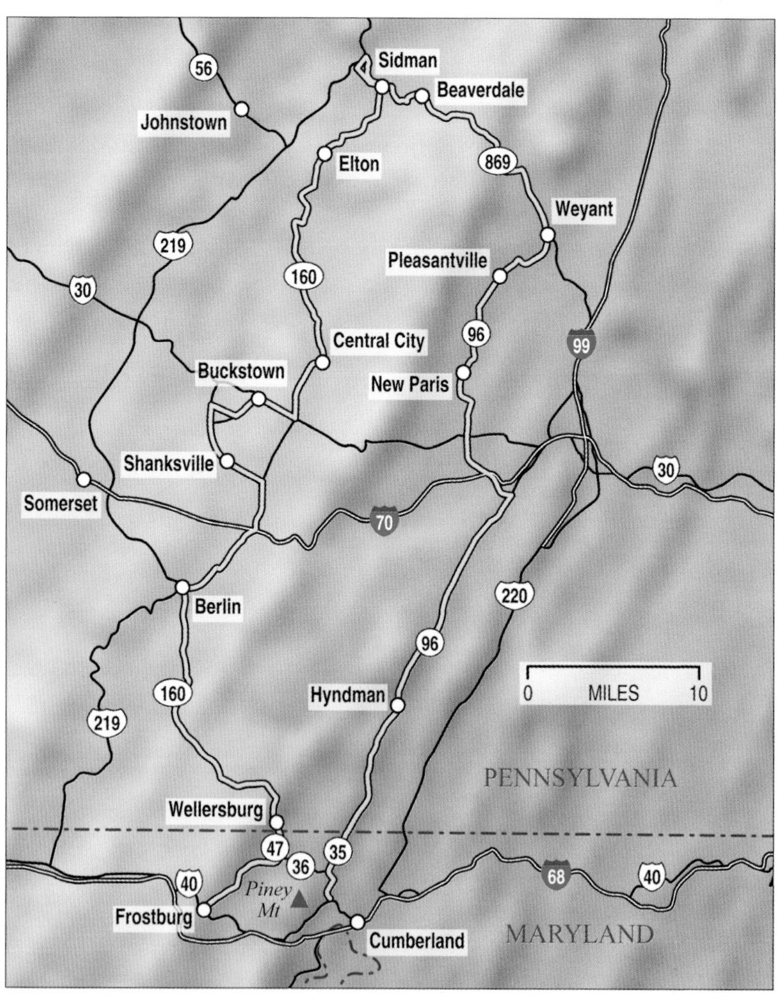

**THE ROUTE FROM CUMBERLAND**

| | |
|---|---|
| 0 | Begin at MD 36 at The Narrows on US 40 Alt |
| 2.1 | Right onto MD 35 |
| 4.5 | MD 35 becomes PA 96 at state line |
| 46.2 | PA 96 becomes PA 869 |
| 62.7 | Right onto Lake Road |
| 64.6 | Right onto SR 2006 |
| 64.8 | Right onto Park Road |
| 64.9 | Arrive Johnstown Flood National Memorial |
| 65.0 | Left onto SR 2006 |
| 65.2 | Left onto Park Road |
| 67.1 | Left onto PA 869 |
| 67.8 | Right onto PA 160 |
| 91.8 | PA 160 to right on US 30 |
| 93.8 | Left on Buckstown Road (SR 1019) |
| 96.8 | Right on Skyline Road |
| 97.8 | Arrive Flight 93 Temporary Memorial Site |
| 98.8 | Right on Buckstown Road |
| 100.0 | Right on Lambertsville Road toward Shanksville |
| 101.1 | Right turn in Shanksville at "Stop, Right turn keep moving" (Bridge Street) |
| 101.2 | Left on Main Street in Shanksville (becomes Cornerstone Road) |
| 104.0 | Right on PA 160 |
| 130.5 | PA 160 becomes MD 47 at state border |
| 132.1 | Right onto MD 36 |
| 138.6 | Arrive Frostburg via MD 36 |

ate that it should be raining as I hopped onto the bike to visit the site of two national disasters. The Johnstown Flood National Memorial (nps.gov/jofl) at Johnstown is the site of the flood on May 31, 1889, that nearly wiped the city off the map. About thirty miles to the south of Johnstown stands the Flight 93 Memorial, a gathering place to remember the United Airlines plane downed near Shanksville, Pennsylvania, on September 11, 2001.

The rain had thoroughly wetted my riding suit after just a mile on the road and as I stepped into Kline's Restaurant at The Narrows, I must have been an entertaining sight for the locals. Lined up shoulder-to-shoulder at the counter, several gave me that friendly-but-meaningful once-over that

*Route 869 offers a great run through rural Pennsylvania.*

says "What'n the hail is a-draggin' in here now?" I elected to forgo the last seat at the counter and take a table instead. That gave me a chance to shed the gear and fit in just a bit better. A hearty bacon-and-eggs breakfast outfitted me for the wet ride ahead.

The route for this tour begins just above Kline's. Maryland's Route 36 turns north over Wills Creek at the point where Alt 40 passes through The Narrows. Route 36 ambles through the clutter of the greater Cumberland area for a few miles. You'll make the right onto Route 35, which becomes a nice two-lane country road as you enter Pennsylvania. You don't need a sign to tell you when you've crossed the state line. The quality of the pavement drops sufficiently to tell you. At this point, you really can't make a wrong turn. Dozens of roads branch off to the right and left of Route 96, winding their way through Allegheny farm country, and you'll find something special on each one, whether it is an Amish farmer working the fields with a team of draft horses, or an eight-sided schoolhouse (they were built that way so children couldn't be trapped in a corner by the devil), or a pretty vista from one ridge to the next.

Pennsylvania's backroads are an odd lot. Somewhere past the hamlet of Weyant, Route 96 becomes Route 869. Following Route 869, there are times when it narrows to practically one lane. You would expect it to turn to dirt at any moment. (Actually, there's a corollary to Murphy's Law that governs this: any unexplored backroad between two points will turn to loose gravel and mud one mile past the halfway point.) Fortunately, this one doesn't. The section that threads its way through Blue Knob State Park (www.dcnr.state.pa.us/stateparks/parks/blueknob.aspx) is beautiful. The roadbed is surrounded on both sides by steep hills; moss-covered boulders loom on either side. Towering trees crowd the roadway in places and when the leaves are out fully, you pass through the forest in near twilight even at mid-day.

After a few miles you leave the state forest area and run through a host of small villages and hamlets. You can start looking for the sign for the Johnstown Flood National Memorial. At Sidman, Pennsylvania, Route 160 intersects with PA 869. This is advance notice that you are close to the turn. Continue on PA 869 for about another seven-tenths of a mile to Lake Road. This road takes you directly to the national park site.

It takes a few minutes to acclimate yourself and determine if there is anything here to see. Perched high on a hillside is a National Park Service facility with a collection of artifacts, articles, and displays related to the flood. Nearby is a perfectly restored wooden frame house above a large open field.

Nothing seems particularly amiss here, until you look to the right side of the field, see the remains of a broken earthen dam, and realize this huge meadow was once a lake. In late May 1889, after several days of soaking rain, that dam gave way and millions of cubic feet of water ran through the Conemaugh Valley like water down a waterslide. All the trees, telegraph poles, houses, barns, businesses, and 50 miles of railroad track with locomotives and trains of cars were dumped in a huge jumble of debris against a large stone bridge in downtown Johnstown. Just as the flood waters began to subside and relief was near, the massive pile caught fire, and those who could not scramble to freedom were consumed by the fire.

After surveying the grounds, be sure to check out the visitor center and the electric map. A ten-minute narrated presentation gives you a clear pic-

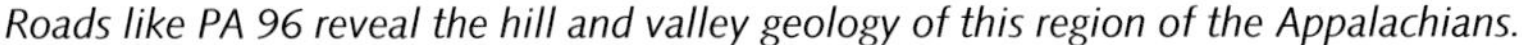

*Roads like PA 96 reveal the hill and valley geology of this region of the Appalachians.*

ture of exactly what happened. One hundred years later, it will still send shivers up your spine.

Departing the park, return to PA 869 via Lake Road. Then turn right on PA 160 to head south.

For my last visit, rain clouds had finally given way to a perfectly clear, sunny day. I knew Route 160 was an enjoyable road, and so I took to the task with some eagerness. I'd been on 160 for about 30 miles and had just passed Interstate 70 when I glanced at a side road. Instinctively my right hand grabbed the front brake and the bike ground to a halt as I stared at the name—Shanksville Road.

Four flights were downed on September 11, 2001, including United Airlines Flight 93 (flt93memorial.org) in rural Pennsylvania. I had no idea this was THE rural Pennsylvania I had read about, but when I saw Shanksville Road, the recognition was instant.

The easiest way to reach the Flight 93 Memorial is to turn right on US 30 west. Two miles ahead, make a left on Buckstown Road. Three miles ahead, a right turn on Skyline Road will bring you to the memorial.

*A portion of the temporary Flight 93 Memorial in Shanksville, Pennsylvania. Photo by Robert Van Allen*

*PA 160 winds through rich pasturelands below Johnstown. A primo route for laid-back touring!*

The emotional reaction of visitors to Johnstown and Shanksville dramatically represents how our reactions are tempered by the passage of time. At Johnstown, the work done by the National Park Service to preserve, document, and interpret what happened gives you a sense of finality and closure. People stroll about the park, visit the museum, and listen to interpretive lectures.

There is no similar sense of closure at the Flight 93 memorial site. I can't describe it to you. It's a feeling you'll have to experience and interpret for yourself.

Following your visit, return to Buckstown Road via Skyline Road. A right turn on Buckstown Road brings you to Lambertsville Road. Turn left to enter Shanksville. Make the left on Main Street. This becomes Corner Stone Road which leads back to Route 160.

Just below Wellersburg, you re-enter Maryland and 160 becomes Route 47. Turn right on Route 36 as it follows Jennings Run through the gap between Piney Mountain. In this direction, MD 36 returns to US 40 in downtown Frostburg and your loop is complete.

# Trip 9 Romancing the Stone

**Distance** *99 miles*
**Terrain** *Sweet stretches of West Virginia backroads and an unsurpassed section of twisties over Cheat Mountain*
**Highlights** *Fairfax Stone, Backbone Mountain Wind Farm, Cathedral State Park*

It was 9 a.m. on a Thursday morning as I rolled into Oakland, Maryland. Traffic in the downtown area had yet to build as I made my way through to the starting point for this loop. Perhaps some folks looked out the window as I did, saw the all-encompassing fog and decided it wasn't worth the effort to get up.

I tapped the digital temperature readout on my Wing as if doing so would urge it to reconsider what it was telling me. Here it was, nearly June, and temps were struggling to get into the forties. I coaxed the gauge a bit more but knew my effort was in vain, so I set off. I knew some good riding

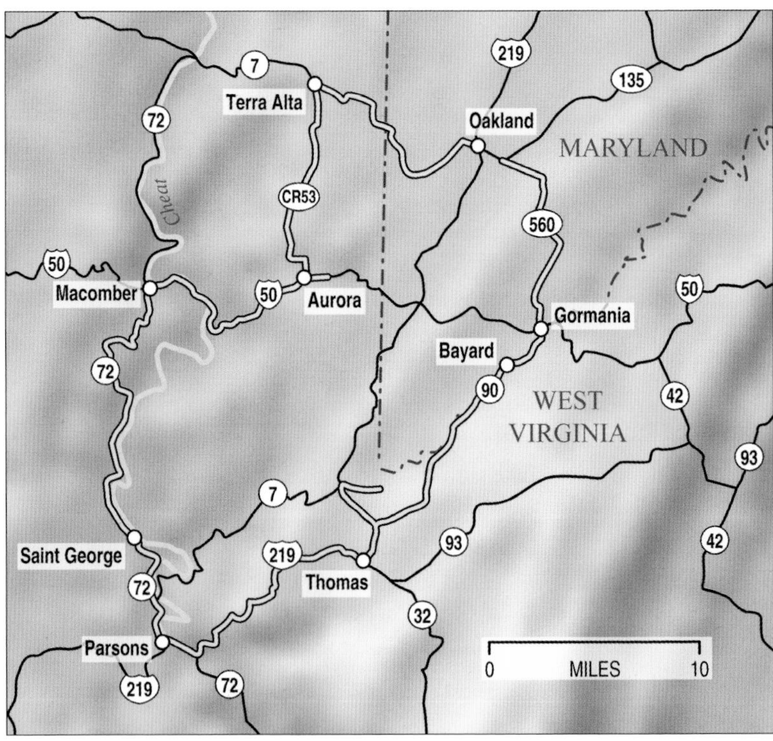

**THE ROUTE FROM OAKLAND**

| | |
|---|---|
| 0 | Start at intersection of MD 135 and MD 560 in Oakland, Maryland |
| 9.2 | Left onto US 50 at Gormania |
| 9.3 | Right onto WV 90 |
| 22.2 | Right onto US 219 north |
| 24.4 | Right onto CR 9 |
| 26.5 | Arrive Fairfax Stone |
| 28.6 | Left onto US 219 south |
| 45.6 | Right onto WV 72 north |
| 65.8 | Right onto US 50 |
| 76.8 | Arrive Aurora State Park |
| 77.7 | Right onto CR 53 (Terra Alta Road) |
| 87.9 | Right onto WV 7 east |
| 98.4 | Arrive Oakland, Maryland |

awaited me and that thought was enough to compensate somewhat for the chill. But I was darn sure wishing I had taken a few extra minutes at home to install the harness for my electric vest.

This route and its mileage estimates are based out of Oakland, Maryland. Oakland (pop. 1,900) is the county seat for Garrett County. Like other towns in western Maryland, Oakland's heydays coincided with the fortunes of the railroads. When timber and coal industries thrived, so did the town. Later, it became a tourist destination as one in a string of high-mountain resorts. With the advent of automobile travel, the area fell into decline. But there are some towns that refuse to give in to hard times. Folks still take pride in their town and find ways to adapt to new economic realities. I've seen that pride in places like Webster Springs, West Virginia, and it's visible here too.

On the east side of Oakland along MD 135, Route 560 turns due south and cuts through a series of undulating hills arriving at Gorman, Maryland, and US Route 50. The left turn onto US 50 brings you into West Virginia and Gorman's counterpart, Gormania. (Sounds like the title of a Friday night, horror show, triple feature, doesn't it?) Gorman and Gormania were once the location of a large tannery operation. The brick smokestack base is all that remains of the tannery now.

Turn right on WV 90 to continue the route. Route 90 loosely follows the

*Giant hemlocks dominate the Aurora State Park in Aurora, West Virginia. Some specimens are more than 500 years old.*

North Branch of the Potomac and toward its end, culminates in a long, straight stretch of road topping out over a few low hills. As you stop at the intersection of route 90 and US 219 you might well see a person or two on the left shoulder with a car full of milk jugs collecting water from a roadside spring. Scenes like this are fairly common in the Appalachians. Clear mountain water gushing out of a pipe sure looks like a source for a refreshing drink, but it's probably not a good idea. Even if the water looks crystal clear, it can contain contaminants from mine run-off or other man-made chemicals used in the area.

Turn north on US 219 and in just about two miles you'll see a sign showing the turnoff for the Fairfax Stone marker, County Route 9. The road into the marker isn't great, but is easily manageable on any bike.

The story of the Fairfax Stone (gowv.com/attractionsfairfaxstone.htm) goes back nearly 400 years to 1649 when King Charles II granted a tract of land to Lord Culpeper, one of his allies during a period of civil war in England. From his exile in France, King Charles couldn't make the grant legally binding until he returned to the throne eleven years later. It was a hundred years before Culpeper's heir, Thomas, the Sixth Lord of Fairfax, actually got his hands on the land.

According to the grant, all the land between the headwaters of the Rapidan and Potomac Rivers were to be included. Survey parties were sent out by several sides with an interest in the matter and in 1746 all parties finally agreed on boundaries that awarded Fairfax a swath of land over five million acres in size.

The marker is a replacement for the original which lasted about a hundred years, but the spring that served as the boundary marker still gurgles away. The westernmost border of Maryland is marked by the stone, but the stone doesn't actually represent the Maryland-West Virginia border. The spring at this spot flows west, then doubles back to head east. So the boundary is at a point about a mile north of the stone, where the creek passes the line drawn north from the stone.

You probably noticed something out of the ordinary on your way to the Fairfax Stone marker. That would be wind-powered turbines that are part of the Backbone Mountain Wind Farm. These are a few of about 40 turbines that line the ridges in this area comprising what is currently the largest wind

*Fairfax Stone marks the headwaters of the mighty Potomac. At this point, you can straddle the river.*

*WV 72 north of Parsons is one of hundreds of great routes in West Virginia.*

farm on the East Coast. One blade on the turbine weighs about 15,000 pounds and at peak operating speed, each turbine can crank out about 1.5 megawatts. Running continuously, that would power about five hundred homes.

When CR 9 returns to US 219, turn left to head south. We haven't talked much about the roads on the route thus far, but this is the part of the route where points of interest take a back seat and the riding becomes interesting. I've ridden many sections of US 219 and the stretch from Fairfax Stone to Parsons is a great one. There are a lot of well-cambered turns that invite you to work the sides of your tires.

In Parsons, follow US 219 through a short stretch of downtown area. At the light, US 219 makes a left. You'll want to turn right and follow WV 72 north out of town. This stretch of WV 72 is a sharp contrast to the other stretch of 72 between Canaan Valley and Hendricks, West Virginia. That section of road is barely one lane wide in spots. This 72, though hardly a primary road, is a good stretch of road and positions you well for a fun run to come next on US 50. At Macomber, turn right on US 50 and head east.

This section of US 50 follows the Cheat River and after a couple of miles begins an ascent of Cheat Mountain. You'll encounter a series of high-speed sweepers with great sight lines that encourage an assertive riding style. Continue through Aurora and start looking for Cathedral State Park (cathedralstatepark.com).

Cathedral State Park features 133 acres of old-growth forest including virgin hemlock trees standing up to 90 feet tall and 21 feet in circumference. Stands of forest like this once dominated the Appalachians and the few pockets that escaped the saw offer you a rare opportunity to enjoy the mountain forest as it once appeared. The park is laced with easy hiking trails, so I encourage you to hop off the bike and explore this unique area.

The return to Oakland begins by following US 50 west out of the park back to Aurora, a distance of about one mile. In Aurora, make a right on County Road 53, also known as Terra Alta Road and Aurora Pike. On your turn it looks as if you're heading down someone's private driveway, but after a few tenths, the road widens a bit. Curves abound on this stretch, but the pastoral scenery is the real attraction along this road.

Aurora Pike ends in Terra Alta (prestoncounty.com) at which point you'll turn right on WV 7 to head east toward Oakland.

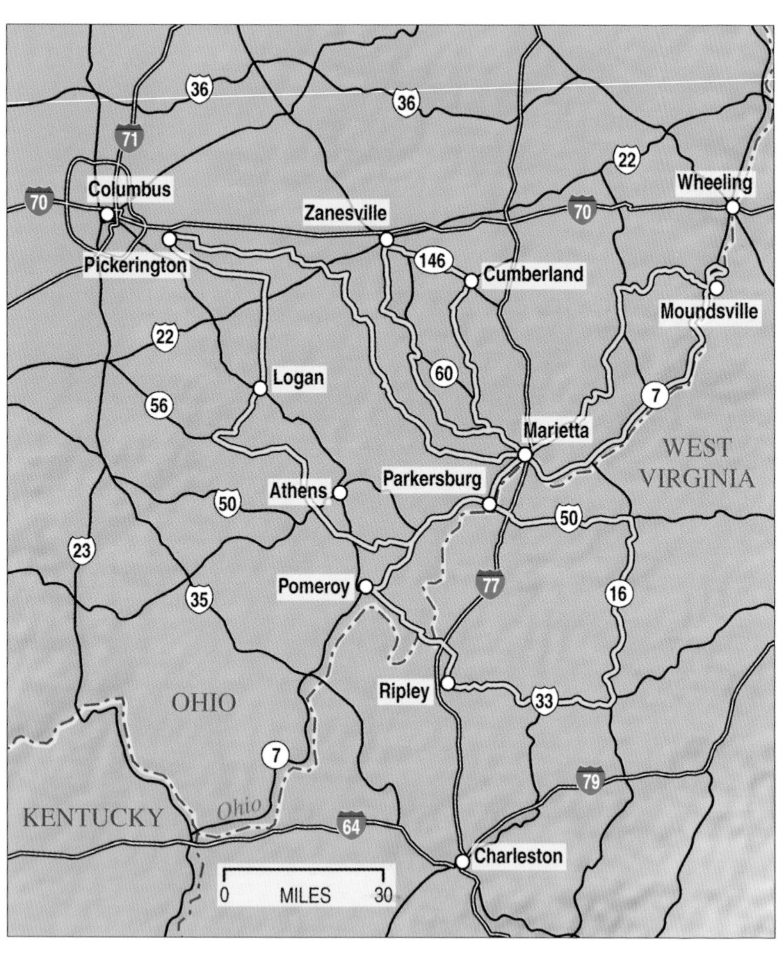
36
36
71
70
Columbus
Zanesville
70
22
Wheeling
Pickerington
146
Cumberland
Moundsville
22
Logan
60
56
7
Marietta
WEST
VIRGINIA
Athens
Parkersburg
50
50
23
Pomeroy
77
16
35
Ripley
OHIO
33
7
79
KENTUCKY
Ohio
64
Charleston
0 MILES 30

# The New Frontier

## *Home Sweet Home*

Imagine you're a settler beginning the great migration to the west in the late 1700s. You're bone-weary, having coaxed your team of horses over dozens of mountain ranges through a primeval forest following little but a footpath. You've fought off bears and jaguars, and exchanged more than a few mean glances with angry natives. Half your possessions are floating down the Youghiogheny River because your wagon fell into a hole and broke a wheel during the crossing.

It's been an arduous journey, but you're the lucky one, right? Your neighbor was washed away the week before in a flash flood. Another woman on the journey went blind after eating poisonous berries. Children have vanished in the night, stolen by local tribes. You've had your share of hardships, but it could be worse.

*Downing House Inn in Middleport is a great place to launch your journeys.*

At least your family is intact. They're mad as hell for being uprooted from their comfortable farm home in the Cumberland Valley, but they're all with you. And besides, you were told that once you got over the mountains and reached the Ohio River, all your troubles would be over. There'd be nothing but flat, fertile farmland ahead, ready for cultivating. Soil so rich, seeds would practically sprout on contact. Why, to hear tell, it's practically a farmer's paradise.

Now, after weeks of sweating, swearing, shooting, and sawing your way through the woods, you've just descended the last hill and stand at the eastern bank of the Ohio. Ready to take that view you've been waiting for. Wait just a minute. As you look across the river, all you can see beyond are more hills. There's no rich farmland waiting for you. Only more dense forest. Presumably, more bears, wildcats, natives, and bad berries. Turning around is not an attractive option, but neither is going forward.

Guess what, honey. We're home.

That place called home by some of the earliest pioneers was Marietta, Ohio. Formed in 1788 as the first permanent settlement west of the Ohio River, Marietta marked the first incursion into the Northwest Territory. The town lies along the banks of two rivers: the Ohio and the Muskingum. Towns like Marietta often formed at strategic intersections like this because waterways were the interstate highways of early American history.

For us though, what makes the whole region worth visiting on a motorcycle, is the distinct difference in riding experiences on either side of the Ohio river. As you explore east of the river in West Virginia, you'll find the usual great Appalachian riding experience. Twisty roads over high mountain passes, switchbacks, scenic vistas, the works.

The Ohio riding experience is vastly different and a heck of a lot of fun. That difference is largely due to the height and shape of the hills. In the higher mountains, it's often necessary to shape the land in order to have enough flat land to lay a road. The road is often carved into the mountains.

That's not the case west of the river. In southeastern Ohio, the mountains are noticeably lower, yet the landscape remains restless. Look at the area on a map and you can clearly see the terrain undulates with countless hills and valleys, joining and countering at endless angles like waves trapped in a bottle (tinyurl.com/motojourneys23).

Rather than carving out paths for roads, the routes around here were simply draped across and around the hills as you might decorate a cake. The end result certainly tastes like dessert. The southeastern region of Ohio offers, flat-out, some of the most purely-for-fun motorcycle riding I've experienced.

*Something old. Something new. Something borrowed. Something loud.*

The ups, downs, twists, and turns come non-stop, one after another, requiring you to pay constant attention to what lies ahead. You may find this hard to believe, but there are many portions of road you can ride at 40 mph and feel fully entertained. Yes, in Ohio. I don't know where else in the Appalachians I can say that about, save US 129 at Deal's Gap and Virginia's Route 16.

If you are looking for a vacation with a focus on riding, or a great spot for a club outing, southeastern Ohio is the ticket.

This riverside location makes Marietta distinctly different from other landlocked towns in our Appalachian journeys. Bridges, boats, and waterways are common themes, replacing the hills, valleys, and vistas of the mountains. Downtown Marietta is filled with mom-and-pop shops, dining, and hotels.

A popular destination for refreshment is the Marietta Brewing Company (mariettabrewingcompany.com). Marietta's strategic river location made it

*There's more square footage in my moto-camper than there is in my home office.*

a popular spot for pre-prohibition breweries. MBC carries on that tradition with an ever-changing lineup of craft-brewed, adult beverages.

Walk through the downtown area and you'll find other dining options. Austyn's (740-374-8188) is a casual upscale restaurant on Front Street near the waterfront. Just a block up is the Town House, a well-known local watering hole (740-374-5073).

If you don't mind floating and eating, take advantage of the weekend dinner cruise on the Valley Gem Sternwheeler (valleygemsternwheeler.com). It's a good idea to reserve your spot ahead of time because the dinner cruise, typically offered on Saturday evenings, is often sold out. The Valley Gem also offers a sightseeing tour daily during the summer months and a number of special cruises throughout the season. Check the Valley Gem's website for exact dates and times.

Lodging options are plentiful in the immediate Marietta area. A dozen or so chain hotels are in the immediate city vicinity or located along the I-77 corridor just across the river and east of town.

If you're looking for something more upscale and in the center of things, the Lafayette Hotel (lafayettehotel.com) is the landmark hotel in downtown Marietta. Its triangular configuration is built along the confluence of the Muskingum and Ohio Rivers, offering you a nearly guaranteed river view. The hotel, one of the last built during the riverboat era, opened July 1,

1918, and was named in honor of the Marquis de Lafayette who visited the area—in 1825. That must have been a memorable visit.

The area surrounding Marietta offers an interesting mix of private accommodations. For example, you could spend the night in the farm home of a Revolutionary War solider at the Bramble Creek Bed and Breakfast (ohioriverinn.com) or bed down with the alpacas—or more accurately, near the alpacas—in the Cottage at Windswept Farm (windsweptfarmalpacas.com). Downtown options include The Cottage on Washington (740-374-4439) and the elegant Victorian House on Hamar Hill (740-374-5451).

Camping offers some interesting options. On my last tour of the area, I stayed at the Forked Run State Park. This park is situated along the Ohio about thirty miles southwest of Marietta (In these parts, by the way, "Forked" is a two-syllable word "fork-ed").

This time I was traveling with a pop-up camper, so I opted to stay in a section of the campground with electrical service. This allowed me to power the satellite radio at night to pick up baseball games and enjoy the comfort of a fan. Mid-August is just what you would expect—hot. However, being near the water, the campground cooled off nicely at night, an aid to keeping the mosquitoes at bay. Setting up the camper, I was surrounded by a black cloud of biters, wondering if I'd made a terrible mistake. By early evening, between the cooler air and the constant breeze created by the fan, the buggers had left to find an easier snack.

Camping is allowed in designated areas in the Wayne National Forest northeast of Marietta. A primitive spot like the Haught Run Recreation Area offer no facilities, but campsites are located along the creek in the shadow of a covered bridge. And you can hardly beat the price.

I know, your non-riding friends and co-workers are going to laugh when you tell them you're headed to Ohio for vacation. Obviously, they've only seen Ohio from the interstate. Get off the well-worn paths of the Buckeye State and you'll enjoy some of the most twisted trails of pavement you'll find anywhere in the United States.

You won't find as many grand vistas as the eastern slopes and you won't have the mile-high riding experiences of the southern mountains, but you'd best have a fresh set of rubber shoes on that iron pony of yours. Because here, in these crazy, jumbled western foothills of the Appalachians, you're gonna need 'em.

# Trip 10 Why Ohio? Loop

**Distance** *133 miles*
**Terrain** *Low hills, relentless curves, and 90-degree turns*
**Highlights** *Zanesville Pottery, the "Y" Bridge, Muskingum Locks, the Wilds*

Larry Grodsky was right. Ripping through the first five miles of my first route in southeastern Ohio, I immediately understood why Larry had waxed so eloquently about this region which is little known among riders. A bead of sweat was beginning to form on my brow as I found myself working the bike from side to side. Not what I was expecting.

Larry, who'd penned *Rider* magazine's Stayin' Safe column for decades was a vocal proponent of this hilly region where Pennsylvania, West Virginia, and Ohio meet. Pennsylvania and West Virginia I understood, but

**THE ROUTE FROM MARIETTA**

| | |
|---|---|
| 0 | Leave Marietta on Route 676 |
| 22 | Turn right on SR 792 |
| 27.5 | Continue straight on SR 266 |
| 29.8 | Continue on SR 377 |
| 36.9 | Right on SR 78 |
| 38.9 | Left on SR 669 |
| 52.6 | Right on SR 555 |
| 64.0 | Right at bridge |
| 64.2 | Left on SR 60, arrive Zanesville |
| 66.0 | Leaving Zanesville, turn right on SR 146 |
| 86.0 | Right on SR 340 |
| 91.3 | Left on SR 284 |
| 99.0 | Bear right on SR 83 |
| 99.2 | SR 78 joins. Continue southeast on SR 78/83 |
| 102.0 | At split, turn right on SR 83 |
| 111.5 | Left on SR 60 |
| 113.2 | Right on SR 339 in Beverly |
| 121.7 | Left on SR 676 |
| 133.0 | Arrive Marietta |

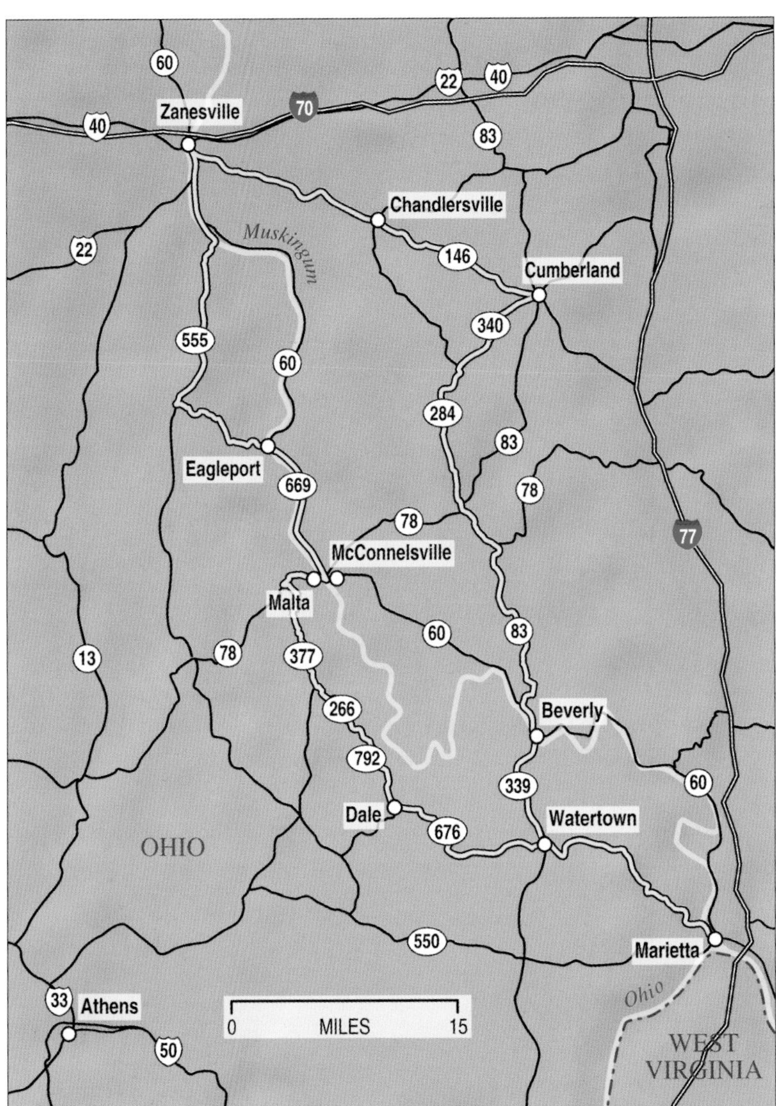


Ohio? Who rides in Ohio but Ohioans? After years of hearing other riders echo his sentiments, I decided to put my assumptions and prejudices aside and visit the area, just for kicks. Maybe I'd map a ride out of it. Maybe not.

Looking over my stack of maps, I decided to put together a tentative route that would hit a wide sampling of the region's offerings, a mixture of state and county roads from Marietta to Zanesville and back, on opposing sides of the Muskingum River. From what I could see on topographical maps and satellite images from Google Maps, it looked like a good trial run.

Those first five miles were the beginning of a trip that turned my Appalachian experience upside down. Already, simple little County Route 676 heading due west out of Marietta was providing more entertainment than I was expecting. More times that I could count, already I was gettin' jiggy with it: heel the bike over to the left, accelerate, now lean right. Downshift, now turn. Upshift—no, downshift—lean, steady throttle, throw bike the other way, roll on, roll off. Rarely could I predict what was coming next. What I could see clearly was this would be a workout. And a thoroughly enjoyable one at that. I decided to call this tour the "Why Ohio? Loop" because after you ride this route, you'll know.

As I learned, and as you may notice, establishing an easy riding rhythm along these Ohio backroads requires more skill and observation than roads in other parts of the region. Ridden at speed, they are technically challenging. Elsewhere, along the Blue Ridge Parkway, for example, your riding style relaxes to match the contours of the road. Almost without thinking, the bike seems to aim for the perfect apex and rolls through the curves without effort.

That's just not going to happen on an Ohio byway until you've spent some time adjusting to tricks like the unmarked 90-degree turns, the relentless up-and-down, roller-coaster hills, and my favorite, the off-camber right-

*John takes a moment to adjust the landslide detector on his FJR.*

*Marietta is situated along the Ohio and Muskingum Rivers.*

hander, or left-hander, or left-then-right-hander, that lies out of sight just beyond the crest of the hill. You'll become very good friends with that one.

So, as I was saying, Route 676 is just a little taste of what the rest of Ohio riding is all about. From the outset, as you motor up a steep hill and out of town, you'll notice the road wanders aimlessly across rolling plains and hills in repeated succession. Indications of town life—people, buildings and traffic—disappear almost immediately and you're soon into the farming heartland of the Midwest.

At the point where Route 676 intersects with Route 339, turn left and follow the combined route for a few tenths, then turn right to resume your ride on Route 676. At Dale, turn right on Route 792. When you arrive at the intersection with State Route 266, continue straight through the intersection. You will now be traveling on Route 266 through Morgan County.

You might not know the name if I said the county was named for Daniel Morgan, a successful Revolutionary War general. But if I told you Morgan developed the Kentucky long rifle, that might ring a bell. Morgan's innovative rifle was accurate enough to allow colonial soldiers to pick off British redcoats at a longer distance than with older muskets, giving the rebels a significant tactical advantage.

As you motor along, you'll notice you are offered a fresh view to the horizon every time you top a hill. This land uniquely combines the characteristic rolling hills of eastern states with long vistas common in western states.

*Leave early on this ride so you can spend time strolling through Zanesville. It's a pretty and walkable town.*

This is due to the fact that much of the land is cultivated, so as you top out on a hill, there is little to obstruct your view.

Route 266 ends on Route 377. Bear to the right at the stop sign and continue north on Route 377 and when this route meets State Route 78, turn right toward Malta. If you need a breakfast bite, follow Route 78 across the river into the town square in McConnelsville and stop at the Blue Bell Diner.

Retrace your steps to Malta on the west side of the river and turn onto Route 669 north. This route follows the Muskingum for a few miles. The Muskingum River wanders through the low foothills of the Appalachians for some 110 miles before it joins the Ohio River at Marietta. Translated roughly by some as "eye of the elk," the Muskingum has long played an important role in the development of the region.

One of the benefactors of that river travel was Zanesville, Ohio, our next stop. To get there, continue following Route 669 north. When it connects with Route 555, turn right and follow 555 into town. If you ask someone who's ridden southeastern Ohio, one of the most often mentioned roads is this one. The northern portion that's part of this route is entertaining but brief. Trip 13, the Hall of Fame Loop, covers the majority of Route 555.

To most folks rolling by on I-70 just north of town, Zanesville is just another spot to grab a bite and gas up, but coming in from the south of town offers a different perspective. Zanesville's downtown features wide avenues, striking and varied architecture, and dozens of small shops to explore. I caught a light lunch and ran up and down some of the streets to check out the city.

Zanesville is billed as the "Pottery Capital of the World," owning largely to the abundance of high-quality clay in the region. You'll see public examples of regional pottery all around and a number of pottery shops downtown. If you're looking for the end-all pottery shop, that would be the Zanesville Pottery (www.zanesvillepottery.com), located just a bit east of the downtown area on Route 40. Go north through town on Route 60, then turn right to head east on US 40 just before you get to the Interstate. Follow US 40 about five miles east and you'll see the well-signed entrance on your left.

Zanesville is also known for an unusual feature in its downtown area, a Y-shaped bridge that is one of only two examples in the world. The span bridges the confluence of the Muskingum and Licking Rivers. For a great view of the bridge and downtown Zanesville, drive to the middle of the bridge (West Main Street, US 40) and turn left. Just over the bridge, turn left on Pine Street, then the second left which is Grandview Avenue. Follow Grandview Avenue for a block or two and the entrance to the overlook will be on your left.

Riding out of Zanesville, pick up Route 146 to the east. In a matter of just a minute or two, you'll be out of town and ready to kick out the highway pegs. Route 146 is straighter than some of the other roads you've ridden, but the high-speed sweepers encourage you to wick it up just a little. Unlike some of the backroads, there will be no hidden surprises or unmarked hairpin turns.

As you near the next turn just outside Cumberland, Ohio, you'll pass by an unusual facility called The Wilds (www.thewilds.com). The Wilds is a wildlife conservation center housed on nearly 10,000 acres of reclaimed mine land. Surrounded by rolling hills, The Wilds land is nearly table flat. This created a landscape similar to savannah, so you'll find animals common to that type of environment, including rhinos, antelope, and giraffes. The center offers dozens of programs throughout the year as well as safari

*Zanesville is home to one of only two Y-shaped bridges. The other is in China.*

tours throughout the day. Not only that, a small group can rent the twelve-person lodge. Imagine having a weekend club ride with a stayover here!

Just past The Wilds, you'll come up on Route 340. Turn right and follow this road over a portion of the reclaimed land. Coming across this section of road for the first time is a real surprise. Cresting a hill, the land suddenly turns completely flat and the road stretches straight ahead. It's like you've blinked and found yourself mysteriously transported to the high plains of Montana.

You'll be happy to know that some of the day's best riding is near at hand. Route 340 ends on Route 284. Turn left on 284 to follow it south. From the high plains, you'll re-enter dense forest and resume the familiar roller-coaster ride that you came to enjoy. When you join up with Route 83, stay straight and pick up 83. After a short distance, Route 83 intersects with Route 78. Turn left to stay on the combined Route 78/83. Once again, stay with Route 83 to the right when the road forks a few miles down the road.

What a great stretch of road. Like Route 146, Route 83 had just enough curves and contours to entertain, but was just straight enough that you could dial up the throttle a little and hit the corners harder than other backroads. No kidding, by the time I reached Route 60, I had a grin from ear to ear. I gave serious thought to turning around and riding it again.

Turn left on Route 60 and run the short distance to Beverly. I stopped there for a break and found myself at Lock #4 on the Muskingum River. I couldn't help notice a fellow standing on the lock wall turning a crank, so I walked over to check it out. About 30 feet below, a group of riders on personal watercraft were holed up in the lock, waiting for the water level to drop so they could continue downstream.

This hand-operated lock system is the last of its kind in the U.S. It consists of a series of eleven locks built 1836 and 1841 and was originally developed to allow steamboats to navigate the Muskingum. The development of the lock system contributed to the growth of Zanesville, offering the city an inexpensive way to export goods. The locks are now operated only during temperate weather and on weekends to allow personal boats to navigate the river. All but Lock #11 are still in use.

There were a few of us standing around as Jeff pushed a lever around and around, causing the lower lock gate to open slowly and drain. As he walked in circles, he started telling the "Wedding Story." By the time he finished I was laughing so hard, I was spitting soda through my nose. I can't do the story justice, but it went something like this:

Years ago when boats moved in greater volume up and down the river, the spectacle would draw an audience, especially on weekends. Some 20

*A worker opens one of the last hand-operated locks in the country.*

years back on a Saturday afternoon, a wedding party passed through on Lock #4 as Jeff was tending the lock. Among the onlookers was one fellow who was roaring drunk, yelling catcalls at the bride and tossing whatever he could find. Thinking he'd play the ultimate joke on the wedding party, the drunk lowered his pants began to relieve himself, causing a stir on the boat.

Jeff wasn't sure what to do about this because he had to mind the lock. But he soon realized the problem would take care of itself. "What that guy couldn't see, because he was so drunk, was that the boat was going up river. So it was rising in the lock," Jeff said, his face widening into a broad grin. "When they got close enough, that bride and groom and a couple other people reached up and grabbed the guy by the ankles and pulled him into the boat. I opened the lock as fast as I could and the boat sailed off with that drunk still on board."

And I'm sure they all lived happily ever after.

Speaking of happy endings, at this point in the route, you are nearing your return to Marietta. In town, turn right on OH 339 and follow it back to the point where it intersects with Route 676. Turning left will take you back to Marietta. If you happen to be staying in Parkersburg, continue straight on OH 339. This will come out right at the point where US 50 crosses the river into West Virginia.

By the time you've completed this loop, I think you'll have a clear picture why anyone who's ridden in southeastern Ohio will recommend it. If anybody asks "Why Ohio?" this ride is the answer.

# Trip 11 Big House Loop

**Distance** *156 miles*
**Terrain** *Numerous hill-topping blind curves followed by miles of sparsely populated areas, ending with a river run*
**Highlights** *State Route 26, Moundsville Penitentiary, Wayne National Forest, Sistersville Ferry*

Spooks, spirits, and apparitions play a large role in the folk tales of Appalachian life. Throughout your journeys in the Appalachians you'll encounter dozens of tales of unexplained events and unsettled spirits, haunted mansions, ghostly sightings, strange lights—you know, the usual run-of-the-mill, haunted-house stuff. But once in a while you'll encounter something

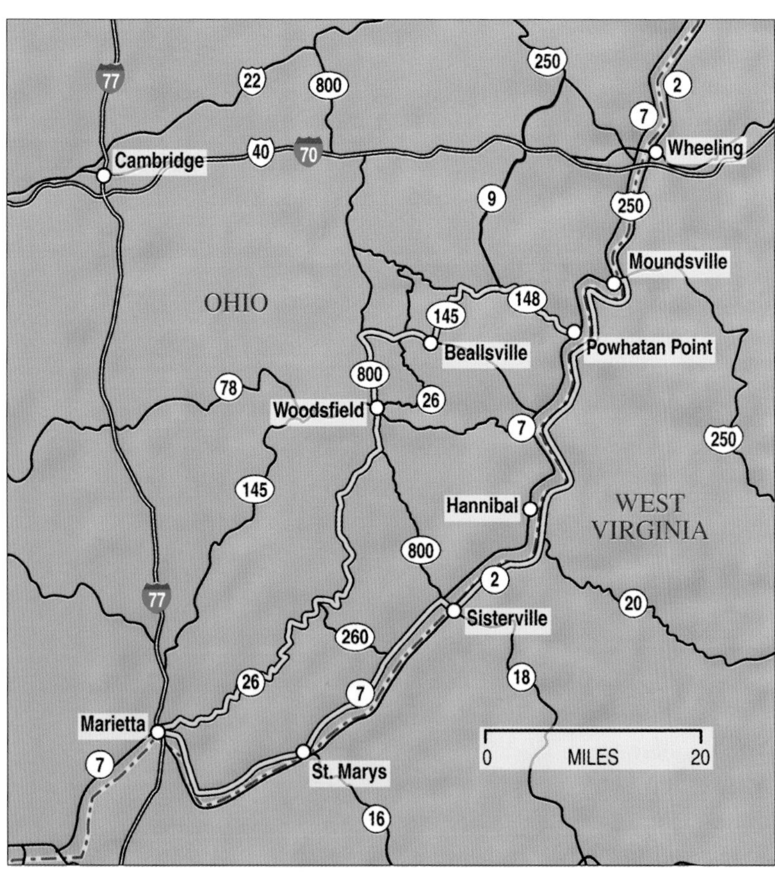

**THE ROUTE FROM MARIETTA**

| | |
|---|---|
| 0 | Leave Marietta on Route 26 |
| 43.4 | Turn left on SR 800 |
| 53.0 | Turn right on SR 145 |
| 59.0 | Turn left to remain on SR 145 |
| 65.5 | Turn right on SR 148 |
| 79.0 | Left on SR 7 |
| 86.3 | Right on 872 (follow signs to Moundsville) |
| 86.5 | Cross bridge into Moundsville, West Virginia |
| 87.0 | Cross Route 2 at light, becomes Twelfth Street |
| 87.2 | Left on Jefferson Street |
| 87.7 | Arrive Moundsville State Penitentiary |
| 88.2 | South to Twelfth Street, turn right |
| 88.4 | Left on WV 2 |
| 123.4 | Arrive Sistersville, right on Elizabeth Street |
| 123.5 | Left on Riverside |
| 123.7 | Arrive Sistersville Ferry |
| 123.8 | Left on SR 7 |
| 156.0 | Arrive Marietta |

that feels real, that genuinely unsettling feeling of an presence not seen. The sensation of cold fingers gripping your neck. Something tugging on your soul. Hey, sounds like a fun trip!

This loop is centered around a trip through the Wayne National Forest in Ohio with a visit to the Moundsville State Penitentiary of West Virginia. From 1878 to 1995, the state pen at Moundsville developed a reputation as one of the most violent institutions in U.S. history. It isn't a pretty picture, but it sure is fascinating.

This is one of the longer loops on the tour and the tour at Moundsville is comprehensive, so you'll want to get an early start in the morning. Right out of the box, State Route 26 out of Marietta aims to please. I'm going to go out on a limb here and say that Route 26 is one of the most relentlessly curvy roads in the nation. It just doesn't let up.

On your ride along Route 26, you'll quickly notice the prevalence of oil derricks along the route. The first commercial oil well in Ohio began pumping in 1859, just a few months after the nation's first modern well began production in Pennsylvania. By 1896, Ohio was riven with well holes,

*Riding pal John Bark tames the curves on Route 26 aboard his smooth-riding Yamaha.*

and had become the nation's largest oil producer, cranking out some 23 million barrels of oil that year. (Current world oil consumption is about 20 million barrels a day.) Ohio's production quickly fell off after 1896, but even today traces of the industry are evident, especially in this part of the state.

Every pumpjack you see marks the head of a stripper well. Stripper wells pull the leftover oil out of a well once the main reserve has been extracted. Most of these wells produce less than ten barrels of oil per day, some just a few barrels per week or month. However, when oil prices run up as they did between 2007 and 2008, even a few barrels a month can add up and a stripper well can produce small amounts of oil for decades. In fact, one out of every six barrels of oil in U.S. production comes from wells of this type.

At the junction with Route 800, turn left and continue to follow Route 26/800 into Woodsfield. Since we were just on the topic of fossil fuels, that reminds me: if you didn't leave Marietta on a full tank, top off in Woodsfield. Remarkably, there are few stations along this portion of the route. Not all have premium gas (my bike needs it) and not all are open on Sundays, as I discovered.

On the north side of town, turn left and follow Route 800 out of town. Between here and Beallsville, the route straightens out. You'll still enjoy long vistas across a mix of farmland and forest, but you won't have to concentrate quite as hard on the turns. It's a nice change after Route 26. Turn right onto Route 145 and continue to follow this road through Beallsville until it ends on Route 148, West Captina Highway. I liked this road because it reminded me a little of the routes in eastern Kentucky, but the roads were in better shape. Route 148 often runs against the edge of a shallow valley, tracing the valley floor at the foot of a hill. Route 148 ends on Route 7 at Powhatan Point. If you've been riding for a long time, this is a good spot to get off the bike for a break and a stretch. It's just a few miles from here to Moundsville.

*Imagine walking through the doors into this place. Many who did never came out.*

*No matter how stern your expression, John, you'll never be a badass. Sorry.*

Moundsville takes its name from the Grave Creek Mound, an Indian burial site. The Grave Creek site is the largest conical burial mound in the U.S. and was chronicled by Lewis and Clark at the beginning of their continental journey. To enter the town from Ohio, go north on Route 7 just a few miles from Powhatan Point and follow the signs for the bridge to Moundsville over Route 872. This becomes 12th Street in Moundsville. Go straight through the first light at WV 2. If you turn left just ahead on Tomlinson, you'll arrive at the burial mound. Or, go just a little farther, turn left on Jefferson, and you'll find the prison.

From the first glimpse you catch of the Moundsville State Penitentiary, you can see it was built to intimidate. Its soaring castellated Gothic architecture with turrets and battlements was modeled after the prison in Joliet, Illinois, featured in the film *The Blues Brothers*. Plans for the prison were drawn up in early days of West Virginia's statehood, gained as a result of the Civil

War. The early capital was located in Wheeling in the northern panhandle of the state. The Moundsville site was convenient, just ten miles downriver.

In its early days, the Moundsville prison was nearly self-sufficient, generating revenue from products produced at the prison and powered by a prisoner-operated coal mine just one mile away. Over time, however, conditions deteriorated and Moundsville gained a reputation for extreme violence. Over the course of its 120-year history, the prison has documented 998 deaths, many of them violent.

Make time in your schedule to take the guided tour. It runs almost two hours and you'll see nearly every aspect of the prison. Even if you aren't a big believer in ghosts, this place will still give you the chills. Between the tiny five-by-seven cells that once housed three prisoners each, to the vivid narrative of past events offered by the guides, you get a clear picture of life in this big house. It leaves little room for wondering, even among skeptics, why the place has such a creepy feel.

Maybe it's the stark contrast in circumstances that makes the ride back to home base so enjoyable. Lingering thoughts about what it must've been like to spend time at Moundsville makes your bike seem a little lighter and faster, and the ride a little more fun.

Or it could be the roads. For the return from Moundsville, you have a few options and they're all a good time. I'd suggest one of two possible routes. If it's later in the day and you're a little tired from the ride and the tour, take it easy and just follow WV 2 south to Sistersville. Then, hop on the ferry to cross the river into Ohio. A ferry has been operating at Sistersville since 1815 and is the last such crossing on the river between West Virginia and Ohio. The Sistersville ferry is open 6 a.m. to 6 p.m. weekdays, and 9 a.m. to 6 p.m. on weekends. Once across the river, you can follow Route 7 into Marietta for dinner and a relaxing evening.

On the other hand, if you're looking for just a little more excitement and have time to cover it, turn right on State Route 800 which is almost right across the road from the ferry. This part of Route 800 is a blast as it rapidly ascends the hills leading away from the river. This returns to Route 26 which you can follow south to Marietta. Or, a few miles farther down Route 7, hang a right on Route 260 for an even prettier backroad return to Route 26.

The bottom line is, you won't be disappointed with just about any return route to Marietta you choose. After all, anything beats spending the night in the Big House.

# Trip 12 The Nickel Tour

**Distance** *187 miles*
**Terrain** *River flats, followed by traditional high-mountain runs through northwestern West Virginia*
**Highlights** *Downing House, Bridge of Honor, Route 16, Berdine's Five and Dime*

Some years ago, my day job had me running back and forth between Washington, D.C., and Cleveland, Ohio. It was a short flight, so we frequently traveled on a twin-turboprop commuter plane.

Flying a prop job wasn't the easiest ride because small planes can't fly high enough to miss most of the turbulence of churning air currents. Over the mountains, there are nothing but churning air currents. Air sickness bags were often missing from the seat back pocket in front of me. However, fly-

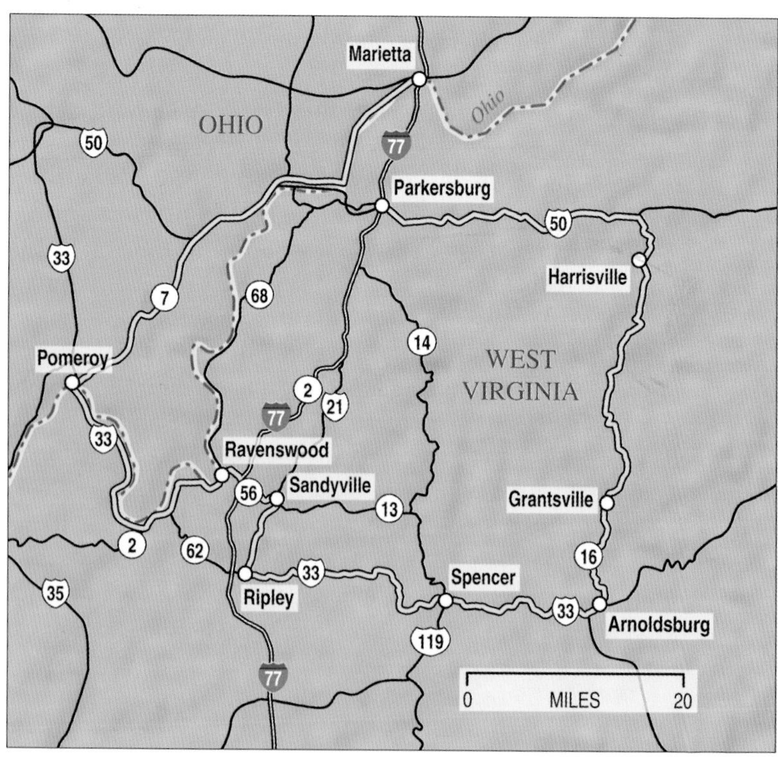

**THE ROUTE FROM MARIETTA**

| | |
|---|---|
| 0 | Leave Marietta on Route 7 |
| 45.0 | Turn left on US 33 |
| 63.0 | Left on WV 68/US 33 |
| 63.5 | Left on US 33 |
| 65.8 | Continue straight to Old WV 56 |
| 69.4 | Right on Old US 21 |
| 75.7 | Left on US 33 |
| 116.7 | Left on WV 16 |
| 160.0 | Left on US 50 |
| 187.0 | Arrive Parkersburg |

ing low did have one perk. As we crisscrossed the Alleghenies, I had the perfect vantage point for scoping out potential rides on the ground.

Everything about this region looked inviting. Even at altitude, the view ahead was an unbroken series of mountain ridges. Mature, blue-green forests and open, lush meadows. Sparsely populated and lightly trafficked. Valleys and passes laced with dozens of little two-lane, blue highways.

If you're up for it, I thought we'd visit there today and see if it's as nice on the ground as it appears to be from the air. This route is mapped to include roads in northwestern West Virginia, looping back into Marietta. Along the way you'll visit a busy riverside town, stop by a business still thriving after a hundred years, and dine at a restaurant where you'll become part of the family when you walk through the doors.

If you didn't catch breakfast on the way out of Marietta, you can grab a bite in Pomeroy at the beginning of this loop. Follow OH 7 south out of Marietta until you reach the junction with US 33. Continue straight onto OH 7A until it ends on OH 124. A left on 124 followed shortly by a right on OH 833 will bring you into Pomeroy, a small town draped along the west bank of the Ohio. (Fun Pomeroy facts: because of it's hilly terrain, Pomeroy is the only town in the U.S. with a courthouse that has a ground-level entrance at each of its three stories. And, it's the only community in the country that has no four-way intersections. You're amazed at my ability to ferret out the essential nuggets on these towns, aren't you?)

This area also makes a good base camp for exploring the region. If you're around in the evenings, try dinner at the Wild Horse Cafe (www.thewildhorsecafe.net). Their steaks stack up with any restaurant outside Kansas City and riverside seats give you a nice view of the Bridge of Honor

*Grab a bite at Carolyn's in Harrisville, then walk around the corner to Berdine's.*

span just to the south. The Bridge of Honor is a beautiful, fan-design, cable-stay bridge connecting Pomeroy, Ohio, and Mason, West Virginia. At night, the bridge is illuminated with strings of blue lights following the lengths of the cables.

A good spot for your headquarters is just down the street in Middleport, Ohio, at the Downing House B&B (www.thedowninghouse.com) owned and operated by Ron and Linda Carpenter. The house was originally built in 1859 by Major John Downing, a steamboat captain. During his time in command, Downing was approached by a fellow who was anxious to learn the art of piloting a steamboat. Downing befriended the eager young man, teaching him how to handle piloting duties, including calling out the depth of the water. When the water was measured at two fathoms, what do you think he would call out? "Mark twain!"

When you're ready to move on, retrace your steps up Route 7A and turn right to follow US 33 into West Virginia. After Route 2 joins US 33 continue north on Route 2 to Ravenswood, West Virginia. Route 2 heading east will join I-77 in about twelve miles. Instead of jumping on the slab, stay on the road you're on and cross through the underpass to continue on Old WV 56, also marked 56/1. This ends on Old US 21. Turn right and follow Old US 21 south to Ripley. This allows you to pick up US 33 heading east, avoiding the interstate and most of the congestion around Ripley.

Heading east out of town, local traffic will drop away, allowing you to dial up to the fun setting on the throttle. This section of 33 isn't as challenging as others we've covered—such as the segment crossing Shenandoah Mountain—but it's a scenic, quiet road with an occasional twist. Just right for getting warmed up for more challenging roads.

*Berdine's Five and Dime is a treasure trove of goodies you thought were long gone. Photo courtesy of Berdine's*

*Berdine's is the longest operating Five and Dime still in business, established in 1908. Photo courtesy of Berdine's*

The fun will begin in earnest as you pass through Arnoldsburg and turn left on WV 16 where it splits off from US 33 and heads north. Some segments of Route 16 are a little rough and you'll have to pick a careful line through the curves to hit the pavement patching strips at an angle that won't upset the bike's handling. They're a nuisance but manageable. Farther ahead, some long sections representing the best of Route 16 have been freshly paved. In these segments, you can run fast and deep into the curves and get on the throttle hard on exit.

Unlike their Ohio counterparts, West Virginia's roads are predictable enough that you will soon develop a leaning and cornering rhythm. In fact, if you want to do a regional tour and stick with smaller state routes; Route 16 is a good choice. Although it's a state route, Virginia and North Carolina keep the Route 16 designation for roads that connect to West Virginia's 16. You can begin at St. Marys in West Virginia and follow a road marked Route 16 all the way to Charlotte, North Carolina. Virginia's Route 16 from Tazewell to Marion is a worthy challenger to Deal's Gap in western North Carolina.

Following Route 16 will bring you through Harrisville, where it might be lunch time, depending on your schedule. When you stop at the intersection with Route 31 (Main Street), you can find a small eatery in the building across the street and to the left, the Sandwich Shop (117 West Main Street; 304-643-2187). Nothing about this place says "swanky," but as you might guess, that's just what's great about it. A burger, fries, and soda will set you back about five bucks.

Now, after lunch you might roll out onto the street in Harrisville, look around, and pronounce your visit complete. Aside from a pretty courthouse tucked behind the lunch room, there doesn't appear to be much going on. Do yourself a favor. Before you blow town, go another half block west on Main Street and turn right on North Court Street (also labeled Route 5/6). Just ahead on the right you'll find yourself at Berdine's (www.berdinesdimestore.com). Open since 1908, Berdine's is the oldest Five and Dime store in the country.

In a store like Berdine's, an hour or two can pass quickly. It's a feast for the eyes and the imagination. The store still has an original pressed tin ceiling, oak shelves, and a confectionary counter. You'll find things in Berdine's you vaguely remember and things you thought no longer existed, like liniment salve, horehound candy, and blue enamelware pots and pans. If you are expected to bring home souvenirs of your trip, this would be the place to get them.

Returning to Route 16 north, follow US Route 50 to begin the return journey. On this section of the route, you'll notice a marked change in the lay of the land. The hills are decidedly lower, the road straighter. It's a pleasant ride as you descend steadily toward Parkersburg and the Ohio River.

I like to eat as much as the next person or, judging by my expanding waistline, maybe a little more than the next person. The end of the ride for this loop brought me to Jimmy Colombo's Italian Restaurant (1236 7th Street, 304-428-5472) in Parkersburg. It's easy to find if you follow I-77 to US 50. Head west on US 50 and make the first exit at 7th Street. Colombo's is about a mile down 7th Street on the left at the intersection with Camden Street.

From the moment you step into Colombo's you feel like you've joined the family. It could be the hundreds of family photos lining the walls, the attentive wait staff, or the satisfying carbohydrate rush from a plate of pasta and meatballs.

It's a fitting end to a fine day on the road and I can tell you with great certainty that riding these roads is a lot more fun than looking at them from above.

# Trip 13 Hall of Fame Loop

**Distance** *257 miles*
**Terrain** *Rolling hills diminishing to the eastern outskirts of the midwest prairie, marked by a return to the hills on the way back*
**Highlights** *AMA Hall of Fame Museum, Route 555, Hocking Hills*

What self-respecting journey through southeastern Ohio would be complete without a visit to the American Motorcyclist Association Heritage Museum? Not this one, friend. That gets done today. Our loop includes not

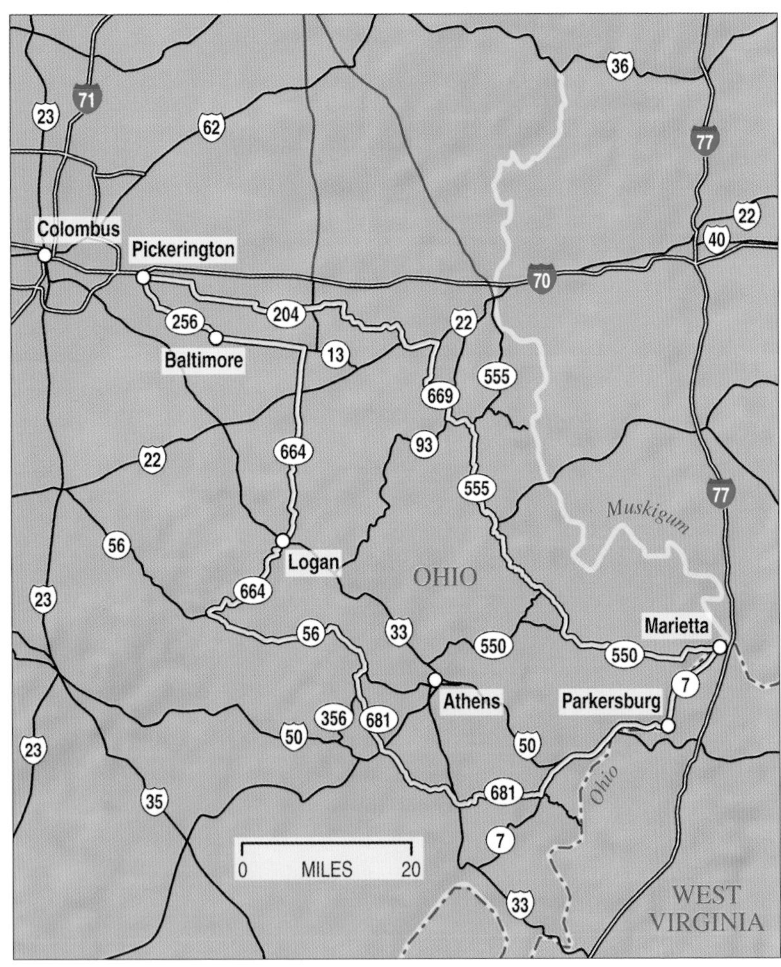

**THE ROUTE FROM MARIETTA**

| | |
|---|---|
| 0 | Leave Marietta on Route 550 |
| 20.0 | Turn right on SR 555 |
| 54.3 | Left on SR 669 |
| 57.7 | Right on SR 669/93 |
| 60.0 | Left on SR 669 |
| 63.2 | Right on SR 345 |
| 67.6 | Left on US 22 |
| 72.1 | Right on SR 204 |
| 109.5 | Arrive AMA Museum. Departing museum, turn right on SR 204 |
| 109.7 | Left on SR 256 |
| 113.4 | Left on SR 256 in Pickerington |
| 132.0 | Right on SR 664 |
| 169.0 | Left on SR 56 |
| 192.5 | Right on SR 356 |
| 195.7 | Left on SR 681 |
| 227.2 | Left on SR 7 |
| 257.2 | Return Marietta |

only a Hall of Fame museum, but Hall of Fame roads, too. And, as part of the return loop, we'll pass through the Hocking Hills region which offers such a diverse range of outdoor activities, it could serve as its own base camp.

Technically, the area we'll visit today lies outside the Appalachians, but there is a lot of good riding on both sides of the museum. The AMA's headquarters lies conveniently on the southeastern side of the greater Columbus area in Pickerington. That means we can easily reach our destination traversing just a smidgen of heavy traffic to get in and out. You've probably encountered more stop-and-go traffic in a McDonald's drive through than we'll see today.

Today's loop begins by heading out of Marietta on State Route 7 to pick up the beginning of Route 555, also known as the Triple Nickel. If there's one Ohio byway that has developed a national reputation among motorcyclists, it is OH 555, a road that begins along the Ohio River near Little Hocking and runs through to Zanesville Ohio.

If you have ridden any of the other routes in this book, Route 555 will be a fun ride, but you'll know something first-timers won't. There are hun-

*The AMA Hall of Fame Museum in Pickerington is home to dozens of cool bikes on exhibit. Photo courtesy of the American Motorcyclist Association.*

dreds of miles of roads in southeastern Ohio just as good as this and many are even better. Still, Route 555 has all the things I enjoy about these roads. Some stretches roll and rise over the landscape like waves while a few sections feature great sections of twists, all against a colorful backdrop of Ohio's scenic fields and farms.

Passing through Chesterhill, you'll find a plaque documenting the history of the Quaker meeting house and a brief mention of the role Quakers played in the Underground Railroad.

Members of the Religious Society of Friends are more commonly known as Quakers outside the religious order. The Quaker movement began in 17th century England and members of the society migrated to the religiously tolerant colonies. Quakers are well known for their silent, unplanned worship services—so well known, one of my school teachers used to recite a children's rhyme about Quakers to quiet the class. As I rode past the meeting house, the words came back as if I'd just heard them yesterday.

*Quaker meeting has begun,*
*No more laughing, no more fun.*
*If you laugh or crack a smile,*
*You will have to walk a mile.*

It never worked on me. My mouth was genetically wired in the wide-open position. But I digress.

What most folks don't know about the Quakers was the important role they played in the Underground Railroad. The Quakers are pacifists, meaning they do not believe in war and actively work to achieve peaceful solutions to any conflict. In colonial days, during the beginning the Quaker movement, founder George Fox urged his followers to release their slaves, even though they had been treated well. By the onset of the Civil War, Quakers were well established as staunch abolitionists who worked to help slaves escape from the South.

Slaves followed the Underground Railroad, a series of safe houses and hiding places to the Free States and Canada. In moving along the route, passengers traveled mostly by foot and covered 10 to 20 miles per day. Those who offered shelter often knew nothing about other locations, and routes were communicated by word of mouth. It's a fascinating operation when you consider how such a complex system evolved and how well it worked. Although only a small fraction of slaves were able to escape, many of them

*A group of riders enjoys a stretch of fabulously curvy slab of pavement in southeastern Ohio. Photo by Dan Bard*

*Riding buddy Steve Fowler shows me some favorite roads in the area.*

were able to buy their family members out of slavery, so the efforts of the Railroad were greatly magnified.

At the intersection with Route 669, turn left. When Route 669 joins Route 93, turn right and continue to follow 669. Again, in Crooksville just ahead, turn left to continue on 669 when it leaves Route 93. By now, you can clearly see a transformation in the terrain beginning to take shape. There's a much greater proportion of flat land to hilly, so at least you can forget about unexpectedly off-camber turns. There is no camber!

Make the right on Route 345, then a left on US 22. Follow this a short distance to Route 204 and hang a right. This road will take you all the way into Pickerington and is the street you turn off of to reach the AMA. Just before you reach the intersection with Route 256, you'll turn right onto Yarmouth Road and follow the signs for the AMA.

The AMA Motorcycle Hall of Fame and AMA headquarters (www.motorcyclemuseum.org) are tucked away on several acres, giving the impression the campus is secluded when, in fact, it backs up to the interstate. As you roll into the parking lot, you'll find dedicated, covered parking for your bike. I guess it shouldn't be a surprise to find that at a motorcycling organization, but it's still a nice touch. Lockers are provided for your gear, if you need them. Show your AMA membership card for half off the ten-dollar admission.

The Motorcycle Hall of Fame opened in 1990, dedicated to telling the stories of motorcycles and their riders. On entry, one look around will tell you your visit is going to take a while. Just think of it this way: when you went to visit that _______ (insert name of place you found boring), you waited patiently, watched the clouds roll by, took a nap. You were building credit for this visit—now it's time to use it.

The museum's two floors contains an ever-changing display of antique and historically significant motorcycles, profiles of riders and industry members who've made important contributions to the sport, and a few displays of evolving motorcycle technology. On my visit, I found a display of motorcycles that either belonged to celebrities or played a starring role in a movie. The MV Agusta F4 ridden by Will Smith in *I, Robot* was there, along with the LAPD bike from *Terminator 2: Judgment Day* represented in a special section of the museum, with eleven of Arlen Ness's most striking creations, including one called Mach-Ness, a bike powered by a helicopter turbine engine. You think that thing can get off the line? Drop the clutch too fast at a light and it'll probably launch itself.

If you're a vintage-bike lover, you can expect to see some rare and unusual models on display. I'm always fascinated by the different arrangements of controls. It's so easy today to move from one bike to the next and, except for how the turn signals work, everything is about the same. But check out the 1909 Royal Pioneer. Imagine stepping off your Dyna Wide Glide and onto this handsome machine. How many hands do you need? Four? Five? The Pioneer has four twist grips, plus a hand pump on the side to supply oil to the motor. And some ideas that seem new can be found on machines decades old. Think shaft drive is a new innovation? Check out the 1911 Pierce Four.

When it's time to saddle up and bid goodbye to the museum, roll back out to Route 204 and turn right. At the intersection with Route 256 just ahead, turn left and head south. There are a few miles of suburbs to trundle

*It's like this all day folks. All day. Who woulda thought?*

through, but it won't take long. In Pickerington, turn left to continue on Route 256. Route 256 to Route 664 to Logan is a sedate ride, but as you near town you'll once again notice that you're entering hill country. Stick with Route 664 through Logan and pass over Route 33. This takes you directly by Hocking Hills State Park.

No other region of the state features as much unique Ohio geography as Hocking Hills. This state park is situated on more than 2,000 acres on top of Blackhand sandstone some 150 feet thick. Sandstone, as you probably know, erodes much faster than other types of rock and is often responsible for unusual and dramatic rock formations. You'll find that true here, too. The park features deep gorges and large outcroppings, hemlock forests and towering waterfalls. Hocking Hills has lodging to suit any requirement, whether you're traveling one- or two-up, in a small or large group, moteling it or camping.

If you decide to complete the loop, continue on Route 664 to Route 56 and turn east. Continue until you reach the split with 356 and follow that to the right. A few miles down the road, make the left onto Route 681. This is a classic southeastern Ohio backroad, threading its way for dozens of miles through the narrow farm valleys wedged between rounded, old hills.

Take your time and enjoy this part of the ride, it's a real keeper. Just remember, it's always a good idea to keep your brake lever covered and keep an eye out for . . . DEER! The thought had no sooner entered my mind, when I caught a flash of white out of the corner of my eye. Almost before I could process what was happening, I was on a clear collision course with a full-grown whitetail doe. Even as I instinctively grabbed a handful of brake and felt the tires chirping at the edge of maximum adhesion, I saw nothing but a frame full of eyeballs and nostrils headed right at me. Inevitably, I was about to T-bone my first deer. The front wheel twitched as I made first contact and then—it was over. Somehow, I'd managed to scrub off just enough speed to avoid a full-scale collision as the deer leaped clear of the front of the bike. The deer and I both came away from that encounter wondering, "What just happened?"

I hopped off to inspect the bike and to let my mind settle down. I felt such a sense of relief, I couldn't help but laugh. I kept replaying the scene over and over in my mind, wondering if there was some way I could have seen that deer sooner, but judging where it came from, it just wasn't possible. Another fraction of a second and it would have toppled me from the bike without warning, or I'd never have seen it at all. *Phew.* Let me tell you about this great little liquor store I found shortly thereafter . . .

I'm kidding, of course. As I rolled down Route 681 and turned left on Route 7 to head back to Marietta, I quickly decided there was nothing unique or surprising about that incident. I've probably had a dozen close calls without even knowing it. My close call did, however, reinforce my decision to wear the right riding gear, and strengthened my resolve to be more aware as I ride, and to check out new riding safety courses that would help me refresh my skills. There is no glory or honor in becoming a member of the Road Kill Hall of Fame.

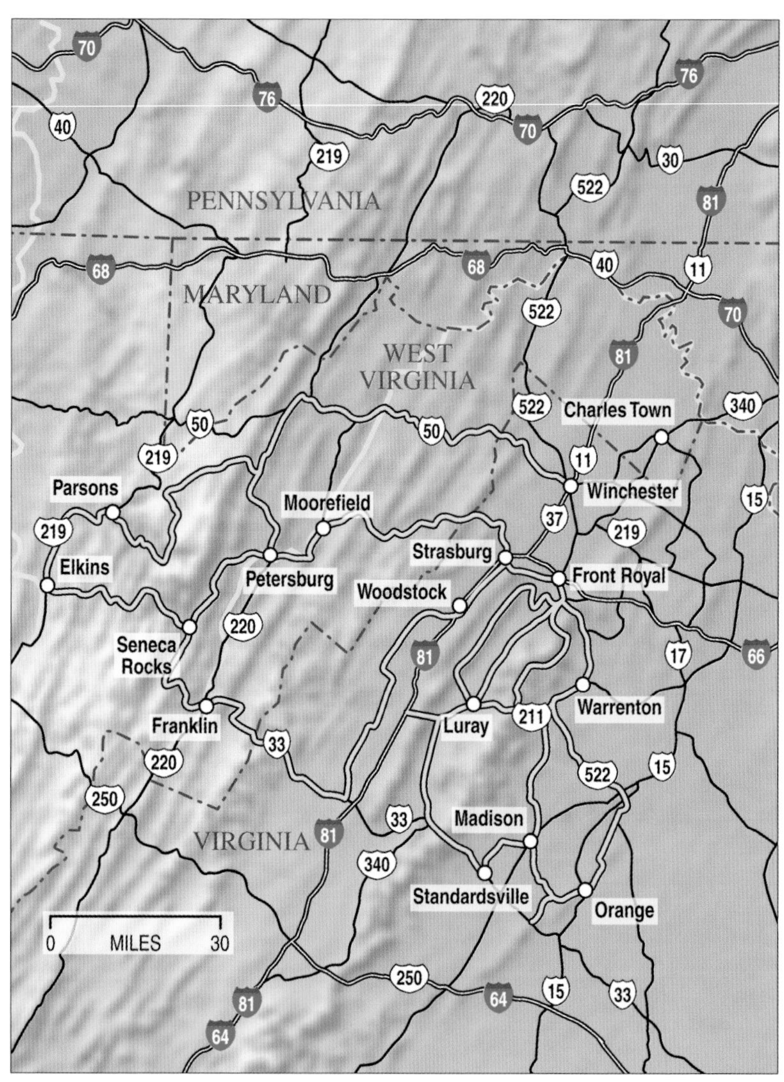

PENNSYLVANIA
MARYLAND
WEST VIRGINIA
VIRGINIA
Charles Town
Winchester
Parsons
Moorefield
Elkins
Petersburg
Strasburg
Front Royal
Woodstock
Seneca Rocks
Franklin
Luray
Warrenton
Madison
Standardsville
Orange
70
76
220
40
219
30
522
81
68
11
50
340
15
37
17
66
211
33
250
64
0 MILES 30

# Gateway to Skyline

## *Front Royal, Virginia*

In Front Royal, you'll find more riders arriving from other areas of the country to ride Skyline Drive than any other spot we'll visit. (Blatant commercial plug coming: be sure to show them your copy of this book so they'll see what they're missing!)

It is said that the name Front Royal (frontroyalva.com) is derived from the story of a British field officer who once attempted to mold rough frontier men from this area into a passable militia. They weren't very good soldier material; getting them to march in a straight line was a tall order. Time after time, the officer drilling the troops would shout the same order—"Front the royal oak! Front the royal oak!"—trying mightily to get his troops to face a large oak tree at the end of the drilling field. He shouted his order so loud and so often, it became a joke among the townspeople. No matter what the topic of conversation was, "Front the royal oak!" was the

*Stone fences and rolling pastures abound in the Virginia Piedmont near Middleburg, Virginia.*

*Two boys discovered the Endless Caverns while rabbit hunting. I always hoped I would discover something like that.*

punch line. The joke passed into history, but the label stuck and the town eventually became known as Front Royal.

The hub of activity in Front Royal is around Chester Street. Here you will find the town common area, including the Warren Rifles Confederate Museum (vaudc.org/museum.html) operated by the local chapter of the United Daughters of the Confederacy. The cottage of Confederate spy Belle Boyd is just down the street. Belle's demeanor and grace were good cover for the work she did, making friends of federal soldiers and learning their secrets. She would often visit her aunt and uncle who lived in Front Royal and who operated the Fishback Hotel. Once Belle hid in a closet in the hotel over the room where Generals Shields and Banks were discussing tactics for Union maneuvers in the area. The information she gathered helped the Confederate Army win an opening round of the first campaign in the Shenandoah Valley.

Just outside of town is one of the valley's limestone caverns open for public visits. Skyline Caverns (skylinecaverns.com) are as large as their cousins in Luray to the south, but they have an unusual formation called anthodites found nowhere else in the world. Anthodites grow from an odd mix of minerals and look like big flowers with delicate, sharp petals that grow in all directions.

Of course the big draw in these parts is the Shenandoah National Park (nps.gov/shen) and Skyline Drive. If you want to really enjoy Shenandoah at its finest, plan your visit here for either late spring or mid-autumn. In May, the temperatures have warmed enough that nearly all the trees have gained their leaves and spring flowers still carpet the forest floor in abundance. The weather will be a bit more settled with fair skies and pleasant temps for touring and hiking. If you plan to come down for the fall foliage season, do not expect to ride on the weekend and have a good time. There are just too many cars, trucks, and recreational vehicles to make the journey anything more than frustrating. The trick is to go during mid-week, say Tuesday or Wednesday. Go earlier in the morning and you'll have the road nearly to yourself.

The big secret that few people know about is riding Skyline at night. You can witness some spectacular sunsets here, but when the western sky darkens, the heavens open before your eyes and you'll understand why Shenandoah means "daughter of the stars." After about 9 p.m., the ranger stations close up and you won't pay a dime to ride. There is one danger in-

*Visit the Apple House in Linden, Virginia, and try the apple smoked pork barbeque. Superb!*

*Germany Valley overlook is one photo-op you won't want to miss.*

volved in riding at night: deer. After a while you'll have seen so many deer lining the highway you will lose count. It is best to keep your speed to an absolute minimum here, no more than 25 mph at the very most. Just enjoy a very slow, leisurely cruise along the parkway. Once you get out of the lights of the Front Royal area you can pick an overlook, park the bike, and enjoy it. Something about the night air, the darkness, and the sense of isolation makes conversation with your co-rider or riding buddy seem even more enjoyable. Savor it. In today's age you don't often have an opportunity like this to enjoy the company of a friend.

You can't stay in the Front Royal area without paying at least a half-day visit to neighboring Winchester (ci.winchester.va.us). By happenstance it didn't fall along any of our tour routes in the region, but leaving it out entirely would be a mistake. By most definitions, Winchester marks the head of the Shenandoah Valley, and this position made it an alluring prize for opposing armies during the Civil War. In addition to Civil War era sites, George Washington's office, the tomb of Lord Fairfax, and even Patsy Cline's (patsycline.com) gravesite and memorial are nearby.

The town's location means there are plenty of travel services to choose from. For campers, the Front Royal KOA Campground just south of town has a great location. After turning off US Route 340, you'll ride about half a mile down a dirt country lane through a pasture to get to the campground. When you start down the lane you can't help but think, "Gee, is there really anything back here?" It is a beautiful location and well off the beaten path.

In the center of town you can find an easy half-dozen small independent motels and several bed and breakfasts. The Blue Ridge Motel (1370 North Shenandoah Avenue; 703-636-7200) is a safe choice. Or, if you have something a little fancier in mind, try the Chester House Inn (43 Chester Street). Although it is outside the immediate area, the restored log building that is the Inn at Narrow Passage (innatnarrowpassage.com) offers some of the finest accommodations in the area. Still farther out are the cabins, lodges, and campgrounds along Skyline Drive. All the accommodations on Skyline Drive are often booked months in advance, so be sure to call well ahead of time if you plan to stay there. Contact ARAMARK, the park's official facility management company, for reservations and information at 800-999-4714.

Restaurants will be all over town. If you're looking for an authentic American dining experience, drive just a little east of town on VA 55 and stop at the Apple House (theapplehouse.net) for some apple smoked barbeque. The applewood smoke leaves a slightly sweet flavor in the meat. It's a real treat. For dessert, bring home some home-made apple donuts. The Knotty Pine Restaurant (540-635-3064), a bit further into town on North Royal Avenue, is a good stop for breakfast or lunch although the lack of a separate smoking section might give you pause if you're sensitive to second-hand smoke. If you're in the mood for steak, the hottest ticket in town is Dean's Steak House (deanssteakhouse.com) close to the entrance to Skyline Drive.

# Trip 14 Home Country

**Distance** *140 miles*
**Terrain** *Pass through Chester Gap followed by small Piedmont towns and villages, a small mountain ascent, scenic byways, and a valley run*
**Highlights** *James Madison's home at Montpelier, Clarks Mountain, Barboursville Ruins, Baby Jim's, Culpeper Museum of History*

The route begins with Route 522 south out of Front Royal over Chester Gap. This particular gap should probably be called the Chester End-Run, because it doesn't amount to much of a gap. Route 522 is a wide, smooth, and relatively empty road, so take your time as you tour through horse country. Enjoy the wide, open vistas, the big green pastures set against the Blue Ridge. In the spring, the fields are awash with yellow buttercups and dandelions, a beautiful setting for our tour. This is Virginia's Piedmont (an Italian term meaning "little mountains") region. The Piedmonts are commonly called the foothills of the Blue Ridge, but the two are actually from different geological epochs. The Piedmonts are the remnants of an older mountain chain that was eventually eroded away, much as the Blue Ridge and Appalachians are worn down compared to the Rockies.

When you enter the town of Sperryville, follow Route 522 through town until you see a sign for Route 231, heading due south. Turn right and follow 231, the Blue Ridge Turnpike. This scenic byway will take you past the entrance for the Old Rag Mountain Trail and the Whiteoak Canyon Falls Trail

*Like the postcard says, "One more payment and it's all ours."*

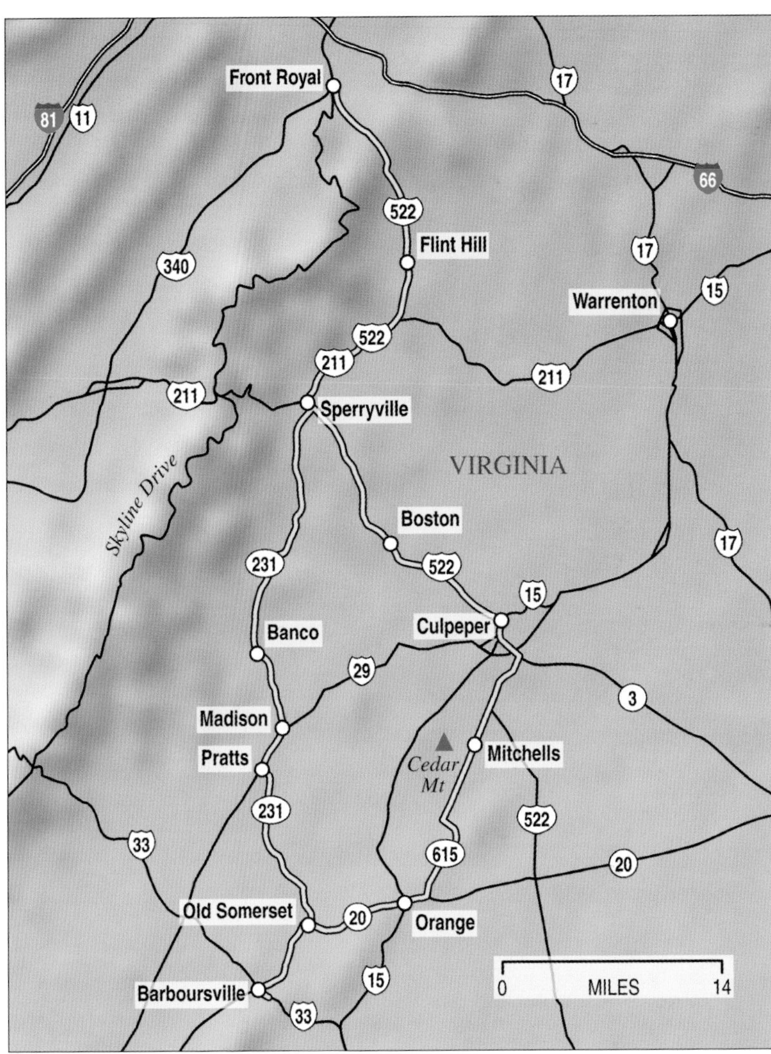


in Etlan (see Trip 15, Skyline Loop, for more information about these trails). The riding is easy along this Virginia Byway, and the long, fast sweepers will make your bike beg to roll on the throttle and lean a little harder than you might otherwise. There aren't many tricky curves here to fool you, all are well marked and properly banked.

By the time you arrive in Madison, you're probably hungry for more. It comes quickly. Continue following Route 231 through the downtown area (don't panic, this isn't downtown Manhattan), past stately old brick homes and the corner drugstore to join the fast and furious pace of Route 29, but

**THE ROUTE FROM FRONT ROYAL**

| | |
|---|---|
| 0 | Start at US 522 and VA 55 in Front Royal |
| 14.8 | Right onto US 211/US 522 at Massies Corner |
| 22.8 | Left onto US 522 at 522/211 split in Sperryville |
| 23.6 | Right onto VA 231 |
| 44.1 | Right on US 29 Business south in Madison |
| 45.4 | Rejoin US 29 south toward Charlottesville |
| 47.3 | Left onto VA 230/VA 231 |
| 48.0 | Right onto VA 231/Blue Ridge Turnpike |
| 57.8 | Right onto VA 20 |
| 63.4 | Left onto US 33 east |
| 63.6 | Right onto VA 20 |
| 63.7 | Left onto VA 678 |
| 64.2 | Right onto VA 777 |
| 64.5 | Right onto Mansion Road (Barboursville Vineyard Entrance) |
| 64.7 | Arrive Barboursville Ruins |
| 64.9 | Left onto VA 777 |
| 65.2 | Left onto VA 678 |
| 65.7 | Right onto VA 20 |
| 65.8 | Left onto US 33 West |
| 66.0 | Right onto VA 20 |
| 78.1 | Arrive Orange and continue straight |
| 78.2 | VA 20 becomes VA 615/Rapidan Road |
| 91.3 | Left onto US 522 |
| 94.8 | Left onto VA 3/Germanna Highway |
| 96.4 | Enter Culpeper and turn right on US 29 Bus/US 15 Bus/ US 522 north |
| 97.4 | Arrive Baby Jim's, then left out of parking lot |
| 97.5 | Right on US 522 north |
| 116.6 | Right on US 211/US 522 in Sperryville |
| 124.6 | Left on US 522 at 522/211 split |
| 139.4 | Arrive Front Royal via US 522 north |

only for a few moments. After just about two miles, Route 231 takes a sharp departure south, splitting from the busy highway and returning to a more genteel pace.

Where Route 231 and Route 20 meet at Old Somerset, turn right and follow Route 20 for a few miles to Barboursville. Follow the Virginia sign for a vineyard—a bunch of grapes—to the Barboursville Vineyard (barboursvillewine.net). You'll turn left onto US 33 east and follow it for a very short distance then right where VA 20 heads south again. The next left will be VA 678. Turn left on 678 and follow it to VA 777. A right on VA 777 will bring you to the vineyard's entrance.

The vineyard is on what was once the estate of James Barbour, governor of Virginia during the early 1800s. Prominently featured on the grounds are what's left of the mansion, which burned on Christmas Day 1884—the Barboursville Ruins. Amaze your fellow touring partners by pointing out that Barbour's mansion was designed by none other than Thomas Jefferson. "Note the remains of the columned portico," you begin, "and the octagonal front room, Jefferson's signature design." Also point out to them that the earthen ramp at the edge of where the portico used to be was built in lieu of steps, a feature not commonly seen. You are free to roam about the outside of the burned-out shell, but the interior is closed to visitors. Huge, overgrown boxwoods indicate where formal gardens once stood, though standing among them now, it is easy to imagine that you have been shrunk to a fraction of your normal size.

It seems appropriate that a home designed by Jefferson should reside on the grounds of an estate now cultivated as a vineyard. Jefferson is widely credited for making the first attempts to create a wine growing region in

*Time passes slowly in the formal gardens at Montpelier.*

central Virginia. The climate is suitable enough, but a native parasite prevented European vines from growing during Jefferson's time. Twentieth-century research eventually yielded disease resistant root stocks that allowed vineyards to flourish in the Mid-Atlantic and the vineyard at Barboursville has produced internationally recognized and award-winning wines.

Returning to the trip, follow Route 20 north toward Orange, James Madison's hometown. The roots of the Madison family run deep in this area and this was the fourth President's only home. Montpelier (montpelier.org) is now part of the National Trust for Historic Preservation, a group that restores and preserves important American homes. To tour the home, you need to sign up at Montpelier Station at the general store across the road from the perfectly restored railroad depot. A tour bus will drop you off at the front of the estate, where an ultra-efficient tour guide will escort you through the interior.

The main part of the home dates back to 1760. Through the years different owners have had different ideas about how the house should be configured; your tour guide will show you where some entrances have been blocked over and others added. The house is currently covered with scaffolding while a major restoration project takes place, part of it to replace the

*Riding buddy Red Fehrle observes the ruins of the Barbour mansion. "Must have been some party," he says.*

*A backroad between Culpeper and Sperryville provides a scenic photo op. Photo by Mike Sprung*

all-copper roof. After your tour is finished, you will be free to walk around the grounds until the last tour bus runs in the late afternoon. One place you must visit is the formal garden at the back of the house. The Garden Club of Virginia has taken care to restore it to its former glory. Here you can get an idea of what the gardens at the Barbour mansion must have looked like in their day. Don't forget to stroll along the front lawn, visit the garden temple, and sit on the front portico. The view of the Blue Ridge is striking, rising like a mighty blue tidal wave on the western skyline and cresting over the Piedmont.

Madison's home and most of his possessions were sold off by his wife, Dolley Todd Madison, to satisfy the debts of her ne'er-do-well son, John Payne Todd. John Todd was often so desperate for money he would rifle through Madison's papers and tear off his signatures to sell them. As a result, most of Madison's papers were destroyed and his possessions scattered. (I discovered that a square piano that once graced the halls of Montpelier now stands in the front room of the Boal Mansion near State College, Pennsylvania. See Trip 5, Lion Country.) Eventually the Madison home and grounds became the property of the DuPont family. It was during this time that it saw its most aggressive expansion, including the show grounds at the front of the estate.

The railroad station was built in front of Montpelier by the DuPonts, who often traveled to New York for business. The only railroad stop was at Orange, some five miles to the east—and though the DuPonts were filthy rich, rules were rules and the engineer would only allow DuPont to get off

*Despite an influx of fast-food restaurants, Baby Jim's has been serving up good food since 1947.*

the train at a railroad station. When you have that much money, though, you don't let a trifling rule stop you from getting what you want. So a station was built at Montpelier to save DuPont the carriage ride.

When you resume the tour, follow Route 20 into the town of Orange. If you'd like to learn more about the fourth president of the United States and "father" of the Constitution, stop by the James Madison Museum (jamesmadisonmus.org). When you enter town, turn right on Caroline Street. The museum will be on your immediate left. The route returns to Main Street and goes through the small downtown area.

In downtown Orange, Route 20 becomes Route 615, which you will take to Culpepper. Along the way you will pass Cedar Mountain on your left. Cedar Mountain was the scene of a sizeable skirmish between Union and Confederate forces in the summer of 1862. Confederate General Robert E. Lee was alarmed by the advances and threats of Union General John Pope, so he ordered Stonewall Jackson to find an opportunity to strike Pope. Poor roads and communication problems hindered Jackson's plans, but his chance came in early August. An aggressive Union force of 12,000 men nearly defeated the Confederate contingent of 22,000. Jackson's advance was threatened to the point that he drew his own sword to lead his troops by example. His rally and the arrival of A. P. Hill's division swept the federal ranks from the field and liberated the town of Culpeper.

At the junction with US 522, go straight to take 522 into Culpeper (visitculpeperva.com), my hometown. At the south end of town, stop by the Museum of Culpeper History. The museum features state-of-the-art exhibits that chronicle the history of the area, from the time of the dinosaurs through settlement by Native Americans, the Civil War, and the town's evolution since the 1900s. Culpeper's downtown area has undergone a transformation in recent years making it an appealing area to hop off your bike at the corner of Main and Davis for a little walking tour.

The best place in town for a good hot dog is Baby Jim's. It has been in operation since 1947 and has never advertised—it never had to. I don't think they've ever worried too much about the parade of fast-food restaurants that have come to town in the last 20 years, either. Nobody beats a Baby Jim's hot dog—nobody. If you want to order like a native, park your bike, walk in to the window and mumble "I'd like two dogs with the works, an order o' fries, and a RC." You can order something else, but no authentic Baby Jim experience is complete without a hot dog. To find Baby Jim's, follow Route 522 all the way through town to the point where it turns left to head west. Go straight through the light instead of turning, and Baby Jim's will appear just ahead on your right. Get there before 3 p.m., though, because they only serve breakfast and lunch.

Fountain Hall Bed and Breakfast (fountainhall.com), in the old residential section of town, welcomes riders. Otherwise, if you're ready to mount up and move west, follow Route 522 through Sperryville back to Front Royal. As the sun sets over the Blue Ridge, the tall hills cast long shadows across the road, and the sunset is regularly spectacular. I think you will find it a fitting end to a fine day.

# Trip 15 Skyline Loop

**Distance** *135 miles*
**Terrain** *Plenty of curves in the first 40 miles along Skyline Drive, then a mountain pass descent, and a Virginia Byway. Another pass at Stanardsville and return via Skyline Drive.*
**Highlights** *Skyline Drive, Shenandoah National Park, hiking trails with remnants of old homesteads, Sperryville Emporium, Misty Mountain Vineyard*

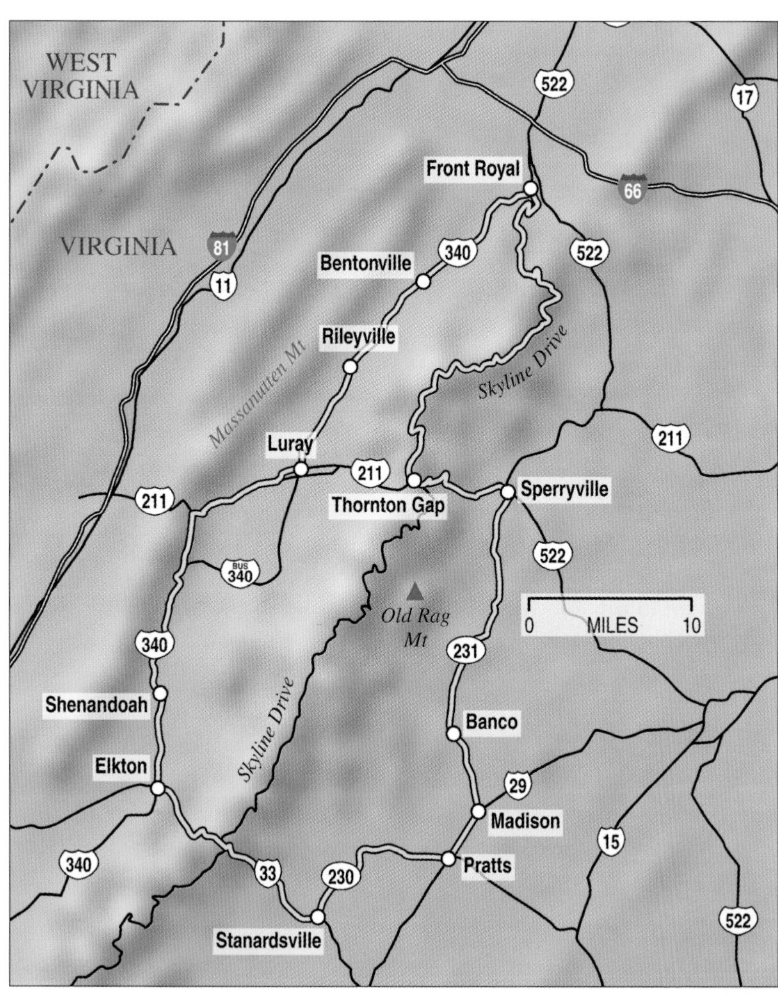

**THE ROUTE FROM FRONT ROYAL**

| | |
|---|---|
| 0 | Start at entrance to Skyline Drive on US 340 in Front Royal |
| 30.7 | Left on US 211 east at Thornton Gap |
| 37.7 | Right on US 522 in Sperryville |
| 38.5 | Right on VA 231 |
| 59.0 | Right on US 29 Business south in Madison |
| 60.3 | Join US 29 south toward Charlottesville |
| 62.1 | Right on VA 230 north |
| 72.9 | Right on US 33 west |
| 87.4 | Right on US 340 north at Elkton |
| 135.0 | Arrive Front Royal via US 340 |

This tour is best suited for a day when you have ridden a lot in days past and want to take a break. There are ample opportunities to get off your bike and explore the dozens of hiking trails along Skyline Drive. We will also pay a visit to a couple of quaint mountain towns and stop off at a vineyard for a

*Skyline is a popular destination for riders. An early start will put you ahead of most cars. Photo by Dan Bard*

personal tour—perhaps by the owner himself. We will then return over the Blue Ridge via Route 33, a popular run for riders.

The tour begins at the north entrance to Skyline Drive in Front Royal, about two miles south of town on Route 340. Admission to Skyline depends somewhat on how the ranger views your mode of transportation. There are different rates for cars and bicycles, and I have been charged both at different times. I think the bigger your smile, the better your chances of getting the bicycle rate!

Be sure to keep your speed at or near the posted limit of 35 mph. Motorcyclists have a mixed reputation on this road, so we should do our best to improve it. It may be tempting to lean into some of the curves, but considering the hiking trails that cross the road and curves you can't see around, 35 is the speed to go. Besides, the purpose of this drive is to relax and enjoy the view.

Skyline Drive is a thin ribbon that traces the length of the 200,000 acres comprising Shenandoah National Park (nps.gov/shen). Each year the park attracts hundreds of thousands of visitors, many of whom ride from one end to the other and pronounce themselves satisfied, riders included. Too bad. In addition to the 75 overlooks along the way, there are about 500 miles of hiking trails, waterfalls, black bear, ancient hemlock forests, fern-shrouded pools, and the ruins of pioneer homesteads, all awaiting your discovery.

Trails range from a few tenths of a mile, to dozens. The terrain is gentle, so you can hike with a minimum of equipment; sturdy shoes, clothing to suit the season, and a supply of water are adequate for a few hours. Bring lunch or a snack to boost your energy along the trail, and you'll be set for a full day.

If you get an early start, watch out for deer. An estimated 6,000 deer live in the 400 square miles of Shenandoah National Park, so the question is not *whether* you will see deer, but rather *how many*. The first few miles of the park climb to the crest of the Blue Ridge. The first pullover looks down on the Front Royal area and will give you a hint of what is to come. Next is the Dickey Ridge Visitor Center, where the 1.2-mile Fox Hollow Trail begins.

The trail passes through part of the 450 acres once owned by the Fox family. Along the trail are large rock piles, now covered with gray-green moss that makes them look like burial mounds. These stones came out of the fields under cultivation. You will also see the Fox family cemetery, and a low stone wall that ran along the property line between the Foxes and their neighbors, the Merchants.

The Merchants and the Foxes weren't the first to settle this area. It had been a prime hunting ground for Native Americans as far back as 1000 BC.

*It's easy to find the road less traveled in Shenandoah National Park.*

The first few waves of European settlers washed ashore in the 1600s and used the seemingly limitless supply of wood to build their homes and villages. By the early 20th century, the entire area was a wasteland, stripped of all its resources. Congress designated the area a park in 1924, but didn't authorize any money to be spent. For twelve years the state of Virginia slowly bought land and accepted donations from private individuals until the park was finally established on the day after Christmas, 1935. When you gaze up the trunk of a mighty oak, hickory, or black locust that grow here so thick, it is hard to imagine that these trees are only 50 to 70 years old.

Before you leave the visitor center, be sure to go inside and collect your National Parks Passport stamp.

The rolling contours of the gentle Blue Ridge are the perfect setting for building a world-class scenic parkway, and a heck-of-a-fun motorcycle ride! The Drive itself weaves along the crest of the Blue Ridge joining its kin, the Blue Ridge Parkway, 105 miles south at Afton Mountain. The Civilian

*Dickey Ridge trail is an easy hike and offers spectacular views of the Shenandoah Valley.*

Conservation Corps did most of the work, with much of the stonework done by expert Spanish and Italian stoneworkers who had just arrived in the United States. The result is an unforgettable mix of flora, fauna, and twisty pavement.

As you sweep through the curves, be sure to stop occasionally at the overlooks to enjoy the view. You can see farthest during the late fall, winter, and early spring when weather patterns move clear northern air through the Shenandoah Valley. On a good day, you can easily see 60 or 70 miles across the Valley to the Shenandoah and Allegheny Mountains on the other side. To the east, the Piedmont region is clearly visible, gradually giving way to the coastal plain. Small towns and villages dot the landscape on both sides; those little specks you see moving through the fields are probably tractors.

Motorcycle campers will find campgrounds at Matthews Arm, Lewis Mountain, Loft Mountain, and Big Meadows, the latter available by reservation. There are also lodge and cabin rooms available. To camp in the backcountry, you'll need to get a permit at any entrance to the park. If you want a campsite, my advice is to set up camp early and then go exploring, especially during the summer season. These campgrounds fill up fast. For a room reservation, call well ahead—many months ahead.

On our tour, exit from Skyline at the Thornton Gap exit. Turn left on Route 211 toward Sperryville. This is a fast, five-mile descent with hairpin turns sharp enough that you can really grind the floorboards. Your arrival into the hamlet of Sperryville begins with a collection of roadside stands selling a wide variety of "must-haves," including apples, peaches, and cider; lawn ornaments of distinction; furniture; fajitas; "I Love Virginia" toothpick holders; and Elvis commemorative hand towels and bed linen sets.

You can have a fun time just stopping at different stands and looking over the goods. The most impressive collection is at the Sperryville Emporium (540-987-8235). It is packed from floor to ceiling with furniture, fruit, a vast array of concrete lawn ornaments, and decorative cedar plaques with moving quotes for those times when a thank you card just isn't enough. A seasonal flea market operates along the perimeter, and a local barbeque joint operates a stand. In the early fall during apple season, the place is so packed it takes on a carnival atmosphere. You'll often run into other riders here who are passing through on their way to the Drive, and many of the local riders will offer tips on other roads to try.

Modest old homes line the street that is downtown Sperryville, each with its own picket fence and front porch. Some have been converted into shops that sell locally made crafts, antiques, and even Native American jewelry. There are plenty of surprises to be found in the antique shops, including pieces and parts of old motorcycles. A rider friend told me he entered a shop one day just as a fellow wheeled an old Indian out the door with a smile on

*Riders often gather at the Sperryville Emporium after conquering US 211. It's a kitsch collector's paradise.*

*Sometimes I get so distracted by the scenery, I just pull over for a while and enjoy.*

his face as wide as Texas. "Four hundred dollars," the proud new owner told my friend before the question could form in his mouth.

When you've done all the wandering you want, it's time to suit up and head out. Follow Route 522 south out of Sperryville toward Culpeper and into the lush Piedmont. The right turn for Route 231 comes up just on the outskirts of town. Turn right and follow it. Route 231 is designated a Virginia Byway, and we know what that means—more great riding! Route 231 isn't as curvy as it is scenic. I discovered this road one day by accident, being lost and simply looking for a way to get from one point to another. I quickly discovered that getting lost out here is a good thing. The smooth pavement tempts you to slip into top gear and tilt your head back to smell the air. It's so fresh and sweet, you can almost taste it (tinyurl.com/motojourneys12). There's nothing to hear but the drone of your motor and the rushing wind. Just make sure you don't relax so much you miss that next curve!

On your right, Old Rag Mountain appears from behind the trees, with its bald, rocky top, looking somewhat out of place among the tree-covered hills beside it. Old Rag is a little different, because geologists say it is an extinct volcano. Old Rag is a popular day trip for weekend warriors who want to test their mettle in the outdoors (and want to be assured a victory). If you decide to conquer it, be sure to bring along the essential gear, plus a little extra food and water. To get to the parking area, turn right on Route 643 and follow this bumpy little cowpath to the foot of the mountain and Route 717, the road which leads to a parking area. Don't park along the side of the road at the trailhead as it'll rile the neighbors. You don't want to rile the neighbors in these parts.

Finishing out the first leg of Route 231 brings you into the town of Madison. Here the homes are more stately, and the folks are more likely to give you a second look than they would in Sperryville. Don't worry, they don't mean anything by it. They just don't see too many dashing, leather-clad figures like yourself darting through town. Madison is another appropriate place to climb off the bike for a look-see. Whether it be this journey through the Appalachians or another, you're always passing some kind of craft shop of one kind or another, and after awhile they all begin to look alike. If you want to purchase a genuine, locally sourced, handmade souvenir without wondering if it wasn't really "Made in the Far, Far East," check out Madison's own, That Little Quilt Shop (thatlittlequiltshop.com). You won't find any Elvis towel sets here, just some of the best handiwork anywhere in the region, and at affordable prices.

To depart Madison, continue to follow US 29 Business/VA 231 west toward Charlottesville. A few miles west of Madison, make a right turn on Route 230 west. Here, the straights are long and the view of the Blue Ridge rising in front of you invites your imagination to speculate what it will be like to attack the ridge. Entering the town of Stanardsville, turn right on Route 33. Your answer will come quickly.

First you enter a series of warm-up curves to get your tires scuffed. Then the road suddenly turns tame, and the immediate fun seems over. This doesn't last long; the more serious curves are just ahead. The road widens, giving you two lanes to set up your lines, and you can really give your cornering a good workout. If you have anything left of your footpegs from Route 211, you're liable to wear them out on this stretch. Your ascent will be smooth, like you're gliding on some of the low-hanging clouds that brush the ridge when they pass. Tight curves, wide pavement, and little traffic offer you the opportunity to set up wide and lead hard into the curves.

Follow Route 33 down the mountain and pick up US 340 north at Elkton. This is an easy return ride to Front Royal offering clear views of the Blue Ridge to your right and Massanutten Mountain on your left. You'll also see several long, steel truss railroad bridges, some of them a few hundred feet long. The ride is pretty similar to what you experienced on Route 231 and 230, with long straights and an occasional town.

# Trip 16 Stonewall's Valley

**Distance** *125 miles*
**Terrain** *Narrow river valley—an exciting, scenic ride, followed by several mountain passes*
**Highlights** *Fort Valley, New Market Battlefield, Luray Caverns*

During the Civil War, the Shenandoah Valley was a much fought-over piece of land because of its strategic location between the warring capitals of Washington and Richmond, and rich farmland that fed Confederate troops. Lose the Valley, and the South would lose the war, but as long as Thomas J. Jackson commanded the Confederate Army of the Shenandoah, this vital region was safe.

Jackson was considered by many to be second only to Robert E. Lee in his ability to achieve victory in battle against superior Union numbers. He

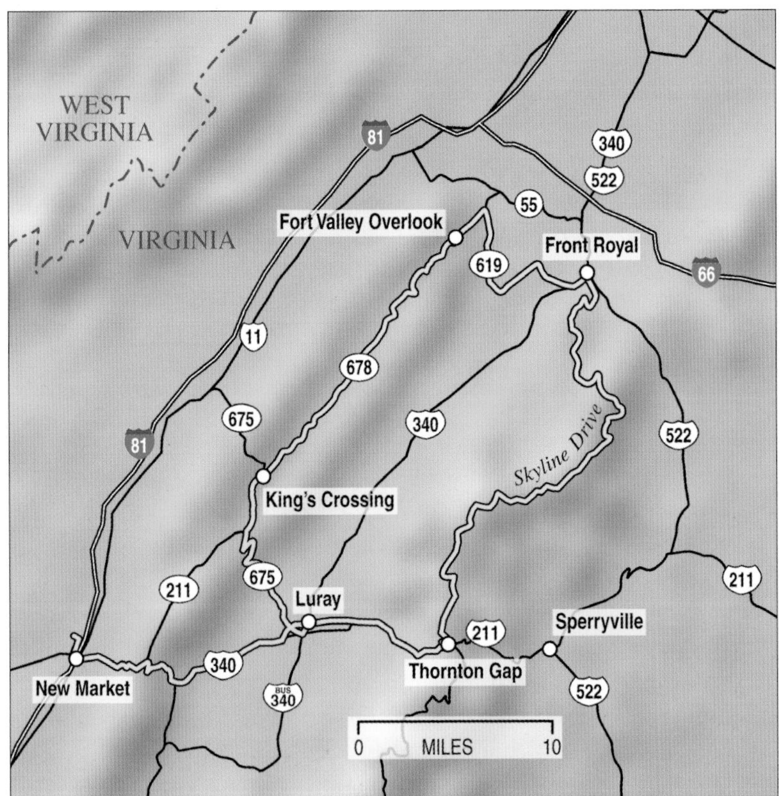

**THE ROUTE FROM FRONT ROYAL**

| | |
|---|---|
| 0 | Begin at the junction of US 340 south and VA 619 just south of the entrance to Skyline Drive and take VA 619 |
| 8.7 | Left on VA 678/Fort Valley Road |
| 27.4 | Bear left on VA 675/Fort Valley/Camp Roosevelt Road) |
| 38.8 | Left on US 340 north in Luray, then right on US 211 |
| 53.2 | Right on VA 305 in New Market |
| 54.5 | Arrive Hall of Valor Museum (see text about tourist traps along this road) |
| 55.8 | Left on US 211 |
| 78.9 | Left on entrance to Skyline Drive at Thornton Gap |
| 109.6 | Return Front Royal via Skyline Drive |

had a habit of being found in the thick of the action, rather than safely behind the lines, and this was a source of inspiration for his troops. At the Battle of First Manassas, his men rallied around him, with one shouting "There stands Jackson like a stone wall!" Soon after, the men simply called him "Stonewall," and the northern Shenandoah came to be known as Stonewall's Valley.

Our trail through Stonewall's Valley begins out of Front Royal following Route 619 west through the outskirts of town. The road soon narrows, and Massanutten Mountain looms in the distance—a portent of good riding to come. But even before reaching the mountain, the road begins dipping and twisting, skirting several small hollows. Near the northern base of the mountain, the trailhead of a popular hiking trail can be jam-packed with cars. I did this ride in March one year after a hard winter in the Valley and though fully cleared, the roads were still lined with snow, several feet deep in some places. With temperatures reaching into the fifties in March, the normally placid Passage Creek was swollen by the runoff of melting snow, leaving its banks and spilling into the narrow river valley. It still didn't quite feel like spring here yet. Winter hadn't let go, but it had loosened its grip. March can be a chilly time to make this ride, but it is a rewarding one.

When Route 619 ends, make the left turn on Route 678. This is the entrance to Fort Valley. The first few miles follow the course of the river bend for bend. High, sheer cliffs rise on either side, in stark contrast to the time-worn, rounded shoulders of the Blue Ridge. Those who never venture from Skyline will think they have seen everything the Valley has to offer, but hav-

*There's plenty of good riding in the region, even in the winter.*

ing ridden the backside of Massanutten, you will know just how much they missed.

Rounding a curve, I came upon a collection of forest service vehicles blocking the road, lights flashing. Had someone fallen in the creek? In the middle of the pack of cars, a large tanker truck was parked with men crawling along the top and removing poles. What the heck is this? I saw that at the end of each pole was actually a net full of anxious trout struggling to get out! Each man carefully walked over to the stream and released his cargo into the roiling waters, stocking Passage Creek for the year's trout fishing season—a sure sign that spring would make its annual appearance after all.

Route 678 continues well into the Valley for another twenty-odd miles before arriving at Kings Crossing. Here, follow Route 675 ahead as it veers off to the left. Route 675 crosses the Valley and then makes a sudden turn and it's up the mountain! Somewhere, I remember reading that only Route 211 crosses directly over Massanutten Mountain, but that's not true. Route 675 dives directly into the George Washington National Forest and then straight up the side of the mountain without the benefit of a gap to lessen the climb. There are several switchbacks along this section of road, tricky hairpins with a steep ascent in the turn. Gravel wash can make it even more of a challenge, especially on a big rig. When you top out on the ridge, make a stop and climb off the bike. On the side of the road facing the east will be a beautiful view of the eastern portion of the Valley with the Blue Ridge in the distance and the town of Luray directly below. The south fork of the Shenandoah River glistens in the foreground. The view alone is reason enough to make this ride—it's something you can take with you that few others will ever see. The descent down the eastern face of the mountain is standard fare with a few moderate switchbacks. You will quickly arrive in the town of Luray. When Route 675 ends in town, make a left turn on Route 340 north, then a left on Route 211 west. This is the road to New Market.

Route 211 passes over Massanutten again at New Market Gap. The grades are considerably smoother and properly banked for a fast, fun ride. In just a few miles you will be deposited into the town of New Market, one of a host of small towns that played a small part in the Civil War. Continue following Route 211 until you pass under Interstate 81. Make a right turn on Route 305 and follow it to the end of the road to the New Market Battlefield Park (www2.vmi.edu/museum/nm/index.html).

Throughout the war, Stonewall's men had repulsed each Union attempt to invade the Valley and destroy the breadbasket of the Confederacy. But in 1863, Stonewall was wounded by friendly fire at Chancellorsville and died. His passing dealt a blow to the Southern forces of Robert E. Lee. Could anyone be as able a protector of the Valley as Stonewall? The test came in 1864 when Ulysses S. Grant began throwing men and munitions at the bat-

*The visitor's center at New Market chronicles the battle pitting teenage cadets against the Union Army.*

tered Southern ranks in three strategic points across Virginia, including the Shenandoah Valley. General John Breckenridge, though a capable man, had few resources and men to hold off the advancing Union forces. In a desperate attempt to bolster the ranks, he called upon the entire cadet corps at the Virginia Military Institute—240 boys, ages 15 to 18—to join the battle. They marched for four days to supplement the ragged Confederate ranks. It was the first and only time cadet forces in the United States have been pressed into live combat. Though they were hardly prepared for the fight, the cadets accounted well for themselves, capturing an enemy cannon and helping the Rebels slam the door once again on the federal battering ram.

While you are on the grounds, you can tour the museum and walk down to the farmhouse around which the troops rallied before marching into hand-to-hand combat. The entire grounds have been well preserved and you can walk throughout the entire battlefield. It is peaceful, though it is not quiet. The roar of the cannons has been exchanged for the roar of the interstate which passes by within a few hundred yards—an interstate which, ironically, is a critical link between the two regions of the country which once fought each other to the death on this very spot.

Lunch is an easy choice. Drive back into New Market, make a right turn on Route 11 south. Down the road about three long blocks is the Southern Kitchen Restaurant. Do not go to New Market and eat anywhere else. This is the real thing. I don't know anywhere else where you can find peanut soup on the menu as a regular item, and their Virginia fried chicken puts the Colonel to shame. The decor is strictly '50s, which is part of the charm, but rather than seeming time-worn, it looks as clean and fresh as if it opened for business yesterday. Anytime I travel the Shenandoah Valley corridor, I'm going to be taking one of my meals at the Southern Kitchen. Whatever they're serving, I'm eating.

The route returns over Massanutten again via US 211 east with a stop at Luray Caverns (luraycaverns.com). The floor of the Shenandoah Valley is predominantly limestone, and over the course of hundreds of thousands of years, underground streams and pools have eroded large caves. Subsequent water dripping through the valley floor caused great limestone formations to grow undisturbed in subterranean isolation. Once settlers moved into the region, folks who began exploring the haunts and hollows would occasionally stumble upon a cave, or—in the case of Luray—a truly remarkable cavern. Unlike other caverns I have visited in the course of this writing (we won't mention any names), this one is worth the price of admission. The hour-long tour follows a trail through a vast maze of stunning formations. Many of them are hollow, and if gently tapped (don't actually do this), will

*At the Southern Kitchen Restaurant in New Market, Virginia, try the peanut soup. You'll thank me for it.*

make a musical tone. There are so many musical stalactites that the cavern developers created an organ that plays them. It was impressive when I was a wide-eyed eight-year-old, and it still is. After you finish the tour of the cavern, you are also invited to take a tour of the transportation museum in the same building. I didn't see any motorcycles, though, just four-wheelers.

There are three ways to return to Front Royal from Luray. The easiest way is to follow Route 340 up the western side of the Blue Ridge. Pretty, but no major challenge. You can also return via the Parkway. When you reach the summit of the Blue Ridge on 211, you'll arrive at the Thornton Gap entrance to Skyline. If you have ridden it within the last seven days and still have your receipt, the trip will be free. You can also pass Skyline and continue into Sperryville. When you reach Route 522, follow it north.

# Trip 17 Seneca Rocks

**Distance** *224 miles*
**Terrain** *Ridges, passes, and river runs characterize this route*
**Highlights** *Seneca Rocks, Germany Valley, and curves, curves, curves*

You've got to promise you'll keep this one a secret. Well, okay, you can share it with your riding friends, but please don't tell any four-wheelers about this route. Of all the roads I've traveled throughout the Appalachians, this route covers two of my all-time favorites. This is the one route I would recommend to even the most jaded "I've ridden 'em all" rider as a showcase of the best riding the Appalachians have to offer. Let's get to it.

From Front Royal, pick up Route 55 west and make your way through Strasburg and over Interstate 81. From this point, Route 55 becomes a plea-

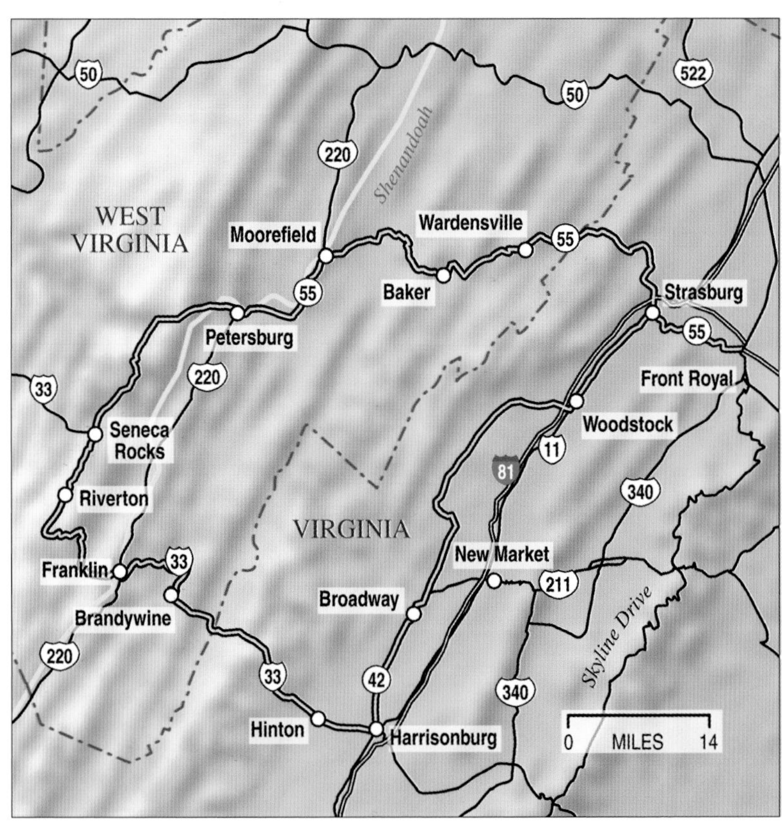

*The overlook at New Germany gives you a good view of the region's geological formations.*

sure to navigate, with virtually no traffic and perfectly banked curves that come rapid-fire, over and around the contours of the Shenandoah and Allegheny Mountains. Just before you enter Wardensville, there's a sign along the road indicating the point which was at one time during the mid-1800s the geographic population center of the United States.

First stop on the tour is the Kac-ka-pon Restaurant (kackaponrestaurant.com) in Wardensville. The Kac-ka-pon offers a great value for any meal, and the prices are as down home as the cooking. If you stop in time for lunch, be sure to save room for a slice from one of their homemade pies.

Out of Wardensville, you can either join the new divided highway, which is pretty (and utterly empty), or you can stick to the road now designated "Old 55" for more great ridge crossings.

Route 55 joins US Route 220 at Moorefield and follows it south for a few miles before returning on its westerly course at Petersburg. Route 220 is

**THE ROUTE FROM FRONT ROYAL**

| | |
|---|---|
| 0 | Begin at point where VA 55 departs US 340/522 north of Front Royal toward Strasburg. Follow VA 55/WV 55 to US 33 at Seneca Rocks |
| 94.1 | Left on US 33 east at Seneca Rocks |
| 158.2 | Left on VA 42 in Harrisonburg |
| 201.7 | Left on US 11 in Woodstock |
| 214.3 | In Strasburg, continue straight to rejoin VA 55 east toward Front Royal |
| 224.4 | Arrive Front Royal at US 340/US 522 via VA 55 |

*Seneca Rocks is popular with rock climbers. And they say motorcyclists are crazy.*

a good road itself, following narrow valleys through West Virginia and well into Virginia. It is often hailed by motorcycle magazines as one of the best unknown roads in America.

Starting somewhere before Petersburg and with increasing frequency you'll notice signs for the Smoke Hole Caverns, Crystal Grottoes, Seneca Caverns, etc. There are probably more attractions of this type in this region than any other because many of the ridges in this area bear limestone caves. Spelunking is a popular pastime. It's not unusual to see a couple of parties of cavers parked by the roadside, headlamps in position, ready to venture into the subterranean passages of the Appalachians.

After Petersburg, Route 55 spends its remaining time chasing a series of rivers before intersecting with US Route 33 at Seneca Rocks National Recreation Area (www.fs.fed.us/r9/mnf/sp/sksrnra.html). This is a popular destination for day-trippers who come to climb the rocks. Seneca Rocks' ragged edges stand out from the smooth ridge lines of the hills that surround them. Often in cases like this, the rock that remains was molten rock that was pushed to the surface by geologic forces below. The heat and pressure made it harder than the surface it pushed through and when that surface wore away, the harder rock was exposed.

Next is a great section of Route 33 between Seneca Rocks and Harrisonburg, Virginia. The first ascent you'll make is long by East Coast standards. It will bring you to a fantastic panorama of the Germany Valley. If you're tempted to pull off for a picture, wait until you get to a spot along the road that has a GERMANY VALLEY marker. It's near the top and offers the best view. This view is a good candidate for your widest lens or a recyclable panoramic camera. To the left and right are the high, imposing ridges of the Alleghenies, while below, a series of small, uniform ridges punctuate the valley floor.

From Franklin, the route settles for a minute and then makes another ascent before dropping into Brandywine. Brandywine is home to a popular recreation area that offers secluded primitive campsites and a lake for swimming and fishing. From here, the last great ascent will soon be upon you as you trek up the Shenandoah Mountains. After a few miles of switchbacks, you can pull off to the side of the road and retrace your path, finding Brandywine in the valley below. Once over the hills, it's another 20 miles or so to Harrisonburg. To avoid the traffic, make a left on Route 42 and head out of town.

When you reach Broadway, you'll face a decision. If you're hungry, follow Route 211 to US 11. On US 11 north at New Market you'll run across the Southern Kitchen Restaurant (see Trip 16, Stonewall's Valley, for details) which is the best place in the area to eat, bar none. You can also continue to follow Route 42 north through Woodstock where you will eventually catch up to Route 11 as well. Route 42 is a more scenic, rural ride.

Route 11 crosses paths with Route 55 in Strasburg. If you're inclined, Strasburg is a good place to hop off and walk around for browsing. There are dozens of small shops willing to accept your credit card and ship your purchases to you (No space on your bike? Not a problem!). Return to Front Royal on Route 55 east to complete the Seneca Rocks tour.

# Trip 18 Land of Canaan

**Distance** *290 miles*
**Terrain** *Long sweepers on US 50, incredibly tight turns on a thin strip of pavement called WV 72*
**Highlights** *Blackwater Falls State Park, Canaan Valley Resort, Amherst Diner*

Many of the tours featured in this book are tied together by a series of great roads that run between points of interest. The focus of this particular loop is really directed toward the roads. There are a few spots worth your attention along this route, but mostly this is just a selection of routes for good, long, hard riding.

Breakfast at the Amherst Diner (540-667-8222) is a good way to start

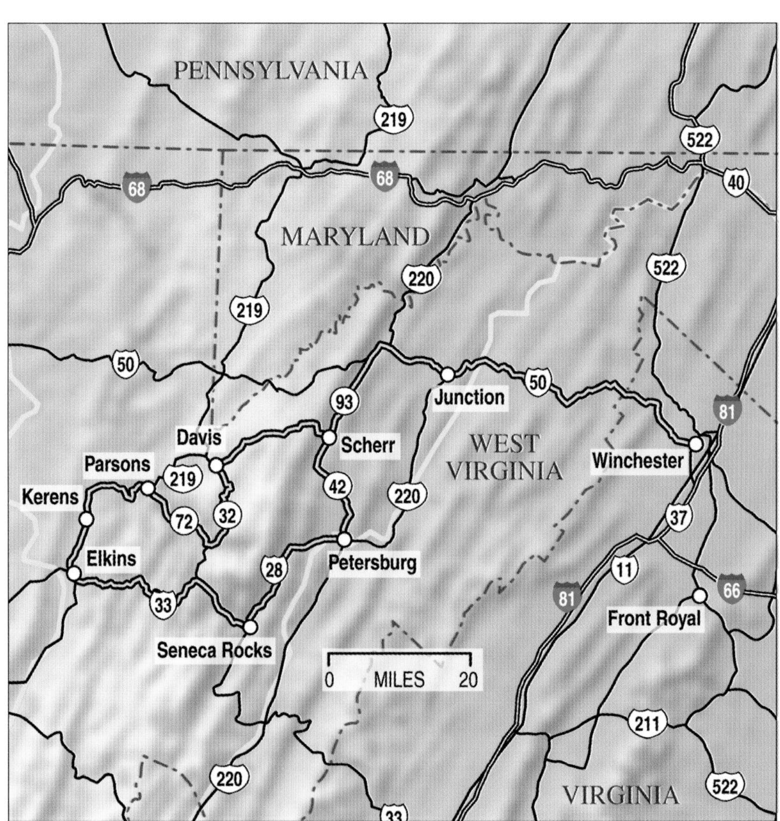

*Ho hum. Just another perfect road, another perfect day.*

this run. You'll find the Amherst on the west side of downtown Winchester where Route 50 becomes Amherst Street. Pick a seat anywhere you like. Robin will likely be your waitress, with Leigh Ann cooking up the victuals. Unlike a lot of other small restaurants in this region, the Amherst is a non-smoking establishment, a welcome development. If you happen to carry

**THE ROUTE FROM WINCHESTER**

| | |
|---|---|
| 0 | Start at US 50/VA 37 junction in Winchester, Va. Take US 50 west. |
| 61.0 | Left on WV 93 |
| 94.2 | Left on WV 32 in Davis |
| 107.2 | Right on WV 72 |
| 123.7 | Left on US 219 |
| 147.8 | Left on US 33 in Elkins |
| 182.6 | Left on WV 28/55 at Seneca Rocks |
| 203.6 | Left on WV 42 at Petersburg |
| 220.6 | Right on WV 93 at Scherr |
| 232.8 | Right on US 50 |
| 293.8 | Arrive Winchester via US 50 |

this book with you on your route, be sure to show it to the gals at the Amherst. They'll get a real kick out of it.

I like US 50 out of Winchester as much as any stretch of federal highway in the Appalachians. Despite the fact that it's nearly all two-lane road, traffic is generally light, and when you do encounter a slowpoke, you're never far from a place where you can deal them out of the picture with a quick flick of the wrist. Route 50 rolls, tumbles, and rocks its way through the thumb of West Virginia.

It's a good 60-mile run along US 50 to reach the first turn on this loop. A long stretch like that makes it easy to find the rhythm of the road. You're not so concerned about when your next turn is coming and what you need to look for. You just ride. Eventually US 220 splits to the north toward Cumberland and four miles later you'll make the left onto WV 93.

WV 93 is joined by WV 42 at Scherr where you'll make the right turn to stay on WV 93. This begins a section of twisty road ascending the mountains surrounding Canaan Valley (pronounced Ka-NAIN as opposed to the biblical KAY-nan). Canaan Valley (canaanvalley.org) is a high mountain plateau, an unusual formation in this area of ridges and valleys. You'll notice something is strange when you enter the Canaan area because you follow a series of curves up, but never come back down. About four miles later, WV 42 splits from WV 93. Turn left, staying on 93 to head toward Davis.

The landscape through this area is so flat it's a little unnerving. The road contains a few gentle curves here and there, but for the most part it's a long, straight path through largely uninhabited wilderness. That large facility you pass on your left is the coal-fired power plant at Mt. Storm.

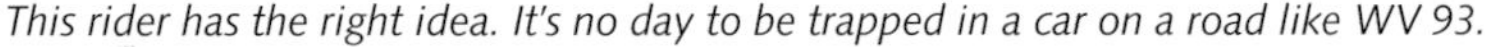

*This rider has the right idea. It's no day to be trapped in a car on a road like WV 93.*

*Park visitors must calculate river flow in cubic feet per minute before they are allowed to leave.*

Arrival at Davis, West Virginia, is sudden enough to take you by surprise after seeing little human activity for so long. Davis is home to Blackwater Falls. It's a spot worth checking out. Turn at the park entrance and follow the signs to the falls. It's a fairly short hike to get to one of several overlooks. The Blackwater River looks amber colored—the result of tannic acid from fallen hemlock trees. After taking a plunge here at the falls, the river continues rolling down an eight-mile gorge. The state operates a variety of facilities here at the falls including a conference center, cabin rentals, and campground. Like other West Virginia parks, the cabins are completely outfitted, so you need to bring nothing but food. Heck, these cabins even have heat!

Continuing on Route 32 south, this route takes you through the middle of the Valley. Toward the southern end, the slopes of the Canaan Valley Resort (canaanresort.com) appear to your left. This retreat is what most people think of when they hear the name Canaan Valley. This is a four-season resort, but it is most widely known for its skiing. If you're not into skiing, you can snowboard, ice skate, or enjoy one of the tube runs. I'm partial to the tubes, because when I ski or snowboard, I spend most of my time on my back anyway.

A few miles south of the resort, make a right onto WV 72. Right away, you know this road will be something special by the NO TRUCKS ALLOWED notice. Route 72 is not for aggressive riding. You'll soon find the road narrows to about one lane with almost no shoulder, and one blind corner after another. In other words, it's great! The first ten miles dodge and twist along

*A slab of West Virginia "interstate" (WV 72). My kind of state.*

a narrow shelf set near the bottom of the hills. This provides for some dramatic views when you break into a clearing and find yourself riding toward the side of a hill that rises nearly straight up. The route is so consistently twisty there are several switchbacks that feel exactly the same. They'll make you think, "Didn't I just run this curve a mile ago?" A little over halfway through the route begins to follow Otter Creek. At this point, the curves calm down a bit, but the views become more expansive.

Route 72 joins US 219 at Hambleton. Turn left toward Parsons. In Parsons, continue to follow US 219 south by turning left at the light. A few miles out of Parsons at Kerens, you are invited to join everyone else on the new, improved, US 219, four-lane highway to Elkins. This is an invitation you can politely decline by continuing straight on Old US 219. The new 219 is part of a controversial route called Corridor H, also known as the "Road to Nowhere."

Many years ago, planners envisioned a series of four-lane roads to be built throughout the Appalachians to open them up to economic development. Some of them made some sense, but few could ever grasp the twists of logic required to justify a four-lane highway connecting Elkins, West Virginia, with Interstate 81 in Virginia. For its part, Virginia took Corridor H off its long-term plan, forcing West Virginia to end its project near the state line at Wardensville.

Old 219 finesses the ridges the old-fashioned way before arriving in Elkins, West Virginia (randolphcountywv.com). Elkins has a sense of busyness that seems out of place for the mountains. It has a thriving art community and features several large festivals each year.

In downtown Elkins, pick up US 33 as it heads east out of town. This section of freeway is known to locals as "the racetrack" because it is so wide-open and straight. This section of US 33 was actually the first part of the original track of Corridor H. Environmental concerns forced the route to be redrawn along its current track. Regardless of which way it goes, Corridor H won't be the kind of road that represents fun riding. The freeway on US 33 dead-ends after a couple of miles, at which point high-quality touring resumes.

At Seneca Rocks, make the left onto WV 28/55, and head toward Petersburg. This section of WV 55 is mostly a straightforward affair. It runs through the upper end of New Germany Valley and gives you a good view of the cliffs. You'll also pass by Smoke Hole Caverns (smokehole.com), notable for its enthusiastic display of entrepreneurship as much as the caverns it promotes.

At Petersburg, make the left turn onto WV 42 and follow that north to the point where it intersects with WV 93. Route 42 is flat and fast with a few good sweepers mixed in for fun. At the junction with WV 93, turn north to return to US 50 and close the loop on your run through the Land of Canaan.

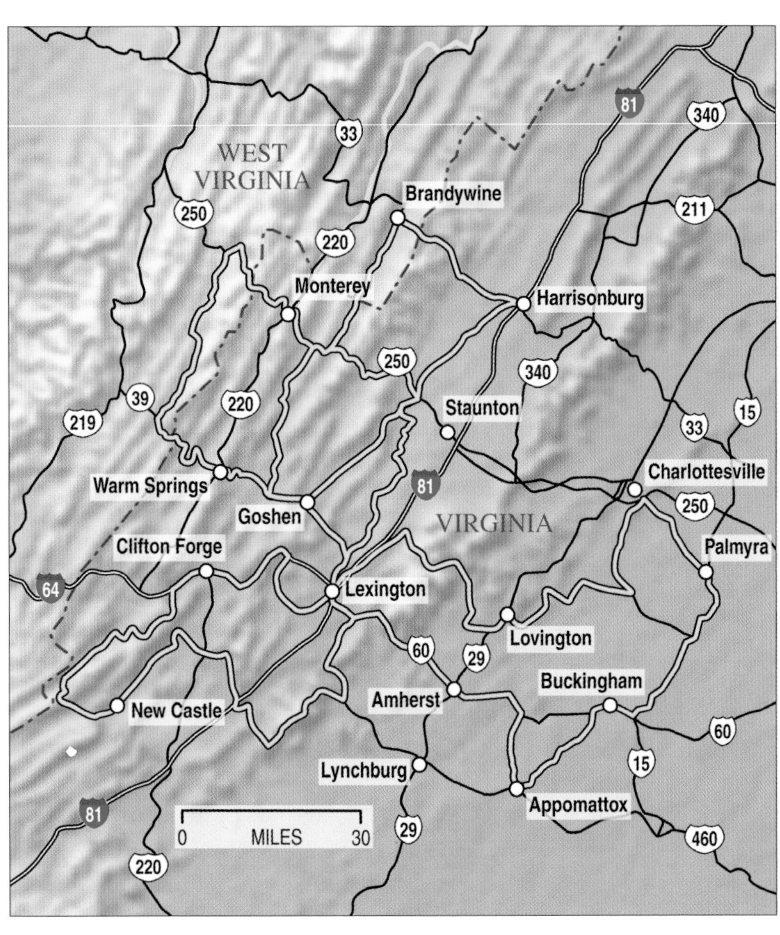
WEST VIRGINIA
VIRGINIA
Brandywine
Monterey
Harrisonburg
Staunton
Warm Springs
Goshen
Charlottesville
Clifton Forge
Palmyra
Lexington
Lovington
Buckingham
Amherst
New Castle
Lynchburg
Appomattox
0 MILES 30
33
250
220
81
340
211
39
219
15
64
60
29
460

# Shrine of the Confederacy

## *Lexington, Virginia*

Lexington is a town motorcyclists should find on their maps and circle with a big red marker. It has all the right features to make it a fine destination for a week of exploring the hills and hollows of the Appalachians. Lexington is an old Southern town with a heritage that it displays with great pride. It is located at the intersection of two major Interstates, I-81 and I-64, making it a breeze to get to and assuring you of a wide range of travel services. It is a college town, too, which means you can always count on something happening around town (lexingtonvirginia.com).

With all these benefits, the town is still relatively small. Somehow, Lexington has managed to hold onto an atmosphere long since lost in many American towns. As you tour the oak-lined avenues and look at the stately old houses, you get a sense of security and serenity, a sense of feeling at home.

Lexington is also in the center of some of the finest, most pleasurable touring I have found anywhere in the region. Five minutes on the road and

*If this is the Hampton Inn, what the heck does the Hilton look like?*

*Downtown Lexington offers a vast array of specialty shops and great dining.*

you will be touring the vast Virginia countryside on well-paved, scenic roads, with little traffic to contend with at any time of the year.

Few people seem to realize the true value of this area, though. In the time I've spent here over the years, most riders I've spoken with are just passing through, on their way to somewhere else. Too bad. In their rush to make it to their destination, they forget about the journey and miss all that good riding. I did occasionally cross paths with a few riders who were out enjoying themselves. They all had one thing in common—big smiles on their faces.

I like staying in downtown Lexington because it's a great walking town. Even the Hampton Inn is historic. A few years ago, the chain renovated the manor house at Col Alto just a couple of blocks off Main Street. Originally built in 1827, Col Alto was the social center of Lexington for many years. It was eventually given to Washington and Lee University. When W&L felt it could no longer maintain the property, Hampton's developer purchased the tract. You can understand that a lot of folks in the area were concerned about what would happen to the estate, but many now believe, as I do, that Hampton did a great job with the property.

Lexington is also home to two motorcycle-friendly B&Bs: Riders Rest and Llewellyn Lodge. Riders Rest is on VA 39 just outside the downtown area, operated by Bernie and Sue Shaw. Bernie has been riding for longer than he cares to remember (sounds like me), and offers not just accommodations for you, but your bike, too (ridersrestbandb.com/motorcyclists.htm). Downtown, innkeeper and Lexington native John Roberts and his wife Ellen enthusiastically welcome riders to Llewellyn Lodge. Ellen's award-winning breakfasts will start your day off right. John is an avid outdoorsman and an expert fly fisherman. A stay with John would be the perfect opportunity to enjoy some of the world-renowned trout streams that run through the Lexington region.

Looking for a lunch or dinner destination? The Southern Inn Restaurant (southerninn.com) in downtown Lexington is an attractive place to dine, especially when prime rib is on your mind. High-backed, wooden booths and the huge, pocket-watch clock on the wall behind the bar are distinctly from an era past. I've also enjoyed lunch and dinner at The Palms (540-463-7911), located downtown at the corner of US 11 and US 60

To the east just a few miles on Route 60 is Buena Vista (pronounced BYEW-na Vista; you, too, can sound just like a native). Buena Vista runs Glen Maury Park, a clean campground perched on a hill just outside of town.

Lexington is home to the Virginia Military Institute (www.vmi.edu), a considerable source of Southern pride. VMI was the first state military college in the nation, founded in 1839 on the principle of perpetuating the model of citizen-soldiers. It has a great legacy of producing soldiers who have accounted well for themselves in the Civil War and both World Wars.

During the Civil War, 240 cadets at the institute—none older than 17—were organized to march against Union forces at New Market (see Trip 16, Stonewall's Valley, for details). The institute also graduated George C. Marshall, who later became Chief of Staff of the Army during World War II, and authored the Marshall Plan for reconstructing Europe after the war. He was awarded the Nobel Peace Prize in 1953, the first professional soldier ever to win the award.

VMI has two museums on campus, the George C. Marshall Museum and Library, and the VMI Museum. Both are free and are well worth taking time to see in order to better understand the role this institute played in shaping world history. Then there is what I can only describe as the Shrine of the Confederacy, the hallmark of the South known as Lee Chapel and Museum.

Robert E. Lee spent his final years in Lexington as president of Washington College (wlu.edu), a small school which had been nearly destroyed

*Lee Chapel in Lexington, Virginia, is considered the Shrine of the Confederacy.*

along with VMI after the Battle of New Market. Lee was hesitant to lend his name to the effort for fear that an association with a fallen general might spell final doom for the struggling college. When all was said and done, it was his name that saved the school.

In the reconstruction of the South, Lee's enduring sense of duty to his country elevated his status as a revered leader even more. He accepted the position at Washington College for a salary of $1,500 per year, turning down several more lucrative offers. Rather than stir resentment among his fellow countrymen who lost everything in the war, his words and deeds underscored the necessity for Virginia and the rest of the South to put the war behind them and concentrate on the task of rebuilding and looking to the future. (It was a message that needed to be heard, too, as it was estimated after the war that Virginia alone had suffered nearly half a billion dollars in losses of private and public property and improvements—a figure that few people could possibly conceive of in that day.)

Soon after Lee assumed his duties at the college, students began arriving from both North and South, and enrollment increased from less than a dozen to more than 400. Lee worked hard in his new job despite his declining health. Though he was only 58 when he accepted the position in 1865, he had aged well beyond his years, no doubt a consequence of the great burden he had borne for the previous few years. He raised money to construct a building on campus that served a great many purposes, including Sunday worship services. If you were a student at Washington College, you were expected to attend Sunday services. Otherwise, you risked raised eyebrows from the general—a subtle but powerful reminder that your absence was noted.

Lee's health finally deteriorated and he died in October 1870. He was interred with other members of his family in the crypt below the chapel he constructed. Out of deep reverence for the general, his office was closed without disturbing a single paper and has remained that way since. It is reported that Lee, like his close companion "Stonewall" Jackson, called on A.P. Hill, another gallant Southern general lost during the war, on his deathbed. His final words were "Strike the tent!"

Though he led the forces that threatened to tear apart the fabric of the still-young union of states, Robert E. Lee's unprecedented leadership and supreme valor have secured his place in history, assuring that he will forever remain among the most respected leaders in this nation's history.

Did I mention Stonewall Jackson's House (stonewalljackson.org) was here, too? Jackson was a professor at VMI before the Civil War and the only home he ever owned is in Lexington. Jackson is also buried here with his family and many Confederate veterans in the Jackson Memorial Cemetery downtown.

Just up the road from Lexington is the Cyrus McCormick Farm (540-377-2255). In case you were sleeping through sixth-grade history, McCormick invented the first mechanical harvester which ushered in the industrial age very nearly by itself. Before the reaper, most folks spent their time growing crops and feeding themselves. The reaper allowed one man to do the work of five and our economy shifted from agriculture to an industrial base. Why should you care? Well, this gave people the time to tinker with things in their spare time such as, oh, fitting crude internal combustion engines in bicycle frames to make them self-powered . . .

# Trip 19 Highlander Loop

**Distance** *197 miles*
**Terrain** *Mountain passes, narrow river valleys, a wide variety of high-speed sweepers and tight switchbacks*
**Highlights** *Luscious green farm country, Green Bank Observatory, Goshen Pass, Monterey, Warm Springs*

There is no finer road for motorcycling in Virginia than Route 39, which opens this trip. I make this bold statement at the risk of being proved wrong someday, but I don't look for that to happen any time soon. Route 39 threads its way through a series of small hills and valleys, passing through the peaceful burg of Rockbridge Baths before entering Goshen Pass. The

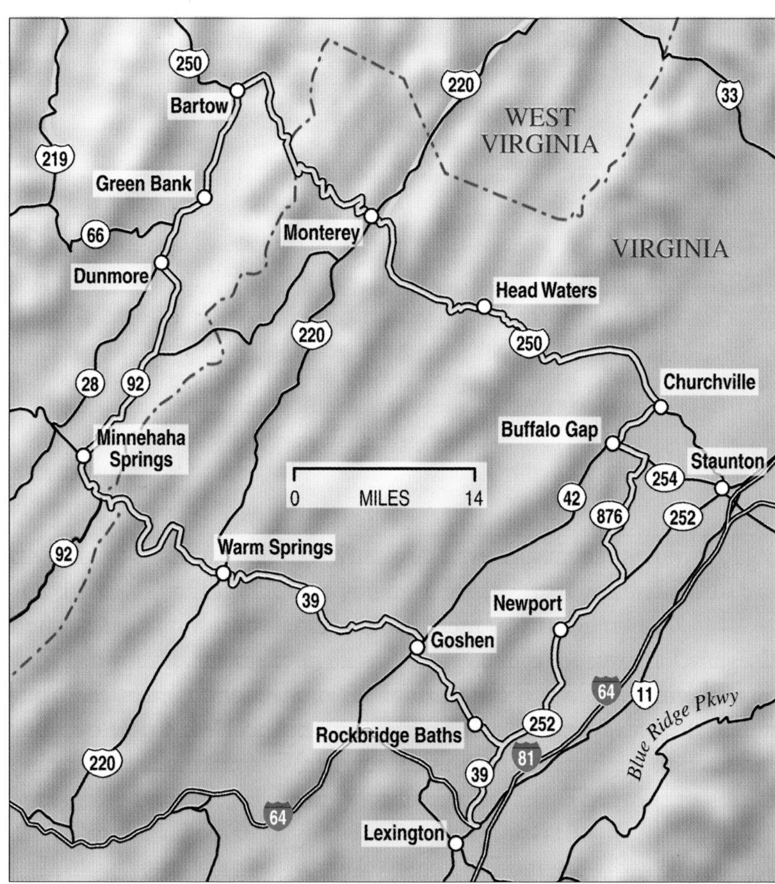

**THE ROUTE FROM LEXINGTON**

| | |
|---|---|
| 0 | Begin on VA 39 west at US 11 in Lexington |
| 62.5 | Right on WV 92 |
| 79.9 | Continue straight on WV 28/WV92 |
| 94.8 | Right on US 250/WV 28 |
| 152.7 | Right on VA 42 in Churchville |
| 158.3 | Left on VA 254 |
| 161.0 | Right on VA 876/Swoope Road/Mish Barn Road |
| 172.3 | Right on VA 252/Middlebrook Road |
| 190.1 | Left on VA 39 |
| 197.4 | Arrive Lexington via VA 39 |

road is cut into the side of the mountain, high above the Goshen River. Near the summit of the pass there is a wayside where you can relax by the river and enjoy a picnic lunch.

The Boy Scouts of America have a large camp near Goshen which you will pass en route. I'm told that the only problem with having the camp in a remote location like this is finding enough old ladies for these spirited young lads to help across the street. There are fewer than 5,000 residents in all of Bath County, and what few candidates there are for street-crossing are likely to be worn out by the time each budding Eagle Scout fills his dance card (tinyurl.com/motojourneys13).

*The annual Blue Grass camp night is a much-anticipated event benefitting the local children's book bank.*

*A contrast between the old and the new; Green Bank's 300-meter scope looms over the landscape.*

When Route 39 runs into Route 220, turn left and head south for a short distance. Just to your right, you will find the Warm Springs Pools (bathcountyva.org). The pools here, and in Hot Springs, have long drawn visitors who wish to relax in the perfect 98.6-degree springs. The Warm Springs pool has separate facilities for men and women. Bring a towel and your swimming trunks.

Follow Route 39 west out of Virginia and into Pocahontas County, West Virginia. The route number does not change. If you happen to be on your way to West Virginia for tours in another section of this book, this is a convenient and scenic route which will pass directly through Summersville, the starting location for those tours.

Shortly after entering West Virginia, Route 92 joins Route 39 for a short distance. When the two separate, turn right and follow Route 92 north. This follows a narrow valley bounded by Lockridge Mountain to the east and Browns Mountain to the west. It's hard to imagine that, even in a remote area like this, you are still within one day's journey of half the population of the United States. Route 28 joins Route 92. After passing the dot on the map called Dunmore, you have an opportunity to visit the Cass Scenic Railroad. It's about eight to ten miles west on Route 66 in West Virginia (see Trip 26, The Gable End of Hell).

This remote area is good for more than just raising cows and making moonshine, it's also good for star gazing. That's why Green Bank was chosen as the site for the National Radio Astronomy Observatory (www.gb.nrao.edu) in the mid-'50s. Radio astronomy is different from the traditional optical astronomy in that it examines the many different kinds of particles and phenomena that generate radio waves, a portion of which strike earth. It didn't become a serious science until radio technology developed significantly in the 1940s.

The telescopes require an area free of any sources of electromagnetic interference. One look around Green Bank will tell you why they located here. In fact, this area has been designated something of a radio-free zone, and special permission is required before anyone can build a facility that might have an effect on the observatory.

Green Bank features a half-dozen big scopes trolling the universe for interesting signals. The largest is a 100-meter telescope called the Green Bank Telescope (GBT). The GBT was built a few years ago after the main scope collapsed under the weight of a heavy snow. Operators tried moving the dish back and forth to clear it, but it gave way. Can you imagine the telephone call that took place when the operator had to call his manager to say that the scope had, er, tipped over?

The new scope looks something like a clamshell rising above the treeline. Each of the 2,204 panels which comprise the dish are independently computer controlled and adjustable so the accuracy of the surface can be maintained to the smallest fraction.

Visitors are welcome at the facility, so be sure to stop by. The observatory's expansive visitor facility features interactive exhibits that highlight the science of radio astronomy. Tours are offered year-round, giving you a chance to see the telescopes up close. Best of all, it's all free.

When you get back on the road, follow Route 28 until it intersects with Route 250 at Bartow. It's time to head east, so make the right turn and follow Route 250 back into Virginia. Route 250 is widely known among area riders for its twists and turns. Things start off pretty gently, but as you ap-

*Nothing but blue skies and great roads in Virginia's Highland County.*

proach the Virginia state line, the frequency of turns quickens, as will your pulse. As you top Lantz Mountain, one of the most beautiful valleys I have seen anywhere will open before you—this is Blue Grass Valley. To the north and south lies a picture postcard valley with big white farmhouses and manicured grounds so perfect they resemble scale models. These are the real thing. All this beauty is framed against a backdrop of Monterey Mountain, a few miles distant. It is a sight that will not disappoint. Highland County lays claim to the highest average elevation east of the Mississippi. The town of Monterey is 3,000 feet above sea level. That kind of elevation means cool summer nights even when the rest of the eastern seaboard is sweltering. It would be pretty darn easy to put the kickstand down in Monterey and set up housekeeping there on a full-time basis. You can really stretch out in these parts—the 1990 census indicated that only a handful over 2,600 people call Highland County home.

Monterey is home to a group of riders who know they're living in the middle of a rider's paradise, and they appreciate every minute of it. Be sure to stop by the Gallery of Mountain Secrets on Main Street and introduce yourself to Rich and Linda Holman. Rich and Linda are avid riders and they really embody the laid-back, people-friendly, Monterey lifestyle. If you happen by the gallery at the same time as local rider Brian Richardson, ask Brian and Rich to recount some of their riding stories, they have a good supply! The gallery is a showcase of items produced by local artisans, but they also have a special bike room featuring items of interest to riders. Rich and Linda also operate the Cherry Hill Bed and Breakfast (www.cherryhillbandb.com) located up on the hillside behind Main Street. I can't think of a better place to recommend to you.

If you're of a mind to stop for a bite, you can't go wrong with High's Restaurant (540-468-1600) on Main Street in Monterey. If you're staying for the evening, be sure you arrive before 8 p.m. There aren't any all-night joints in this part of the country. Right across the street is the Highland Inn (highland-inn.com), a frequent retreat for the region's BMW motorcycle clubs.

There aren't many stretches of road on the East Coast that cross as many ridges head-on as the section of Route 250 between Monterey and Staunton. The next 30 miles have a generous mix of tight, 10-mph switchbacks and double-nickel sweepers. There are three or four main passes interspersed with small valleys, so just as you get tired working the bike from one side to the other, you get a short break, and then another workout. Your trip through George Washington National Forest is like riding an avenue for a king, lined with stately old trees and a brook running on either side. Beautiful!

*Highland Inn is a favorite destination of riders throughout the mid-Atlantic region.*

All too soon you arrive at Churchville. Make the turn south on Route 42 and follow it to Buffalo Gap. Follow Route 254 east to the left at the intersection and after a couple of miles, look for County Route 876 on your right. This is a neat little road that at times threatens to turn to gravel but never does. It is so deserted and open, it almost feels like you're riding along a farmer's private driveway or through the field. You'll need to exercise all your navigational skills on this route because it takes unexpected turns at some intersections with other roads. It is clearly marked, though, so at worst you'll simply have to make a U-turn and pick up where you left off.

This area is so quiet and unhurried, your pace automatically slows. You'll feel a real connection with it—a sense of continuity and stability. Cows march slowly across the field in the evening, keeping their appointment with the farmer as they have day after day, year after year. Folks amble down a back lane, returning from a day at the shop or the office as they have done for the last 30 or 40 years. You could easily fall into the habit of living here yourself.

Eventually Route 876 finds Route 252. Route 252—another well-paved country road—meanders gently through towns with innocent names like Brownsburg, Bustleburg, and Middlebrook. When Route 252 ends on Route 39, turn left to make your way back to Lexington.

# Trip 20 Valley Run

**Distance** *187 miles*
**Terrain** *Rolling farm country, river valleys, and mountain passes*
**Highlights** *Museum of American Frontier Culture, Woodrow Wilson Birthplace and Museum, Valley League Baseball*

Today's tour explores roads of the upper Shenandoah Valley, turning in a counter-clockwise direction. It is difficult to find a road that disappoints, and if your bike is stable on gravel or dirt roads, don't hesitate to explore to the sides. There are surprises around every turn, most of them pleasant.

If you didn't get a chance to practice your lines on the seductive pavement that is Route 39 in another tour, today is your day. After following Route 39 through Goshen Pass, turn right on Route 42 in the town of Goshen and follow it north. Route 42 passes through the village of Craigsville and eventually works its way between Great North and North Mountain to Buffalo Gap. Once through the gap, you'll re-enter the Shenandoah Valley with its wide-open views and green pastures.

Churchville is a good place to turn if you want to check out Staunton (pronounced STAN-uhn by the local folks). Follow Route 250 about twelve miles east into downtown Staunton. The Museum of American Frontier Culture (frontiermuseum.org) is on the east side of town and worth a visit. When the European settlers came to this country, they brought their old methods of living with them and adapted them to a new country. The museum is home to three farmhouses of Scots-Irish, German,

### THE ROUTE FROM LEXINGTON

| | |
|---|---|
| 0 | Begin on VA 39 west at US 11 in Lexington |
| 19.5 | Right on VA 42 in Goshen |
| 69.8 | Left on US 33 west in Harrisonburg |
| 98.0 | Left on CR 21/Sugar Grove Road in Brandywine |
| 115.6 | CR 21 becomes VA 614 at state border |
| 124.0 | Right on US 250 west toward McDowell |
| 128.3 | Left on VA 678/Williamsville Road |
| 158.5 | Left on VA 39 east |
| 186.8 | Arrive Lexington via VA 39 |

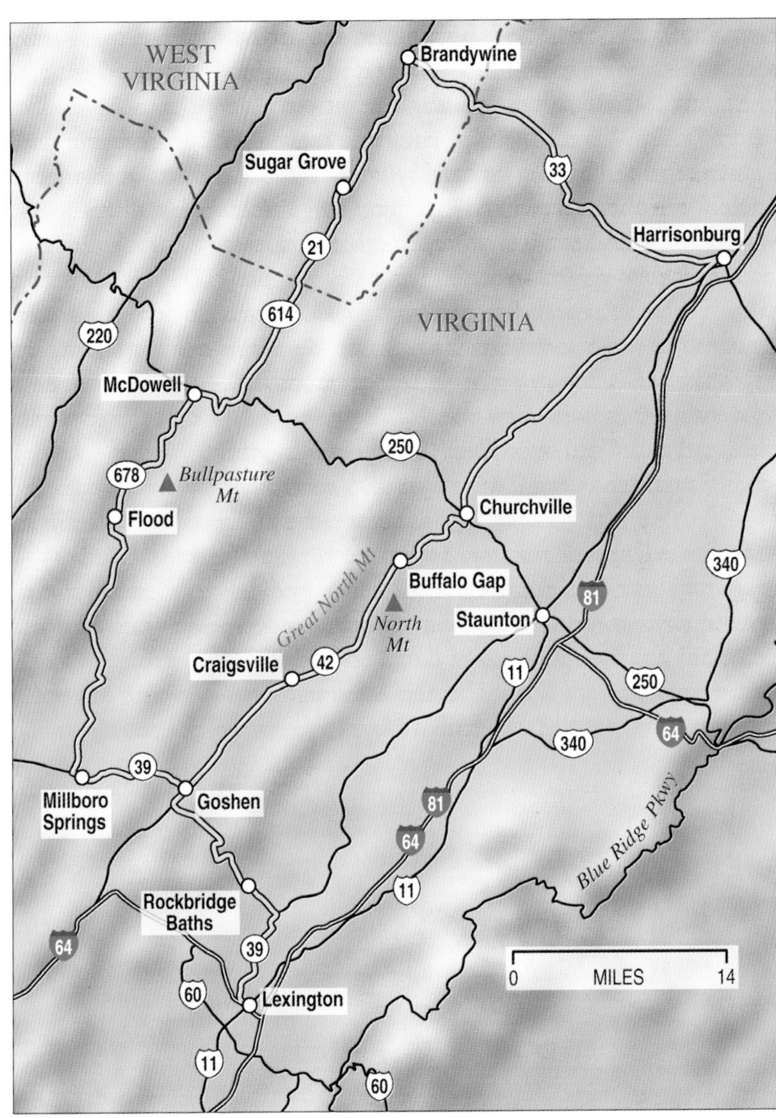


and English heritage, each having been carefully disassembled in its home country and then brought to this 180 acres in the valley where all three cultures began to intermingle in the 1700s. A fourth farm from Botetourt County, Virginia, shows how these European designs were carried over from the Old Country and evolved into an American style.

Speaking of different cultures, there's an old joke about the pioneers that settled the Appalachians, and I have to say, it really rings true. They say that

*There's a Walmart Super-Center around the bend. Just kidding!*

when the English moved into a new territory to settle, they built a church on arrival because they were pious. When the Germans came to a new area, they first built a barn, because they were practical. When the Scots-Irish moved in, the first thing they built was a whiskey still. Those cultural differences exist to this day. Ask me some time about the difference between my family reunions (Germans) and those of my wife's family (Scots-Irish).

Downtown is the Woodrow Wilson Birthplace and Museum (woodrowwilson.org). Wilson, the 28th president of the United States, was born here in 1856. He came from a wealthy family and was well educated, earning a doctorate in political science and rising through the academic ranks to become president of Princeton.

If you're in the area for more than a day, check out the Valley League Baseball game schedule (valleyleaguebaseball.com) for a game in the region. The Valley League is a throw-back to old-time baseball with teams from the local area competing for the Valley League Championship. Chances are good that some of the players you see here will end up in "the bigs." Former Valley League players include folks like David Eckstein, Raul Garcia, Javier Lopez, and Mike Lowell.

When you've had enough looking around, find your way back out Route 250 west, Churchville Avenue. Turn right and follow Route 42 north to

Harrisonburg. The scenery between Churchville and Harrisonburg is nice enough to write home about, and so is the road. What will get you are those occasional straights that give you a chance to look around, and then before you know it—surprise! The road makes an abrupt turn.

Your route does take you into downtown Harrisonburg, but the traffic is usually pretty moderate. Harrisonburg is an active college town, home to James Madison University (jmu.edu). Your next turn will come in the middle of town onto Route 33. Make the left and head west toward the mountains. We've got some dicing to do! Even though US Route 33 is one of just a handful of east-west corridors over the mountains, there isn't much traffic to speak of because, quite frankly, there isn't much to arrive at when you get over the mountain—other than more good riding.

Once you enter the George Washington National Forest, the road unexpectedly straightens for what must be two miles. The Shenandoah Mountains lie directly in front of you, hidden by thick forest, and even with advance warning, the first curve is surprisingly sharp.

The pass over the Shenandoahs begins with some moderate speed switchbacks. The tighter stuff is on the back side—when the downhill slope makes it more of a challenge. The view is so enchanting it can be a real distraction, but there are a few turnouts near the summit where you can stop for a look. The road straightens at Brandywine, site of the Brandywine Rec-

*Folks chat on the front porch on Sunday morning while waiting for a table at The Cabins Restaurant.*

*Mountains ahead, mountains behind—that's a can't-miss combination.*

reation Area. If you're looking for cheap camping in the middle of nowhere, this is a great place. Most of my riding and camping buddies like to come out here to beat the summer heat because you can always count on Brandywine to be about 10 to 15 degrees cooler. Camping is well under 20 dollars per night. Look for a spot along the outside of the loop in the very back of the camp, that's your prime location.

You can hike an easy trail that leads from the camp to an old sawmill site along the ridge. It isn't uncommon to spot a lot of wildlife, especially if you hike early in the morning or at dusk. There's even the off chance you might see a black bear. The lake sports a beach (it's a big pond, really, but I suppose if it has a beach it qualifies as a lake) and a changing house if you need to cool off.

There isn't much doing in the town of Brandywine, but stop by The Cabin Restaurant for a great meal. And make sure you save room for a piece of homemade pie. It's also a good place to catch up on what's happening in Brandywine. On Sundays, there's a good chance you'll be sitting outside on the porch waiting for a table. It's not unusual for folks to get so caught up in conversation, they forget they're waiting to eat!

At the T intersection in Brandywine, make a left turn on County Route 21 toward Propstburg and Sugar Grove—and the naval base. Yep, your U.S.

Navy has seen fit to build a naval base on the south fork of the Potomac River that has barely enough water to float a canoe. Rumor has it the original purpose for the base was the development of a top-secret craft, codenamed "Waterless"—a revolutionary new ship that required no water to float. The secret was to make the boats small enough to hold only a few people and outfit them with tracks like a bulldozer and a big gun on a turret that could spin around in any direction. The project was canceled in 1953 after the Navy discovered the Army had been using a similar device for 40 years, called a "tank." (Okay, I'm just joking. Actually, the naval base is a communications facility. Apologies to my Navy riding buddies . . .)

At Sugar Grove, follow the road to the left to stay on course. Turning right will take you further into West Virginia and eventually you will run into Route 220. Only the cows in the field or a watchful hawk will note your passing. On either side you will be surrounded by mountain ridges. Route 21 often looks as though it will run directly over a ridge only to divert at the last possible moment and find a narrow gap through it. The only indication you have returned to the Old Dominion is a small sign which says, simply, VIRGINIA. Here the road becomes Route 614.

Route 614 continues to follow the south fork of the Potomac. When Route 614 intersects Route 250, turn right and follow 250 west to stay on paved surfaces and to catch some serious switchbacks. Hug the curves back across Bullpasture Mountain and turn left on Route 678 in the burg of McDowell. In a way I hate to say that you'll soon discover "more of the same," because I don't want you to get the impression you will be bored—you won't be! In this case, "more of the same" is something you could handle all the time!

After passing through Flood, the road draws closer to the Bullpasture River until the two are almost one. Somehow both just manage to squeeze through a tight gap and do an end run around Bullpasture Mountain. There are some places where the riverfront is privately owned and stopping along the river would be trespassing. However, there are other areas open to the public where you can stop for a breather and enjoy the rushing water.

From here, Route 678 ends on Route 39 just above Millboro Springs and the journey home begins. You've still got plenty of good riding left; Goshen Pass is yet to come. And if you happen to run into any Navy fellas, ask them to tell you all about the Waterless Project. Remember, you heard about it here first.

# Trip 21 Hollow Hunting

**Distance** *227 miles*
**Terrain** *Mountain roads with sharp turns at odd cambers, main routes mixed with large, fast sweepers and tight hairpins*
**Highlights** *Confederate ironworks ruins, a short section of the Blue Ridge Parkway that includes Peaks of Otter, Natural Bridge*

This tour features some of the roads favored by local riders who have guarded them as a closely held secret until now. There are abundant opportunities to explore roads leading in all directions from the planned route—limited only by your time and imagination. Dual sport riders would have a field day with the tracks that take the high road over some of the ridges, rather than skirt around them like the paved roads.

Begin the route by finding Route 251 on the south edge of Lexington. This road will quickly whisk you out of town on broad curves and into rural Virginia. At Collierstown, the road narrows and for a brief period becomes Route 770, changing after Collierstown to Route 646. The front of North Mountain rises before you like a fortress, and though the road looks as

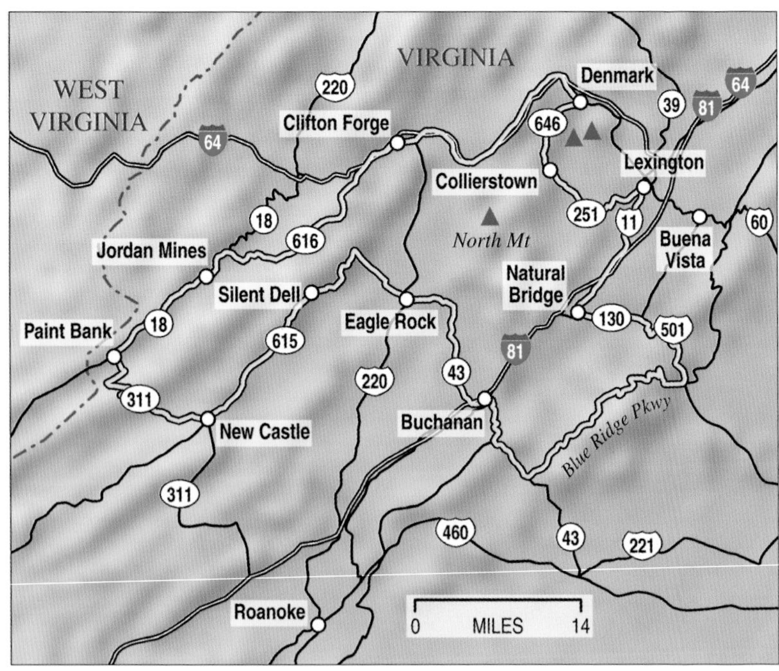

**THE ROUTE FROM LEXINGTON**

| | |
|---|---|
| 0 | Depart on VA 251 west at intersection of US 11 Business and VA 251 in Lexington |
| 9.8 | VA 251 becomes VA 770 |
| 10.4 | Continue straight on VA 646 |
| 17.8 | Left on US 60/Midland Trail at Denmark |
| 35.5 | Continue straight, US 60 becomes VA 269/ Longdale Furnace Road) |
| 37.3 | Left on US 60 Business in Clifton Forge |
| 40.6 | Left on VA 696 toward Selma |
| 43.3 | Left on VA 616/Rich Patch Road |
| 59.0 | Straight on VA 613/Bens Road |
| 60.7 | Left on VA 18 at Boiling Springs |
| 74.4 | Left on VA 311 at Paint Bank |
| 90.6 | Left on VA 615/Craigs Creek Road |
| 116.5 | Right on US 220 south/Botetourt Road |
| 117.5 | Left on VA 810 (To VA 43) at Eagle Rock |
| 118.0 | Right on VA 43 East |
| 137.1 | Left on Blue Ridge Parkway |
| 170.8 | Left on US 501 toward Glasgow |
| 181.0 | Left on VA 130 |
| 197.5 | Right on US 11 at Natural Bridge |
| 227.1 | Arrive in Lexington |

though it will make a direct charge on the stronghold, it turns north at the last moment. There is no paved road directly over the summit. Route 770 does cross the mountain, but this is a route for dual sport riders. I am still apologizing to my touring rig for trying to make it across. Routes 770 and 646 are representative of the country lanes that crisscross the landscape throughout the entire Appalachian region in unending variety. You could spend weeks in Lexington alone, riding in a different direction each day, tracing each little line on the map. I haven't found a bad road out here yet; there just aren't any people to get in the way. If there is any identifiable danger to riding aggressively on these roads, it would have to be the chance encounter of two pickup trucks stopped in the road, with a couple of old-timers talking to each other. They don't often pick the best place in the road to stop.

*This rider seeks the perfect apex along the Parkway.*

The route we follow rides the boundary of the Jefferson National Forest between North Mountain to your left and the twin Big House and Little House Mountains to your right. Route 646 ends at Denmark (passport not required). Turn left on Route 850 to do an end run and finally find your way around North Mountain. The route is an old stretch of US 60 that parallels Interstate 64 and changes numbers a few times, beginning as 850, then 269, and finally 632. Route 850 begins as a lovely jaunt through the woods; you would never know the interstate is just a few hundred yards to your left. Heck, even the interstate is nice for that matter. It isn't a major east-west route for trucks, so it is actually a nice ride.

Just after you reach Longdale Furnace, look for a pair of tall brick smokestacks on your right. These are what remain of the Lucy-Selina Furnace, a Confederate ironworks built to supply Rebel forces during the Civil War. These old stacks stand as defiantly today as they did more than 130 years ago, and they symbolize the pride some Southerners still feel when they speak of the Confederacy.

As you pass through Clifton Forge on Route 60, look for Route 696 and a sign for Selma. A bridge will take you over the track yard and along the foothills of the Rich Patch Mountains. Look for Route 616 on your left. It's one you might easily miss. If you go through a narrow bridge and end up near the interstate, turn around and look for Route 616 on your right. Fortunately the route whisks you away from the industrial section of town quickly and soon you will be meandering through a maze of foothills, hollows, and coves. The roadbed is so crooked it seems to turn in on itself sometimes. Route 616 follows an unending series of small creeks and narrow valleys, and when faced with a hill, resigns itself to climbing over it, sometimes meandering back and forth, other times making quick work of it, but never becoming boring. Be sure to watch for roads intersecting Route 616. Sometimes you have to hunt for the road. This is when a good map is indispensable. At the intersection with Route 613, turn right and follow Route 613 for a few tenths of a mile. Route 616 will reappear on your left (tinyurl.com/motojourneys14).

For decades, the early settlers who came from Europe settled on the eastern side of the Appalachians, the mountains acting as a natural barrier separating the seaboard from the rest of the continent. It wasn't until they were hard pressed to find new land that some began following the trails blazed by Daniel Boone and others through the terrifying wilderness deep in the mountains. You may think you live in the sticks in a small town, but even after 400 years of settled history, this area is still sparsely populated. But you

*Stacks of the Confederate Lucy-Selina Ironworks still stand watch over the Virginia countryside.*

know, something is different about this area now. I think it is the advent of the satellite dish. You see them in the yards of even the crummiest houses. They might have a leaky roof, but they can pull in ESPN, by God.

Eventually the road ends near Jordan Mines on Route 18, a wide, clean road that follows a narrow valley along Potts Creek. Take Route 18 south to where it ends on Route 311 at Paint Bank. Good news: if you're ready for lunch, Paint Bank is a great place to stop. The Swinging Bridge Restaurant and General Store are ready to serve up a tasty lunch or light snack, your choice (theswingingbridge.com). After topping off your bike's tank and yours, you will be ready to conquer Potts Mountain. Follow Route 311 south. The road gets you warmed up with a few switchbacks and sweepers, then starts to get busy as it climbs the mountain. These are curves familiar to all types of motorcycles, so you'll be assured a good time no matter what you ride. There are some occasional gravel hazards caused by our four-wheeled friends who run a little wide in the curves, a luxury they can afford.

After the fireworks, Route 311 meanders peacefully eastward, passing through the town of New Castle.

In town, make a left onto Craigs Creek Road/Route 615. This is a beautiful country road which follows Craig Creek for its entire length through dots on the map such as Given, Oriskany, and Silent Dell. At Silent Dell, check out the unusual footbridge crossing the river. Make a right at your intersection with Route 220 and follow it for a short distance, turning left on Route 43 at Eagle Rock. This is a lightly traveled road, easy for making good time. On our ascent of the Blue Ridge, we once again will cross paths with the Appalachian Trail. Our entrance to the Blue Ridge Parkway is just a few miles south of Peaks of Otter, a small resort area located directly on the Parkway which takes its name from the two matching formations that rise behind it.

The Peaks of Otter Lodge (peaksofotter.com) is a popular base for exploring the twin peaks, so you might time your trip to coincide with an overnight stay here and then set out for some backpacking. If you venture through the area on a fall weekend, be prepared to deal with traffic. The great majority is clustered around the lodge and service center on the parkway. Some folks just can't move fast enough to get out of their own way, so be patient if you're creeping along. Go during the week or at any time other than peak foliage weekends to avoid the crowd.

After the 45 mph speed limit on the Parkway, you'll probably be wanting a little faster pace. Exit at Route 501 and turn left, following it west as it careens down the Blue Ridge. I'll wager you won't go any faster than you did on the Parkway, but it will seem like warp speed! Don't let those fast curves

*Enjoy the pools Thomas Jefferson bathed in over 200 years ago. Yes, it is different water.*

seduce you; there are some tighter surprises lurking ahead, just waiting for you to overcommit yourself.

When Route 130 splits from Route 501, follow 130 into Natural Bridge (naturalbridgeva.com). In 1774, Thomas Jefferson bought Natural Bridge and the surrounding property from King George III for 20 shillings (in today's money, about two dollars and forty cents). Obviously old King George didn't have good advisors working for him; he could easily have gotten twice as much. The natural arch is proclaimed to be one of the Seven Natural Wonders of the World. If you haven't seen it before, it is worth a look. Not wanting a dollar to burn a hole in your pocket, the purveyors of the bridge have thoughtfully erected a few other intellectually stimulating exhibits for your touring pleasure, including a wax museum and a zoo.

The return route follows Route 11 north into Lexington. I like Route 11. I only seem to ride it in small stretches, but I find it rewarding. When you jump on the interstate, you have a tendency to think in miles by the fifties or hundreds. On a road like Route 11, you can anticipate that the next town or village is just a few miles ahead, not fifty or a hundred. I know I'm not making the same kind of time that I would out on the interstate, but running across those small towns makes me feel like I'm getting somewhere. On the superslab, I'm just lost in the crowd. I think you'll notice this, too—when you're out there motoring along the highway—this feeling of getting somewhere, of being somewhere. Let's go home.

# Trip 22 Surrender at Appomattox

**Distance** *231 miles*
**Terrain** *Rolling Virginia piedmont, mountain passes*
**Highlights** *Appomattox Court House, Monticello, Ash Lawn, Walton's Mountain Museum, Crabtree Falls*

This tour features a good dose of history from three distinct eras. First stop on the tour is the site where the Civil War ended, Appomattox Court House. After that, we will visit Thomas Jefferson's famous home, Monticello, and another home made famous by the TV generation, the boyhood home of Earl Hamner, Jr., creator of the television series *The Waltons.*

The loop begins following Route 60 east over the Blue Ridge Mountains at Buena Vista. This is a good start to the day with a dozen or so miles of smooth, twisty pavement. Once over the Blue Ridge, Route 60 straightens and makes a beeline toward Richmond. When you approach the James River, turn right on Route 26 and follow it to Appomattox. A left turn on

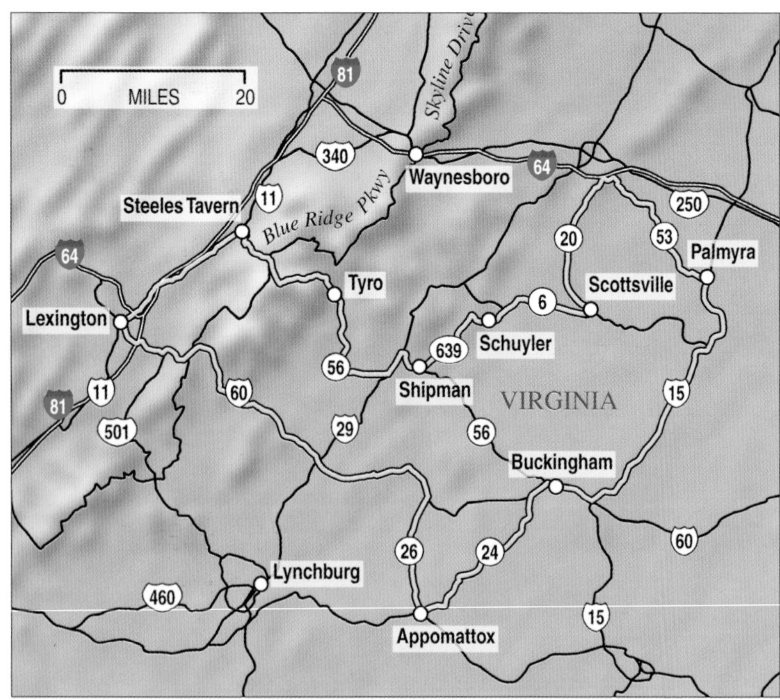

### THE ROUTE FROM LEXINGTON

| | |
|---|---|
| 0 | Depart Lexington on US 60 east at junction of US 60/ US 11 Bypass |
| 46.6 | Right on VA 26 |
| 59.5 | Left on VA 131 in Appomattox |
| 59.6 | VA 131 becomes VA 24 |
| 62.2 | Arrive at Appomattox Court House. Continue on VA 24 north |
| 78.8 | Right on US 60 east |
| 86.6 | Left on US 15 north |
| 117.1 | Left on VA 53 west |
| 135.1 | Left on VA 20 south |
| 152.0 | Right on VA 6 north |
| 162.5 | Left on VA 800 (Schuyler Road) |
| 164.7 | Right on VA 617 (Rockfish Gap Road) |
| 168.6 | VA 639 joins VA 617 |
| 168.9 | Stay to the left with VA 639 when VA 617 splits off to right |
| 177.3 | Right on VA 56 at Shipman |
| 181.3 | Left on US 29 south at Lovingston |
| 184.7 | Right on VA 56 |
| 215.0 | Left on US 11 at Steeles Tavern |
| 231.1 | Arrive Lexington via US 11 south |

Route 24 will bring you to the Appomattox Court House National Historic Park (nps.gov/apco). On your way to and from Appomattox, you pass through rolling farm country which, with the exception of a few more houses, looks pretty much the same as it did in April 1865.

The atmosphere at Appomattox Court House is quiet, reverent. A few visitors speak to each other in hushed tones and walk through the courtyard where two armies once met. Here General Robert E. Lee surrendered the Army of Northern Virginia to Union General Ulysses S. Grant, ending the four-year-long Civil War. Though it was finished nearly 130 years ago, the story of the surrender still tugs at the heartstrings.

After a long siege and years of posturing, Grant's army was finally able to sweep through Richmond, the Confederate capital. The Confederate army retreating to the west was cut off from its supplies and stood little chance of gaining reinforcements. Lee's men were nearly starved and poorly clothed. The wounded suffered even more. In his words, "There was nothing left for

*They say you can run but you can't hide. Wilmer McLean, former owner of this house, will tell you that's true.*

me to do but go see General Grant." Weary but stone-faced, Lee went to meet the general at the town of Appomattox Court House.

The two men met at the home of Wilmer McLean, a private citizen. Ironically, Grant had occupied McLean's house as his headquarters four years earlier at the Battle of Manassas. Wanting to get away from the flying bullets, McLean packed up his family and moved to remote central Virginia. The two generals sat in the parlor of the McLean home where General Grant drafted the surrender. His terms were unusually generous, as an offering to begin the healing process. Word of the surrender spread like wildfire through the ranks. Hardened Southern soldiers, who had suffered so much, wept openly. As Lee returned to his battle-weary men, they swrmed around him, hoping to touch him or his horse, Traveler. Lee's eyes filled with tears as he surveyed his ragtag army. Over and over again, he told his men to go home, plant their crops, and obey the law.

After years of neglect and near ruin, the village of Appomattox Court House has now been restored to its appearance during that era. The home of Wilmer McLean has been fully restored and the reconstructed courthouse holds a museum and visitor center (get your Parks Passport stamped here).

After your visit to the courthouse, continue the loop by following Route 24 until it rejoins Route 60. From here it is a short distance east to Route 15 at Sprouses Corner. The touring is easy and wide open with views of the Blue Ridge some 50 miles distant. At the intersection with Route 15, turn left and head north. This section of road is more frequently traveled, but you shouldn't have too much trouble keeping a good pace. At Palmyra, make the left on Route 53, the backdoor entrance to Jefferson's Monticello (monticello.org) and Ash Lawn, (ashlawnhighland.org) James Monroe's home. As you approach Charlottesville, the road regains its playful quality and dark woods hide your approach to the Jefferson estate.

Jefferson's home is one of the most widely known and visited of all our American forefathers. Jefferson was a Renaissance man with far-ranging interests and expertise in many things, including architecture, agriculture, literature, and political science. He secured his place in history by authoring the Declaration of Independence, founding the University of Virginia, and serving as our ambassador to France and as third President of the United States. Jefferson was also an inventor, tinkerer, and wine lover. Monticello is full of the products of his imagination, including a seven-day clock and a writing machine that allowed him to duplicate his correspondence. Strolling the grounds is as much fun as touring the inside. Jefferson planted extensive gardens and you can walk freely among them. Jefferson's horticultural legacy has helped modern gardeners revive old and rare varieties of plants that would have otherwise vanished by now. Thus, the gardens you see are very similar to how they would have appeared in Jefferson's day.

Out of Monticello, follow Route 53 to Route 20 to Scottsville and turn right on Route 6. This road must have been designed by laying a straight edge across a sheet of paper and drawing a line—it's pretty darn straight. However, it is a pretty ride. When you enter a straightaway there is nothing

*The gals at Boyer Station Restaurant invite you to join them. The food is fresh and well prepared.*

*Route 56 offers a great set of curves over the Parkway at the Tye River Gap.*

to see ahead but a broad tree-lined avenue. Watch for Route 800 appearing on your left and make the turn. This ends on Route 617 in Schuyler (SKY-ler). Things are abuzz these days in Schuyler, thanks largely to the fame of one native son who wrote stories about his family. They called them *The Waltons* for television, but the real John Boy was Earl Hamner, Jr. The enduring popularity of the series brought many people searching for Waltons Mountain and prompted the local community to create the Waltons Mountain Museum (waltonmuseum.org). The museum includes reproductions of some of the famous scenes in the show, including John Boy's room and the kitchen.

Your route out of Schuyler is probably the same one the Walto . . . , er, Hamners would have taken to get to the main highway, and though it is paved, it isn't any busier today than it was sixty years ago. The hills are small but packed tightly together, and the road busily winds through them, following each small opening between them to trace a path. You might feel tempted to drop a trail of bread crumbs, just in case the particular road you're on should dead-end without warning. The easiest way out is to stay on 617 until you intersect 639, a left turn that crosses over a mountain river. When you cross the railroad tracks at Shipman, turn right at the end of the road on Route 56. You are now on your way to another encounter with the Blue Ridge. Stay with Route 56 as it joins Route 29, then splits off again.

Route 56 makes a direct assault on the mountains at the Tye River Gap. This is probably the best crossing of the Blue Ridge and attracts a lot of motorcyclists. The road begins with a long straight, aimed right at the mountain, then takes a sharp turn upward. From Massies Mill, it follows the Tye River Gap through the mountains. From this direction your ride is mostly up, so you can take a more aggressive riding posture. The road gets even wilder after you pass the intersection with the Blue Ridge Parkway at the gap. On your descent, watch for broken pavement and gravel hazards. Some of the turns are pitched at incredibly steep angles.

One of the popular watering holes for local riders is the Country Store at the Montebello Camping and Fishing Resort (montebellova.com). On a sunny day, stop for a sandwich, have a seat on the front porch, and watch the parade of bikes. Feel the need for a stretch? The Crabtree Falls Trail near Montebello is an easy hike of about three miles. There are at least five major waterfalls along the trail and many smaller ones. Shack up for the evening at the Montebello Camping and Fishing Resort in one of their cabins. A trailer is available for rental, too, in case you want to experience life in a trailer park. The Crabtree Falls Campground, located just below Crabtree Falls, features campsites alongside the Tye River.

After descending into the Valley, Route 56 meanders through Steeles Tavern and ends on Route 11. Lexington is just a few miles south. If you happen to be coming into town on 11 north at dusk, keep your eyes peeled for cars stopped in the right lane. That would be folks lining up to enter Hull's Drive-In (hullsdrivein.com). Hull's is unique among first-run, drive-in theaters because the venue is operated as a non-profit, solely to preserve the outdoor movie experience for a new generation. What does this non-profit group call itself? Why, "Hull's Angels," of course.

*Montebello Country Store is a good spot to grab a sandwich and enjoy the scenery.*

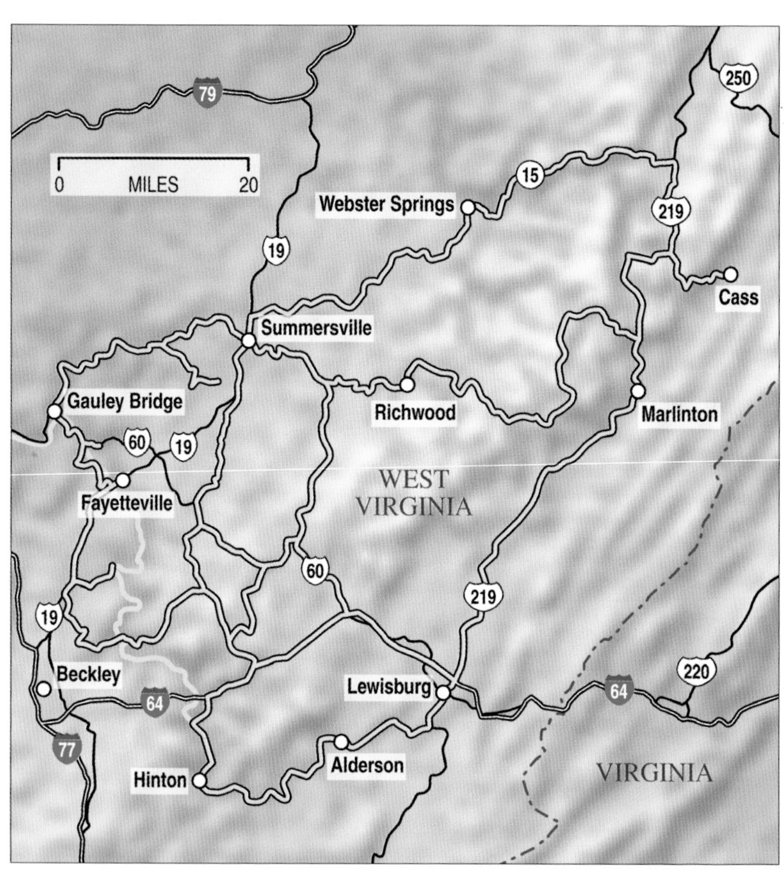

79
0 MILES 20
Webster Springs
15
219
250
19
Cass
Summersville
Gauley Bridge
Richwood
Marlinton
60
19
WEST VIRGINIA
Fayetteville
60
219
19
Beckley
64
Lewisburg
64
220
77
Alderson
Hinton
VIRGINIA

# Mountaineer Country

## *Summersville, West Virginia*

Before I started touring by motorcycle, the only two points of interest I could recall in West Virginia were the historic town of Harpers Ferry and the Charles Town horse-racing track. Owing to what I heard through the news, I pictured it as a big strip mine that flooded a lot. Why would anyone want to go there? To me, the Mountain State was a 24,282-square-mile question mark.

Motorcycling has erased that question mark for me and has exposed me to more pleasurable experiences in this Appalachian wilderness than by any other means except perhaps hiking or bicycling. I have discovered the dramatic beauty of the New River Gorge, the serenity of the Cranberry Wilderness, the oddity of Beartown State Park. And the people here are as memorable as the landscapes. They don't shy away from conversation. They readily accept you. Touring here is a bit like camping out in your backyard—the experience is new, and yet familiar to you at the same time.

When you travel some of the backroads and get deep into the woods, you can easily understand why the first explorers called it a "pleasing tho' dreadful sight." At the time they arrived, the woods were full of bears, panthers, and other wild creatures. Records of the first European expeditions seemed to consider it a good day if an expedition didn't lose someone to a wild beast or a slippery incline.

*Morning fog remains settled in hollows of West Virginia's Greenbrier Valley. Photo by Frank Fox*

The rest of the state's history is much the same—rough and tumble. Settlers in the area quickly grew uneasy with a colonial Virginia government that was more concerned with events east of the mountains than in their neck of the woods. When Civil War broke out, the Union "restored" the government of Virginia in the western part of the state, effectively creating a separate state. Unclear land grants caused many original settlers to sell their claims to enterprising coal magnates for pennies on the dollar, fearing a total loss if their claims were entirely unfounded. And then erupted the much publicized feud between the Hatfields and McCoys that produced the image of the stereotypical, drunken, lazy hillbilly.

In a way, the feud began over the matter of who owned a certain razorback hog. After a jury awarded custody of the hog to the Hatfields, things got out of hand. Over a period of 10 or 15 years, the warring clans exchanged gunfire, killing several members of both families. Things really heated up a few years later when a Kentucky deputy began sneaking across the river into West Virginia, capturing Hatfields, and extraditing them the old fashioned way—tying them up and dragging them across the state line to stand trial. The media got wind of the story and pounced on it. Speculation ran across the country. Would two temperamental backwoods families draw two states to the brink of war? Not really. By that time most of the original parties were dead and the feud just faded away.

Over the past thirty years, the state has found success in promoting the tourism industry. It has established about two dozen attractive state parks and many miles of unspoiled highway and quiet forest byways to enjoy. I

*A pair of riders break in the new pavement along the Highland Scenic Highway.*

*People actually jump off this perfectly good bridge on "Bridge Day" each October.*

chose Summersville as a starting point for tours in this section because it is centrally located in the heart of the state. In addition to its own share of attractions, it is also close to many other points of interest. It is on the northern edge of Summersville Lake (summersvillelakeretreat.com), with 4,000 acres of sparkling blue waters just right for attracting boaters, fishermen, and kayakers. (When the Army Corps of Engineers came around to naming the lake's dam, they faced a problem they didn't anticipate in its construction. It was customary to name dams after the towns located closest to them. Summersville wasn't the closest; the town of Gad was. "Gad Dam . . ." Well, you can figure it out for yourself. The Corps no doubt quickly cast aside tradition in this instance and Summersville Dam it became.)

Downtown Summersville is like most other American small towns, with a block or two of shops, a courthouse, cafe, etc., but you don't see any of this by just passing through. US 19 cuts a wide swath to the east of town and it is along this strip that the vast majority of travel services are located.

The routes I planned fall to the south and east of town, more from circumstance and time than intention. Looking at the places I wanted to visit, most happened to be in that region. I wouldn't doubt though that the areas north and west aren't equally worth exploring, too. If you have an opportunity to do so, I'd like to hear about what you find.

I hope you take the opportunity to explore West Virginia. When I think of the riding I've done there over the past few years, the old cliché springs to mind: "So many roads . . . So little time."

# Trip 23 New River Gorge

**Distance** *154 miles*
**Terrain** *Mostly river valleys and gorges with a small mountain run*
**Highlights** *Summersville Dam, Carnifex Ferry, Hawk's Nest State Park, Mystery Hole, New River Gorge and Bridge, Thurmond ghost town*

The New River Gorge is the perfect place to gain an understanding of both the old and new West Virginia. Once completely dominated by coal and

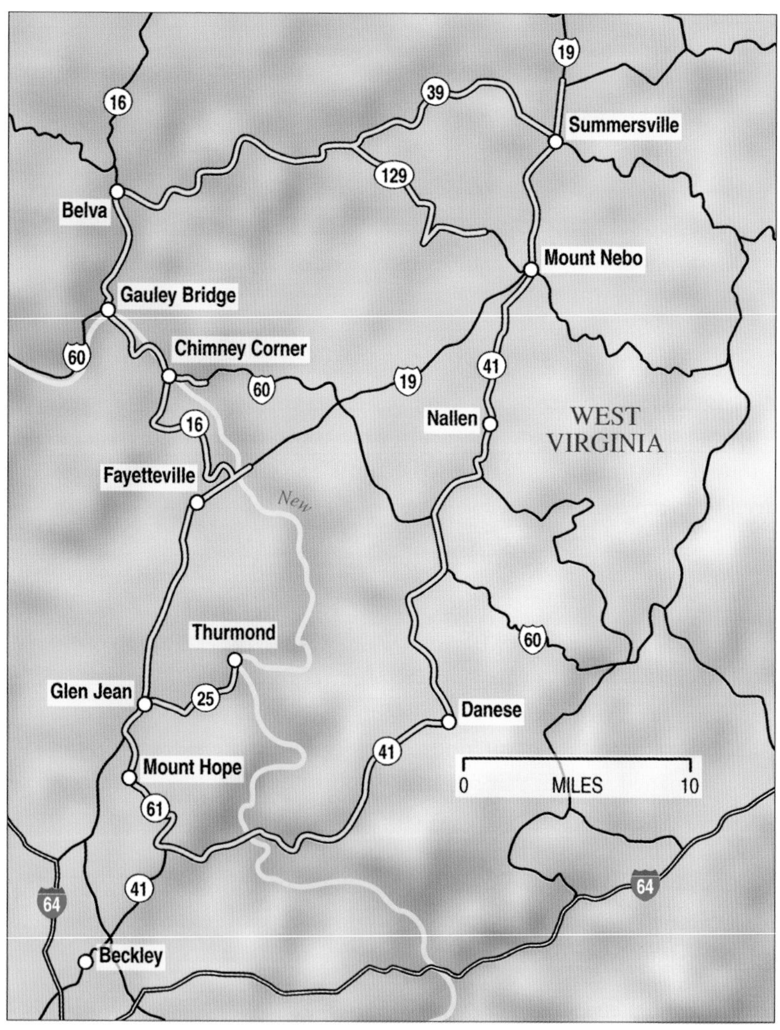

### THE ROUTE FROM SUMMERSVILLE

| | |
|---|---|
| 0 | Depart downtown Summersville on WV 39 |
| 12.0 | Left on WV 129 |
| 18.0 | Right on CR 23 (Carnifex Ferry Road) |
| 18.9 | Arrive Carnifex Ferry Battlefield, then turn around |
| 19.8 | Right on WV 129 |
| 22.3 | Arrive Summersville Dam, then turn around |
| 30.8 | Left on WV 39 |
| 44.6 | Left on WV 16 at Belva |
| 50.2 | Left on US 60/WV 16 at Gauley Bridge |
| 54.8 | Left on US 60 at Chimney Corner |
| 57.9 | Arrive Hawk's Nest State Park, then turn around |
| 61.0 | Left on WV 16 south at Chimney Corner |
| 69.4 | Left on US 19 north |
| 71.7 | Right into New River Gorge Visitors Center on CR 5 |
| 71.7 | Right out of NRG parking lot onto CR 5 |
| 71.9 | Right onto CR 82 (Fayette Station Road). Some portions one-way |
| 78.9 | Right onto US 19 south |
| 89.7 | Left at Glen Jean exit. Signs for Thurmond National Historic Site present at this exit |
| 89.8 | Left onto WV 16 north |
| 90.3 | Right onto CR 25 (Thurmond signs should be present) |
| 96.7 | Arrive Thurmond, then turn around |
| 103.1 | Left on WV 16/WV 61 |
| 106.3 | Left on WV 61 at 16/61 split |
| 110.7 | Left on WV 41 |
| 136.5 | Left on US 60/WV 41 |
| 139.1 | Right onto WV 41 |
| 153.6 | Arrive Summersville via WV 41 |

timber harvesting concerns, the Gorge is now an up-and-coming travel destination. We'll have a chance to see both sides on this loop route.

The route begins in Summersville and follows Route 39 west out of town. Route 39 is fairly typical of most roads in the area: where the valley narrows it follows a creek bed and begins to twist and sway; where the valley

*The New River Gorge Bridge is the highest vehicular bridge in the Americas. Photo by Robert Van Allen*

widens, it stretches out and flies straight. You will see the good and the bad of West Virginia along Route 39. Some communities look clean and prosperous, others look as though they've been bombed. Hang a left on Route 129 to go out to the Summersville Dam and the battlefield at Carnifex Ferry. This road isn't heavily traveled. It runs over the hills and along the ridges just south of town near the Summersville Dam.

Summersville Dam holds back the waters of the Gauley River, creating a 4,000-acre lake. Route 129 passes over the top of the dam. Pull off to one side and you can gaze upon the boulder-strewn back side. Near the bottom of the dam are two pipes, each about 20 feet in diameter, that allow water to pass through the dam and continue down the river. The pressure exerted is so great the water blows horizontally out of the pipes and about 30 feet downstream before landing in the riverbed. At the put-in point near the base of the dam there's a sign warning kayakers that if they hear three short blasts, they can expect a sudden rise in the water level. No kidding.

When you leave the dam, double back toward Route 39. You will have to look carefully to locate the hidden turn to Carnifex Ferry Battlefield (carnifexferrybattlefieldstatepark.com). It isn't well marked. About two miles west of the dam, Route 129 makes a sharp right. A smaller, unmarked road to the battlefield branches off to the left at the curve. (Watch for a large billboard advertising the Mountain Lake Campground—it's located along Route 129 at the curve in question.) Make the left turn along this pleasant country lane to reach the battlefield.

The battle at Carnifex Ferry was one of dozens of moves and counter moves conducted by both sides during the War Between the States. According to accounts of the battle which took place in September 1861, a contingent of about 6,000 Union soldiers swept through Summersville to re-establish a supply line broken by the Rebels in earlier action. The Confederates, outmanned three to one, had time to dig in. They riddled the Union ranks with fire and suffered only 30 casualties themselves.

Despite suffering a rout, the outlook was undimmed for some Union soldiers like Rutherford B. Hayes. According to him, "[West Virginia] is the land of blackberries. We are a great, grown-up, armed blackberry party and we gather untold quantities." I'm guessing Hayes, who went on to become the 19th U.S. president, didn't see much trench warfare.

Exiting the battlefield, return to WV 129 and head west to WV 39. Turn left and continue south on WV 39, passing though a dozen small villages until you reach Gauley Bridge. Make the left turn on Route 16/60 and head east. You will be following the course the ancient New River has traveled for thousands of years. Follow US 60 east at Chimney Corner where 60 and WV 16 split. This spot is marked by the Country Store Craft Shop and Gallery, home to Appalachian crafts including jewelry and crafts made from coal. I don't care much for today's modern tourist traps. Places like Pigeon Forge, Tennessee, are just too crowded and overdone for me. However, I do favor those small, independent attractions that catch the eye along the road. Case in point is the Mystery Hole (mysteryhole.com), located along US 60 a couple of miles up the road from Chimney Corner. I'm more likely to patronize a place like this to chat with the folks who run it and reward their entrepreneurial spirit as I am to "explore the mystery."

Follow Route 60 east from the Hole to Hawk's Nest State Park. You'll enjoy this section of road as you climb out of the gorge. Rising higher, you can see the gorge below and a thin glittering ribbon that is the New River. The best views are from the park. Hawk's Nest has two sections, upper and

*A pair of riders enter Thurmond from a rough, unpaved road that descends from the rim of the New River Gorge.*

lower. The upper portion of the park overlooks the New River Gorge at a point where it forms a lake. Down by the lake, there are the usual water diversions, such as rowboats and paddle boats. You can also arrange a pontoon boat ride upriver to the New River Gorge Bridge. To navigate the rough terrain between the lake and the lodge above, there is an aerial tramway which is an attraction in itself. At the lodge, ask for a room with a view. There's no extra charge.

The lower area features a hilltop museum constructed by the Civilian Conservation Corps (ccclegacy.org) in the early 1930s. What looks like a chalet is perched on top of the hill over the gorge. Massive stonework and tremendous wooden beams inside display the craftsmanship of the CCC workers who assembled it. The chalet is filled with a collection of Indian, pioneer, and Civil War artifacts. If you feel in the mood for a hike there are trails which lead to views of the gorge and range from a hundred yards to about two miles.

When you leave the park, your best bet for a better ride is to simply retrace your steps to the cafe at Chimney Corner and hang a left, continuing to follow WV 16 and the river. In Fayetteville, they still talk about "Five

Dollar Frank," a name Frank Thomas earned for the five-dollar airplane rides he offered over the New River Gorge. I once took a ride with Frank over the gorge, and after that experience, I decided motorcycling was pretty safe by comparison. Sadly, Five Dollar Frank no longer flies over the gorge in his battered old Cessna; he's taken on a new set of wings. However, you can still get a ride out of the Fayetteville Airport from pilot Christian Kappler in his open-cockpit, Stearman biplane. On request, Christian will perform barrel rolls, hammerheads and other aerobatic feats of derring-do. Even if you choose not to go by air, there is still a way to see the gorge and the New River Bridge from a vantage point that few folks know about.

When Route 16 intersects US 19, turn left and head over the New River Bridge to the New River Gorge National River-Canyon Rim Visitor Center (www.nps.gov/neri/planyourvisit/crvc.htm) on the right.

The New River Gorge Bridge is the world's largest steel arch bridge, completed in 1977 at a cost of nearly $37 million. It is the highest bridge in the East, standing 876 feet tall. Before the bridge was completed, the trip from one side of the gorge to the other took nearly an hour; now it takes

*Typical afternoon in downtown Thurmond, West Virginia. "Dear, it says right there, RESERVATIONS REQUIRED."*

*At Mystery Hole, near Hawks Nest State Park, the only mystery is what happens to your money.*

about thirty seconds. You have to see it to believe it—it is impressive. In fact, if you've seen the television commercial where Chevrolet drops a truck over a bridge on a bungee cord, then you've seen it. On the third Saturday in October, the bridge is closed to traffic and a festival is held on the bridge complete with parachutists, bungee jumping ( . . . no, no, after you, I insist), and rappelling.

If you carry a National Parks Passport, don't forget to get yours stamped at the visitor center. There are several trails from the visitor center, including one which will take you down to the river for great photo opportunities. Just remember, every step you walk down, you have to walk back up!

The other popular diversion here is river running. The New River Gorge is widely recognized as one of the best whitewater routes anywhere. In many areas, the river is about a mile wide, but it squeezes down to a few hundred feet through the gorge and the result is a ride that promises to be bumpier than even Frank's ten-minute flying tour. In season, the traffic down the river is nearly bumper to bumper. There are a dozen or more companies that organize raft trips on the New. Two of the more established companies are Class VI River Runners (class-vi.com) and Wildwater Expeditions Unlimited (wvaraft.com).

Out of the parking lot of the visitor center, hang a right and continue down CR 5 for just a couple of tenths, then make the right turn onto CR 82, also labeled in some parts as Fayette Station Road. Route 82 makes some crazy twists and turns as it travels underneath the bridge and picks its way carefully down the gorge to the very bottom. Here you can hop off the bike and take some great pictures of the bridge from your new vantage point. This is the former route of US 19 which now whizzes by overhead. Can you imagine what travel must have been like when this was a major route? Route 82 is one-way at this point, so continue across the bridge at the bottom and up the other side. This returns you to the west side of US 19 just a few tenths up the road from Route 16 where you appeared earlier. Head south on US 19, then turn left at Glen Jean, following signs for the Thurmond National Historic Site. You'll make a quick left onto WV 16 heading north, then you'll see another sign at CR 25. Follow CR 25 all the way to the train depot in Thurmond. You'll cross an open-grate bridge across the New River to reach it. The bridge looks dicey for bikes, but just maintain a slow, steady speed across and you'll be fine. My Wing didn't complain, and I didn't look down. Piece of cake.

The New River Gorge is home to dozens of towns that once flourished during the coal boom of the early 20th century. The richest of them was Thurmond (tinyurl.com/motojourneys15). Mines from this area generated the greatest revenue and Thurmond's banks held the largest deposits in the state. When the coal played out, so did Thurmond. The National Park Service restored the train depot and is working to preserve some of the buildings that remain along the tracks. I think you'll enjoy time spent here. It's an interesting exercise to walk along the row of abandoned buildings and imagine what life was like here during the heady days of the Roaring Twenties.

There are dozens of other sites scattered throughout the gorge though none are preserved like Thurmond. Riding buddies of mine have told me harrowing tales of seeking out these places on their street bikes. I think a dual purpose bike would be well suited to an adventure like that, but I wouldn't even think about it on the Wing.

From Thurmond, head back on CR 25 and turn left on Route 16. Follow this down to Mount Hope and make the left on WV 61, then make a left on Route 41 and follow it north all the way to Summersville. This route also crosses the gorge many miles upstream from the main bridge. It plunges down one side of the gorge, crossing the river on a dilapidated steel bridge near the river, then dutifully climbs the other side of the ridge. The scenery is spectacular on both sides and is a pleasant ride to end the day.

# Trip 24 Greenbrier Valley

**Distance** *183 miles*
**Terrain** *Moderate hills, mostly valley touring along routes following rivers*
**Highlights** *Babcock State Park, White Sulphur Springs, Lewisburg*

The Greenbrier Valley should do much to dispel the notion that West Virginia is one big strip mine. As a touring area, it has much in common with

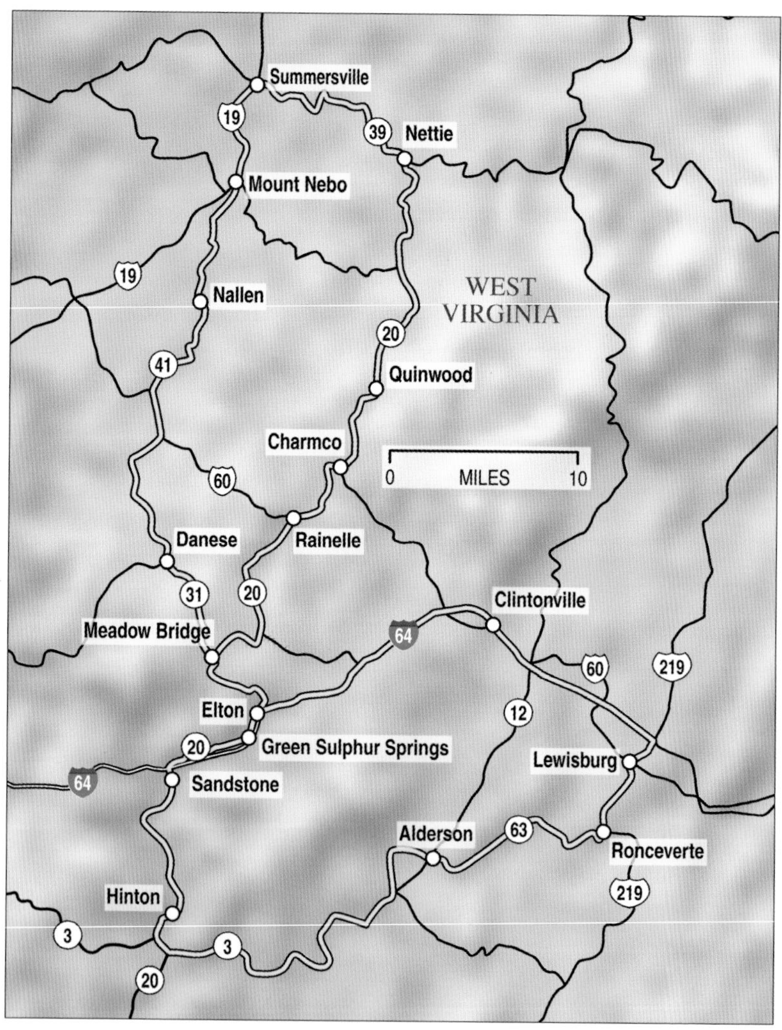

**THE ROUTE FROM SUMMERSVILLE**

| | |
|---|---|
| 0 | Depart WV 41 west at junction of US 19 and WV 41 |
| 14.5 | Turn left onto US 60 east |
| 17.1 | Turn right onto WV 41 west |
| 25.8 | Turn left onto CR 31 (Meadow Bridge Road) in Danese |
| 32.2 | Right onto WV 20 at Meadow Bridge |
| 54.2 | After crossing bridge in Hinton, turn left on WV 20/WV 3 |
| 55.9 | Left onto WV 3 at split of WV 20 and WV 3 |
| 77.1 | Continue straight on WV 12 in Alderson at WV 3/WV 12 split |
| 77.6 | Right onto WV 63 |
| 89.0 | Left onto US 219 at Ronceverte |
| 94.2 | Left onto I-64 at Lewisburg |
| 124.8 | Right onto WV 20 north |
| 171.2 | Left on WV 39 west at Nettie |
| 182.9 | Arrive Summersville via WV 39 west |

its better known counterpart to the east, the Shenandoah Valley. Large farms stretch across the lowland against a backdrop of the ever present Alleghenies. Roads meander through the Valley, bending where they parallel rivers and cross ridges.

Our route through the Greenbrier begins by following US 19 south to Route 41 south out of Summersville. Route 41 is a beautiful backroad that is lightly traveled and an entertaining ride. It intersects with Route 60 and follows that route for a short distance before turning south again.

The first spot you might like to visit along this route is Babcock State Park (babcocksp.com). Located on Route 41 about five miles south of the intersection with US 60, this park is well off the beaten path. It would make a perfect place to set up a base camp for your explorations in this region. In addition to inexpensive campsites, they also rent cabins in standard and economy flavors, the standard having a separate kitchen equipped with appliances and fireplace. All of them feature everything you would need to set up housekeeping. This option will appeal to those who travel by credit card. The park features a number of diversions, including fishing, swimming, boating, and 20 miles of hiking trails.

A gristmill located near the visitor center makes a good photo opportunity. There's a better than average chance that if you've seen a picture of a West Virginia mill, it's this one. This particular mill is actually recon-

*The gristmill at Babcock State Park was assembled from the remains of several other mills around the state.*

structed from several old mills in other parts of the state which had either burned or fallen into disrepair. It continues to grind corn and wheat into products which you can buy at the gift shop.

You can easily get lost in your riding and forget about sticking to the route, as I found myself doing throughout my rides in this area. I guess it was a combination of perfectly warm, sunny days that were just right for cruising and the beautiful scenery that caused me to ride 20 miles past my intended turn at Danese (pronounced day-NIECE). When you're doing this kind of riding, getting lost isn't a big deal; actually it's kind of nice. Realizing my mistake, I made the return to Danese and then turned onto Meadow Bridge Road.

After a stretch of seven miles or so, you'll arrive in the village of Meadow

Bridge. Just across the railroad tracks is a general store which is a good spot to stop for a drink and a dime's worth of conversation. An older fellow named Harold joined me on the porch and we started to chat, trading the usual "nice weather" and "where are you from" tidbits. I found that my new acquaintance was not only a good talker, he could often carry both sides of the conversation. Somewhere in the middle of a long tale about his latest fly fishing trip, a train crawled through town with eight engines on the front and three on the rear. The noise was deafening and conversation was impossible, but it didn't matter to my front porch friend. Harold was lost in his remembrance, somewhere in the middle of the river now, casting as he talked. I just kept nodding at the right times and he kept casting. The noise from the train was just beginning to subside when he reached the end of his tale, exclaiming "Now ain't that the darndest thing you ever heard?"

In Meadow Bridge, pick up Route 20 and follow it south through Elton and Green Sulphur Springs to Sandstone Falls (nps.gov/neri/planyourvisit/the-sandstone-falls.htm). Route 20 is another road made just for pleasure touring. The ride becomes a bit more dramatic once you cross under the interstate at Sandstone and head toward Hinton. First you make a steep climb as you cross one of the higher ridges in the Valley, and the route enters the New River Gorge, paralleling the river all the way to Hinton. Be sure to stop at Sandstone Falls, the largest falls on the river. These falls aren't especially high but their breadth makes them distinct. The entire riverbed looks as though an earthquake tugged at it until it cracked and dropped a few dozen feet.

The outskirts of Hinton arrive long before the town does. When you first see the city limit sign, the only signs of civilization are a few dilapidated buildings and a high school across the river. This, as it turns out, is only the greater Hinton metropolitan area. Downtown is a few miles farther south. Hinton (hintonwva.com) is an old company town. You can tell this by the streets lined with nearly identical houses stacked up the side of the hill like rows of dominoes. The older downtown part of Hinton is a cluster of distinct brick buildings featuring architectural styles that include American Gothic, High Victorian, and Greek Revival. Looking for a place to eat, I caught a glimpse of the now defunct Hinton Hot Dog Stand and decided it might be as much fun just to see what it was like as it would be to eat there.

Five or six men sat around the lunch counter while a young woman behind the counter chatted with them and simultaneously filled lunch orders with a practiced hand. The dilemma of the day was Larry's. He was having trouble with his brother-in-law, Junior, who had recently borrowed Larry's pickup and bass boat. Having run a little wide in a tight corner, Junior had launched the boat and trailer off a steep cliff and into the tops of the trees a few hundred yards below. "Too bad the trailer didn't take the truck and him with it," Larry said.

Across the counter another fellow was complaining about his sister-in-law, Mary Jane, who was getting on his nerves. Someone suggested that maybe they ought to introduce Junior to her. "Let's do that," Larry agreed. "They deserve each other."

Upon cruising through Hinton, I discovered furious activity around a new building being raised on the outskirts of town, and as I passed by, a large sign was just being lifted into place. Yep, when the Golden Arches are raised, Hinton will have officially arrived.

Just south of Hinton on Route 20 are the Bluestone and Pipestem Resort State Parks (www.bluestonesp.com, pipestemresort.com). The latter is famous for its Mountain Creek Lodge, which is tucked away in Bluestone Canyon and is only accessible by aerial tram. Both parks offer the usual array of hiking, horseback riding, and water sports. Pipestem also features 27 holes of golf.

Turning east on Route 3, I began following the Greenbrier River. This area is more built up than I had anticipated, with a smattering of little towns and villages along the riverbank. The road is mostly flat and straight, because the river valley is wide, giving you ample opportunity to enjoy the sights along the road. You run into the darndest things sometimes, especially when you're not looking for them. I sat in a short line of traffic where some road construction was taking place, waiting to be waved through. When our turn came, we proceeded slowly through the work zone and I saw a statue labeled JOHN HENRY. I dropped out of the line of traffic and stopped for a closer look.

The Big Bend Tunnel nearby was one of many railroad construction projects taking place in this area in the 1870s when the introduction of steam-powered equipment knocked many men out of work. Legend has it that Big John Henry believed that he could outwork any machine and made a bet to prove it. Big John beat the machine at laying track, but like any good tragic hero, he then lay down and died, exhausted from the effort.

At Alderson, follow Route 12 when it splits from Route 3. In just a few miles, you'll pick up Route 63 which continues to roughly parallel the river. Five miles later you'll enter the town of Ronceverte (French for Greenbrier) and traffic will increase. It is interesting to note that even though Greenbrier County is a little larger than the state of Rhode Island, its population is only three and a half percent of that state's. Turn left on US 219 and follow it north to Lewisburg.

*Legend has it that John Henry won his contest against a steam-powered drill. Then he laid down and died. There's a lesson in there somewhere.*

Downtown Lewisburg (lewisburg-wv.com) is an historic district that is worth hopping off the bike for a closer look. The district comprises a few square blocks of stately homes and shops filled with antiques, crafts, and quilts. Stop by Food and Friends (304-645-4548) for a hearty lunch and conversation with an accommodating staff. If your server happens to be Patty Vass, tell her Dale sends his best wishes.

If you wish to make a two-day trip of it, this is a great place to stop for the

*The highway department must know that motorcyclists prefer pictures. Photo by David Wiley*

evening. The whole corridor between White Sulphur Springs and Lewisburg is an informed traveler's mecca, featuring the majestic Greenbrier Hotel (greenbrier.com), the antique-filled General Lewis Inn, and the Old White Motel. If you're camping, Greenbrier State Forest offers campsites and cabins. Of course, if you want to go all-out, the Greenbrier is it. The Greenbrier has always been an elegant resort and its size and grandeur will utterly amaze you (so will the price). Remember, though, honored guests such as yourself may be able to find a special deal or get a weekend rate.

One of the lesser known features of the Greenbrier was revealed to the public in recent years. In 1959, during the height of the Cold War era, construction began on a top-secret, underground facility designed to shelter members of Congress in the event of a nuclear attack on Washington, D.C. Although the project was highly secretive, it was just too big an undertaking to keep completely quiet. One contractor working on the facility was told the cavernous room he was working on was an exhibit hall, to which he replied, "We just put in 110 stalls in the bathroom. What in the hell are you going to exhibit?" It became clear that an underground facility just wouldn't be practical to serve the purpose for which it was built. After decades of denying its existence, the bunker was officially decommissioned and opened to public tours in 1992. It'll set you back 27 bucks to see your tax dollars at work.

The return route follows Interstate 64 to Green Sulphur Springs. From here, pick up WV 20 again and turn north. You'll pass through Meadow Bridge once again where you're likely to find my buddy Harold at the general store talking to another unsuspecting passerby he's managed to buttonhole. Continuing north, Route 20 intersects with US 60 just west of Rainelle. Turn right onto WV 20/US 60 east through Rainelle to Charmco. Follow WV 20 north to WV 39 at Nettie, then turn west on WV 39 to Summersville.

While you're in the area, don't forget to keep an eye out for a pickup decorated with tin cans and a JUST MARRIED sign, towing a patched-up bass boat. You can bet two good ol' boys at the hot dog stand will be grinning from ear to ear.

# Trip 25 Cranberry Fields Forever

**Distance** *170 miles*
**Terrain** *Small mountain passes through national forest then high road through Cranberry Glades. More small passes and backroads through Greenbrier Valley on return.*
**Highlights** *Cranberry Glades, Falls of Hills Creek, Pearl S. Buck's birthplace, Droop Mountain State Park, Beartown State Park*

The last Ice Age drew to a close some 10 to 15 thousand years ago and though none of us were around to bid it farewell, we can still see some of the effects of it to this day. On this tour, we will visit the Cranberry Glades, a remnant of that Ice Age heritage, roam the Highland Scenic Highway, and explore the nooks and crannies of Beartown State Park.

This tour is easy to auto-pilot because there are only a few major routes. But there is a lot to see and do. We begin by heading east on West Virginia 39 and pass through the town of Richwood. On passing through, I discovered a couple of interesting tidbits about the town.

For instance, Richwood (richwooders.com) is the home of what was

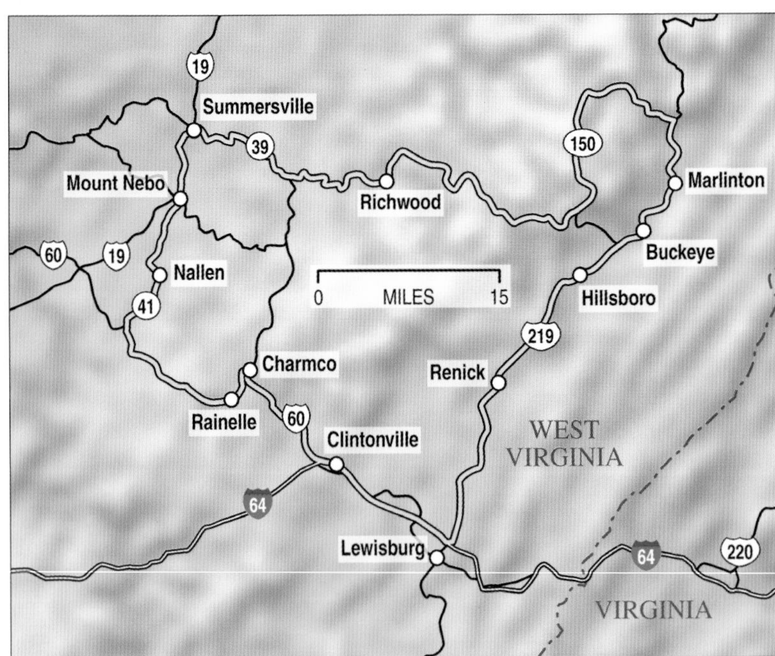

*Highland Scenic Highway is a must-ride if you find yourself in the Greenbrier Valley.*

once the world's largest wooden clothespin factory, surely a fact you will want to readily command as you play Really Trivial Pursuit. Richwood is also known as the Ramp Capital of the World (make that two facts to have on hand). Ramps are actually wild leeks and they are the first growth to appear in the late winter, signaling the arrival of spring.

If you sail into town in early April, you will arrive just in time for the annual Ramp Festival, an old Appalachian tradition dating back to frontier days that heralds the coming of spring. Ramps are gathered in tremendous quantities and served with corn pone, potatoes, and beans. You should be

### THE ROUTE FROM SUMMERSVILLE

| | |
|---|---|
| 0 | Depart WV 39 east from Summersville at US 19/WV 39 |
| 45.9 | Turn left on WV 150 (Highland Scenic Highway) |
| 68.4 | Right on US 219 south |
| 114.6 | Right on I-64 west |
| 128.2 | Right on US 60 west |
| 155.5 | Right onto WV 41 |
| 170.0 | Arrive Summersville via WV 41 |

warned though, ramps linger on the breath like garlic. If your riding partner eats any, you had best have some yourself. One other note, there are plenty of opportunities to have a picnic lunch in the quiet solitude of the Monongahela National Forest on this loop, and few chances to pick up the groceries. Richwood is your best bet for that.

East of town you enter the scenic Highland Trace corridor. This is a soothing ride with no competing traffic and those vehicles you do happen upon can be easily dispensed of with a quick twist of the throttle. The first stop you'll want to make is the Falls of Hills Creek. The full trail is about three-quarters of a mile long and descends a steep gorge to a series of falls.

The entrance to the lovely and popular Cranberry Glades Botanical Area (www.pocahontascountywv.com/cranberry_glades_nature_center.aspx) is just a little farther ahead. It is part of a nearly 53,000-acre wilderness and backcountry area which is closed to all forms of motorized travel. The glades are an unusual feature of the area, dating back to the time when massive sheets of ice moved southward, bringing with them elements of flora more commonly associated with Canadian climates. The bog, a perpetually wet area, became a harbor for cranberries and other plant life uncommon to the surrounding area such as orchids and carnivorous plants like pitcher plants.

The trail through the bog area follows a boardwalk for the entire half-mile route. The chances are good that you will be the only person in the area, especially if you go during the week. The trail begins winding through an area of dense vegetation almost like a jungle. Suddenly, the trail opens into a vast, treeless area where the ground is covered by millions of delicate vines. CRANBERRIES, the sign says. I laid down on the boardwalk and got almost close enough to the ground to kiss it and I didn't see a single blessed one. Your luck may vary.

What impressed me as much as the flora was the sense of isolation: no traffic sounds, no jets overhead, no chain saws buzzing. It's a sense easterners of the concrete jungle rarely experience. I guess that's why I felt like there must be at least a dozen pairs of eyes watching me from the thicket. A grasshopper suddenly lunged from its perch and the sound was loud enough to startle me. I had this strange sense that the last remaining undiscovered panther on the East Coast would bound out of the forest and devour me.

The boardwalk follows the bog for a few hundred feet, then turns into the forest again. Another small clearing appears, and it is here that you will find the insect-eating pitcher plants. These insidious little plants don't capture their prey in the same dramatic way as the Venus flytrap. The pitcher plant grows in such a way that when an insect ventures inside, it can't get

*Visitors of all ages enjoy the labryinth of formations at Beartown State Park.*

out. The leaves of the pitcher plant excrete a digestive juice that dissolves its prey. What an ugly way to go. These are pretty easy to spot, though I couldn't find any unwitting insects to drop into the plant. Where was that darn grasshopper?

The Cranberry Mountain Visitor Center, just east of the botanical area on Route 39, has the standard visitor center stocks-in-trade: museum, bookstore, and restrooms. The book selection is specific to West Virginia and includes a section of West Virginia mountain music on CD. I picked up a copy of some homegrown music by Dwight Diller (dwightdiller.com), a Pocahontas County native whose cover for the album *Hold On* bills his tunes as "Neo-Orthodox Old-Time Mountain Music from West Virginia (without Yodeling)." I should point out that most people would call this bluegrass, but that term didn't originate until the 1940s. This is authentic mountain music, the kind that leaves a lingering taste of sour mash in your mouth. I popped in the disc and set off northward on Route 150, the Highland Scenic Highway, adding my own unique vocal stylings to some of those tunes in a way Dwight could never have imagined.

The Highland Scenic Highway is touring bliss. The roadway follows a high trace through the mountains, affording long peaceful views with nothing but green all the way to the horizon. If you brought a picnic lunch, you'll find several fine places to stop. I counted traffic on two fingers. This is not a curve-hugging road. It's long and straight and open, and the kind of

*Cranberry Glades State Park is an example of an alpine ecology at home in the Appalachians.*

road that makes you slow down to enjoy the ride. Dwight and I were having a right fine old time traveling down that road together singing "Lizards in the Spring," the "Yew Pine Mountains," and that "Cluck Old Hen." Too bad that road couldn't go on forever. It ended on Route 219 all too soon.

Route 219 is good for some thrills as you work your way down toward Marlinton. For lunch, stop by French's Diner (304-799-9910) in downtown Marlinton. A neat place to get lost is the Pocahontas County Historical Society Museum, (304-799-6659) just a mile or two south of town. The museum houses a collection of antiques and artifacts from Pocahontas County. If you like old gadgets and oddities, this is your place. I spent close to an hour wandering the two stories of goodies and browsing through the special Pearl S. Buck room. One display case features postmarked letters and postcards from all the post offices in Pocahontas County, many of which are now closed. It gives you a sense of how many once-thriving towns and villages ceased to exist when the lumber supply disappeared. Another favorite was the table-top flyshooer.

While we're in Pocahontas County, I should mention that Pocahontas is one of a growing number of counties that recognize the economic effect that we riders have when we tour their area. To their credit, the Pocahontas County website at pocahontas.org has a section devoted to riding tours and information on motorcycle rallies held in the area. I picked up a few ideas for some new destinations on their site and was reminded of many pleasant places I've already visited.

The road that leads to Watoga State Park (watoga.com) isn't numbered on any maps, but it is clearly marked as a left turnoff from US 219 as you head south out of Marlinton. It's off the beaten path by an easy eight to ten miles. At 10,100 acres, Watoga is West Virginia's largest state park. Watoga is a Cherokee word meaning "river of islands," which aptly describes the Greenbrier River. Watoga has thirty-three cabins for rent in addition to two separate and fully-equipped campgrounds. It is also strategically located along the Greenbrier River Trail.

Returning to US 219, you'll encounter three stops clumped together. First is the Pearl S. Buck Birthplace Museum. Buck was born in 1892 in this house built by her great-grandfather. Her missionary parents took her with them to China when she was just six months old. Author of *The Good Earth,* Buck won the Pulitzer Prize for Literature in 1932, followed by the Nobel Prize for Literature in 1938. She is only one of two Americans ever to receive both of these awards.

A little farther down the road is the entrance to Droop Mountain State Park (droopmountainbattlefield.com). Droop Mountain was the scene of the largest Civil War engagement in West Virginia. The neatest feature of the park is a stacked-log tower you can climb for views from an elevation of 3,100 feet.

The last stop on the trip is also a state park protecting the unusual geology of the area: Beartown State Park (beartownstatepark.com), just a few miles south of Droop Mountain. Beartown is noted for its unusual sandstone formations. It looks as though a prehistoric gopher dug a series of interconnecting tunnels along the hillside and over the years the tunnels collapsed, creating alleyways through the rocks. An elaborate boardwalk allows you to explore the area without damaging it.

The remainder of the trip through the Greenbrier Valley is easy touring on the big shoulders of Route 219. Entering Lewisburg, follow Interstate 64 west toward Beckley. This is not potholed, high-volume interstate like I-40 or the Pennsylvania Turnpike, this is more like your own personal concrete ribbon into the heart of the Mountain State. However, you don't want to follow it all the way into Beckley.

Your best bet is to pick up Route 60 when it departs from the interstate at Sam Black Church. Route 60 gets twisty when it encounters a sizable ridge; other sections bulldoze straight through the hills. To complete the loop, follow WV 41 north to US 19. Turn right on US 19 north to return to Summersville.

# Trip 26 The Gable End of Hell

**Distance** *178 miles*
**Terrain** *Small mountain passes through Monongahela National Forest, and farming valleys*
**Highlights** *Cass Scenic Railroad*

The lumberjacks who transformed the isolated town of Cass into a wide-open Dodge City each payday are gone. The ringing of axes and the thunder of falling timber no longer echo through this part of the eastern Alleghenies. The sawmill—a massive building packed with belts, pulleys, blades, timber, and men—is gone. Cruising through the town of Cass gives little indication of what used to be the essence of this town's existence—until you reach the Cass Scenic Railroad.

Getting to Cass is a simple matter. Follow Route 41 east out of town through suburbia. Pick up Route 55 east when the two routes intersect. Stay on Route 55 until it joins Route 20 north, and then follow that. I was a little surprised at the amount of traffic on the road in the morning (almost a genuine rush hour), but it was heading in the opposite direction. The northern loop of the route runs out of traffic around Camden on Gauley. Despite the

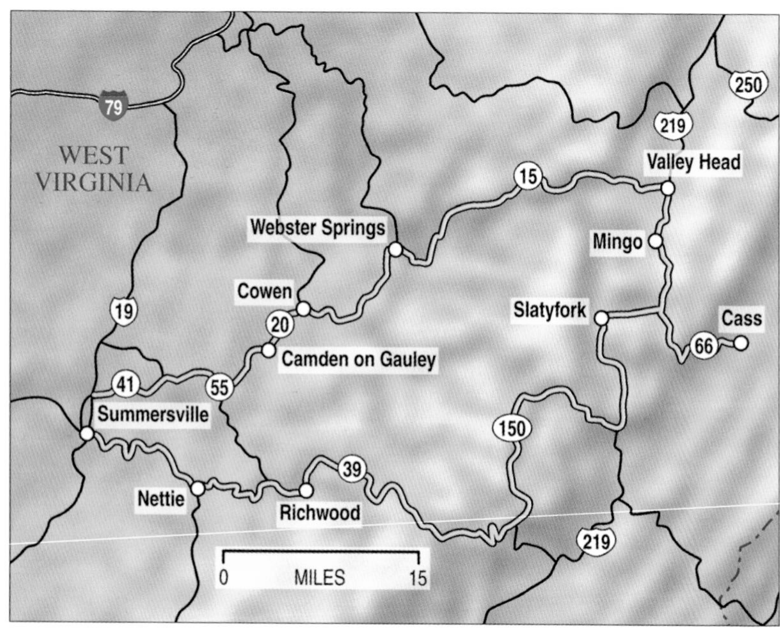

### THE ROUTE FROM SUMMERSVILLE

| | |
|---|---|
| 0 | Depart WV 41 east out of Summersville at junction US 19 and WV 41 |
| 6.5 | Continue straight where WV 41 joins WV 55 |
| 12.0 | Continue straight where WV 20 joins WV 55 |
| 34.7 | Right on WV 15 east in Webster Springs |
| 64.0 | Right on US 219 |
| 75.3 | Left on WV 66 |
| 85.8 | Arrive Cass Scenic Railroad State Park, then turn around |
| 96.3 | Left on US 219 |
| 110.0 | Right on WV 150 (Highland Scenic Highway) |
| 132.5 | Right on WV 39 |
| 178.4 | Arrive Summersville via WV 39 west |

harsh weather and heavy use, West Virginia's state roads are in good condition. Except for the occasional speed zone, you can keep it at full throttle.

Route 20 passes along the Gauley River on the northern border of the Monongahela National Forest and the Cranberry Recreation Area (see Trip 25, Cranberry Fields Forever) before intersecting with Route 15 at Webster Springs. Turn right and follow it east until arriving at Route 219. Turn right here and head south, deep into the national forest. I think Route 219 is perhaps my favorite corridor through this area because the road runs at a tangent to the Appalachians. You get a few miles of mountain passes followed by a scenic valley ride and more mountains. The process repeats itself along the length of US 219, a handy fact to keep in mind if you're planning another ride along this route. The turnoff for Cass is prominently marked as a left off Route 66 near Snowshoe.

The road surface is less refined with some tight, off-camber turns that more aggressive riders will enjoy if only to wear down trailing metal parts. It's hard to believe, but little cowpaths like this were once the main roads through the mountains. They weren't much more than muddy lanes. Can you imagine trying to get through during the spring thaw? Muddy bogs would be more like it.

One of my favorite stories about traveling through this area comes from accounts of two brothers who had more than their share of trouble along this route. The Trotter brothers had the contract to deliver mail from Staunton, Virginia, to Parkersburg, West Virginia. After several complaints

*Pretty little houses all in a row. Rent one for a quiet and pleasant evening in Cass, West Virginia.*

about their sporadic service, the postmaster general sent a reprimand from his cozy little office in Washington, D.C. The brothers had no doubt received some of these complaints in person and this letter was just about the last straw. They responded to the postmaster's letter, "If you knock the gable end of Hell out and back it up against Cheat Mountain and rain fire and brimstone for forty days and forty nights, it won't melt the snow enough to get your damned mail through on time." The Trotters never heard the postmaster complain again.

When you roll into the town of Cass, you'll find rows of identical white two-story houses lining the road into town. Except for activity at the train station, a quiet calm settles on the rest of town. Things were different at the turn of the century when the timber operation was in full swing in Cass. It was by most accounts a den of sin and iniquity which thrived on the appetites of hard-living lumberjacks. After working from dawn to dusk, seven days a week for months on end, these fellas would get their pay and then head into town for some worldly diversions. The town teemed with saloons, women of ill repute, games of chance, and frequent gunplay. By the mid-1900s, the timber gave out and the town was on its way to becoming extinct, just like so many other small lumber towns. However, fate intervened when the state bought the railroad and most of the town and set it aside as Cass Scenic Railroad State Park (cassrailroad.com) in 1963.

The highlight of the park is a ride up the mountain in converted flatbed cars pulled by Shay locomotives. The Shay engine is a wonderfully complex machine and a triumph of engineering which would be tough to match, even today. It was designed to reach timber in the higher elevations that couldn't be reached by ordinary engines. It had to handle heavy loads and negotiate frail tracks laid on steep ground—as much as an eleven percent grade. When you're on the road and see a warning about a nine percent grade, you know the descent will be steep. Imagine descending that kind of grade hauling a few thousand tons of hardwood!

While you can have a good time just gawking at them sitting still, they're even more fun to ride. If you want a really good look at how they work, board the car nearest the engine. The smoke is thick and the noise deafening as one of these giant black beasts gets underway, but the real work begins on the slopes. Smoke and cinders begin to rain down in clouds so heavy the entire mountain range is obscured until you change directions. The smell of

*No jostling required to board your train here at the Prince, West Virginia,, train*

*Gravel road, switchbacks, 800-pound bike—yeah, that could be a good time.*

burning coal fills your lungs and permeates your clothing. And you'll nearly jump out of your skin the first time the engineer grabs a handful of steam whistle as he approaches an intersection.

You can take two different runs, depending on the amount of time you have. One train runs three times a day to an intermediate point at Whittaker Station, which was once a regular stop along the line and is now the place where dinner trains stop during the summer season. That ride lasts about an hour and a half. For a longer ride and even more tremendous views, the ride to Bald Knob leaves once a day at noon and requires four and a half hours to make the run. Fall color runs are nothing short of spectacular.

The Whittaker Station run is nine dollars and Bald Knob is twelve dollars. That price also includes admission to the wildlife and historical museums. You can also walk along a footpath that passes by the old sawmill site and eventually leads to the machine shop where you are invited to visit the engineers who keep these remarkable engines running. Once you debark the train back in the village, take the time to walk around and visit the restored homes and shops. Cass is another company town, with rows of crackerbox homes in varying states of repair (tinyurl.com/motojourneys16). You can rent a restored company home here, and, like at other West Virginia state parks, it comes with everything you need. Be sure to visit their website for a current calendar and rate schedule, because there are many special runs and events. Of the many attractions I have visited in West Virginia, Cass has the greatest entertainment value for the dollar.

While you're in the area, you may wish to visit the National Radio Astronomy Observatory (see Trip 19, Highlander Loop) or visit the Cranberry Glades (see Trip 25, Cranberry Fields Forever). Retrace your steps along Route 66 to Route 219 and follow it south. Turn right and follow the Highland Scenic Highway (Route 150) along the tops of the mountains. When you're touring a route through a remote area like this, it's easy to understand why some people in the Appalachians seem to be from a different time. That kind of isolation also breeds superstition and a deep-rooted belief in witches, demons, and past life experiences.

Around here they still tell the tale of a man who had strong flashbacks of something that happened to him in a former life. He could clearly recall a vision of his two brothers in a past life murdering a man. He remembered helping them move the body into a limestone cave and placing it on a shallow ledge in the cave. He never told anyone about it because he thought it wasn't real. Some time later, his son was exploring limestone caves in the Blue Ridge area, and taking photographs of them. One of the pictures looked remarkably like the vision his father kept seeing, prompting him to tell his family about it. His son revisited the cave with the intention of proving to his father that the vision was only imagination. He entered the cave, walked a short distance, and found a ledge. Shining a flashlight over the edge, he discovered a human skeleton, fossilized by water dripping through the limestone. It was later determined that the skeleton was at least 200 years old. Had any visions of a former life lately?

When Route 150 ends, turn right and follow Route 39/55 through Richwood and into Summersville. Pleasant dreams . . .

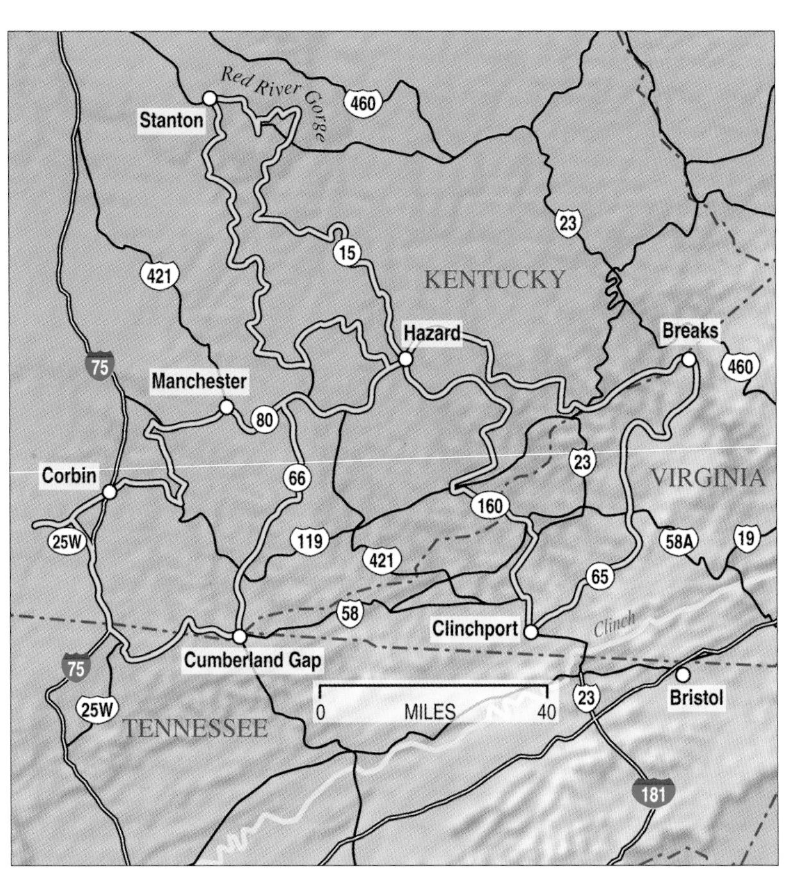
Red River Gorge
Stanton
460
23
15
421
KENTUCKY
Hazard
Breaks
460
75
Manchester
80
23
Corbin
VIRGINIA
66
160
25W
119
58A
19
421
65
58
Clinchport
Clinch
Cumberland Gap
75
Bristol
0 MILES 40
23
25W
TENNESSEE
181

# The Appalachian Question

## *Hazard, Kentucky*

"I'm going to do some riding down in the Appalachians. Eastern Kentucky," I said when a riding buddy asked me recently what I was planning to do for a vacation ride. "Kentucky? What are you going there for?" my buddy replied. "Everyone knows that eastern Kentucky is all torn up with strip mines, coal trucks running up and down all the roads tearing them up, roads slick with coal dust. Why do you want to waste your time down there?" I was sure of my answer. "Well that's what everyone said about West Virginia 15 years ago when I went riding out there and they were dead wrong. I expect the same to be true in Kentucky."

If the regions in this book were characterized as children, some would regard Lexington as the beautiful daughter, Brevard the playful son, and Hazard as the black sheep of the family. It is true that Hazard is not a handsome town as some others in this compilation. Its economic engine is not built on a foundation of tourism, nor on the shoulders of bright young faces like many of the college towns I've visited. It does not draw from a cornucopia of recreational options as do others. No, Hazard is the epitome of a gritty, proud, blue-collar, town.

The key to enjoying and understanding the deep Appalachians lies in its people. I know I've reported people in other areas as "friendly," but com-

*Despite heavy mining activity in eastern Kentucky, plenty of good views remain.*

*Traffic census #1: I counted 15 minutes between cars along this stretch of Route 80.*

pared to folks from Hazard, they're downright stand-offish. You don't ask simple questions in Hazard and expect a bare acknowledgement. You get a full-blown conversation. "Where you visiting from? How long ya staying? What're you going to see? How do you like that bike? How long you had it? How many miles you got on it? Sure is pretty. What do you carry in the trunk, there? What kind of fuel mileage do you get? Sure is a good looking bike. You have a safe ride, now, you hear?" And that's just from nodding hello to someone. At a traffic light.

It shouldn't be surprising that Hazard and other towns in the region bear a worn, scrappy look, it comes natural in this part of the country. From the time this part of the American wilderness was settled and continuing today, making a living in this part of the country is just plain tough.

Much of the struggle to endure in this region has to do with the geography. In other areas of the Appalachians, the ridges rise in a predictable, manageable arrangement. Between long ridges lie valleys of rich soil, readily able to sustain an agricultural economy. In this region, the mountains are jumbled, confused, with the narrowest of hollows wedged at the bottom.

Where development has come to this region, it has usually been to the detriment of the people who live here. Everything that man has taken from this region has had to come with the application of force. Timber clear-cutting and mining disasters have resulted in torrential floods wiping away communities in an instant. Unfair land-rights deals protected the rights of mining companies and left landowners with nothing. Transportation has always been problematic. Poor education and few economic options created a sense of powerlessness in the people who struggled to make a living here. Progress in education, housing, and economic development has been made in recent decades, but much remains to be done. When you tour this area, you will see a huge contrast between the haves and the have-nots.

So, despite that seemingly grim assessment, let me offer you some positive thoughts.

There is good riding to be found here in the region surrounding Hazard. It's almost guaranteed that any road you take is going to have a lot of curves because there just isn't that much flat land to be found. There are at least a couple of routes in this region that hold their own with the infamous Dragon at Deal's Gap.

Worried about getting stuck behind coal trucks? I can count on one hand the number of times I rode for any distance behind a slow-moving coal truck during my travels along one or two roads. I caught up to a few more than that, but at the speed they move, it's usually not difficult to get around them. For the most part, I was free to travel at any speed I found comfortable. Many roads were utterly deserted.

The people in these hills maintain a culture that has resisted the homogenization we see across the rest of the country. Radio sounds different. Time is spent in a leisurely way. People are approachable.

The region is rich in historical sites and places to visit. In the journeys chronicled here, we'll explore the Trail of the Lonesome Pine and the story behind it, stand over the Cumberland Gap, and visit Colonel Sanders's kitchen. We'll encounter the site of a rare moonbow and scrape elbows on a narrow tunnel passage.

I don't know what you're thinking about the inner Appalachian region right now. I've tried to give you an honest assessment of both the bad and the good. I had some misgivings before I ventured there myself and I came back feeling rewarded. All I can tell you is, it's an area that deserves more recognition than it has received.

The way I see it, you can't say you know the Appalachians until you've visited this place for yourself.

# Trip 27 Red River and Rock Bottom

**Distance** *216 miles*
**Terrain** *Scrambles through deep hollows, roads skirting Kentucky Bluegrass Country*
**Highlights** *Daniel Boone National Forest, Boonesborough, Nada Tunnel, Red River Gorge*

This route begins on State Route 451 that departs from Hazard off of the Route 15 bypass. Touring 451 is a bit on the adventure touring side. It's narrow and rough in many places, but certainly passable. Kentucky is full of wide spots in the road with memorable names and you'll pass a few of them on the way out. Spots like Krypton and Busy. Didn't look like a thing was

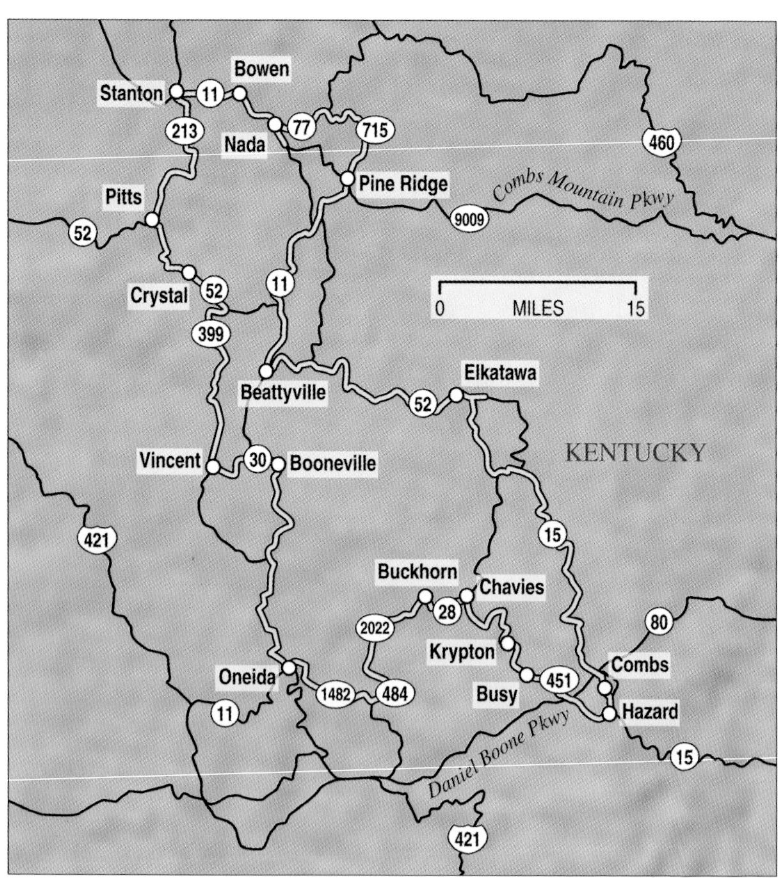

**THE ROUTE FROM HAZARD**

| | |
|---|---|
| 0 | Depart Hazard on KY 451 west |
| 16.1 | Left on KY 28 at Chavies |
| 28.4 | Left on SR 2022 at Buckhorn |
| 39.0 | Right on KY 484 |
| 41.1 | Right on SR 1482 |
| 50.3 | Right on KY 66 |
| 51.0 | Right on KY 11 in Oneida |
| 72.6 | Left on KY 30 in Booneville |
| 76.9 | Right on KY 399 |
| 91.8 | Left on KY 52 |
| 102.8 | Right on KY 213 |
| 116.1 | Right on KY 11 in Stanton |
| 126.5 | Left on KY 77 (Nada Tunnel Road) |
| 131.5 | Right on KY 715 |
| 150.6 | Left on KY 11 |
| 162.1 | Left on KY 52 |
| 183.3 | Left on KY 30 east |
| 184.6 | Right on KY 15 south |
| 216.4 | Arrive Hazard via KY 15 |

stirring or had stirred in Busy in quite some time. Route 451 ends in Chavies on Route 28 where you'll make a left turn.

Route 28 passes by the entrance to Buckhorn Lake State Resort (parks.ky.gov/findparks/resortparks/bk/). The resort is open year-round although most activities are geared toward the summer months. Buckhorn Lake is a good spot to consider as your base camp as an alternative to Hazard, especially if you like water sports. A little past Buckhorn Lake you'll arrive in Buckhorn, the hamlet. Make the left turn onto KY 2022. I like this road a lot, as it seems to lead nowhere. Generally the pavement is in very good condition with lots of tight twists. The forest crowds in from both sides, giving the impression the road is narrower than it is. A few miles in, you'll pass through Doorway, then Rock Bottom. You also just miss passing directly through Whoopflarea and Mistletoe. Darn the luck.

Make the right on Route 484 and then Route 1482, which has some good moments as it passes through Brutus on its way to Oneida. Here's a small valley wide enough to allow some farming. You'll see a fair amount of

*She's seen better days, but she's still a looker.*

tobacco grown in this region. The road hugs the side of the valley, so the route tends to feature a few sweepers followed by an occasional yank to the right or left. At Oneida, make the right onto KY 66. In just a few tenths, make the right again onto KY 11. Route 11 is a main road running approximately in a north-south direction. You'll catch up to a car here or there, but in most cases can get around them easily enough. Route 11 will deposit you in Booneville.

Along the Mid-Atlantic coast, "George Washington slept here" is the claim that many small towns make in a bid for recognition. Around these parts, it's Daniel Boone. So it is with Booneville, Kentucky (pop. 232). The area was once known as Boone's Station because Daniel Boone camped here once (no one knows if he slept). When the town was incorporated in 1846, it was then officially dubbed Booneville.

It's here that we reach a turning point in the tour. In the first part of the tour, you couldn't miss the incredible density of mountain ridges and peaks. Everywhere you looked seemed to be up. Now the country is beginning to open up a bit. At Booneville, you'll turn west on Route 11, which is joined by Route 30. When Route 30 turns left a few miles later, follow it. Another turn comes up shortly on Route 399. On Route 399, you almost feel as if you're in an entirely different country. Sharp ridges have given way to undulating hills. You're now riding around the edges of Bluegrass Country.

The next few roads rival their counterparts in other regions for scenic quality and general riding pleasure. I had a blast on 399. Make the left turn onto 52 for another fun run. This is a fast section of pavement with great sweepers. Route 213 is more like 399. The pavement isn't as smooth as 52, but it's a nice long stretch of road with good vistas. This road will bring you into Stanton. At this point, turn left on Route 11 in Stanton and follow that as it parallels the Combs Mountain Parkway toward the east. In Nada, turn left on KY 77. At this point, you'll also see signs directing you to the Red River Gorge.

The best way to enter Red River Gorge is through the Nada Tunnel. The entire gorge area was logged at one time and the tunnel was built to help expedite the process of removing the timber. Two crews started at opposite ends and began working their way toward one another in 1911. After the tunnel was done, the first train sent into the tunnel got stuck. Ooops! Must have been a metric-to-English conversion problem. Folks stood around scratching their heads a bit figuring on how to get the engine out of the hole

*Duck your head and pull in your elbows before entering Nada tunnel.*

with the consensus finally settling on dynamite. Heck, don't bother trying to winch it out, just blast the darn thing and be done with it! The second engine sent through didn't dare get stuck. It probably observed what happened to the first one. In another mishap, a man was killed when he tried to thaw frozen dynamite over a fire. I had no idea dynamite could freeze, but why would it occur to anyone to try to thaw it over a fire? Now there's a deserving candidate for the Darwin Awards (darwinawards.com).

When I first encountered the 900-foot Nada Tunnel, I got off the bike for a spell to read the sign posted outside the tunnel, but I also had to take a peek inside before I ventured in. From where I stood, it looked like an awfully darn small little hole in the ground! Was the real tunnel somewhere else that I was just missing? Riding through, I not only felt like the sides were closing in a little, but the ceiling also felt like it was getting lower. The tunnel is cut completely straight through, so it is possible to ensure no one else is in the tunnel before you enter. Throw on your high beam and it will help illuminate the sides a little. But be careful to keep your elbows in. You wouldn't want to scrape them along the walls (tinyurl.com/motojourneys17).

A few miles along Route 77, make the right on Route 715. This will take you through the gorge along the river and leads to some of the prominent

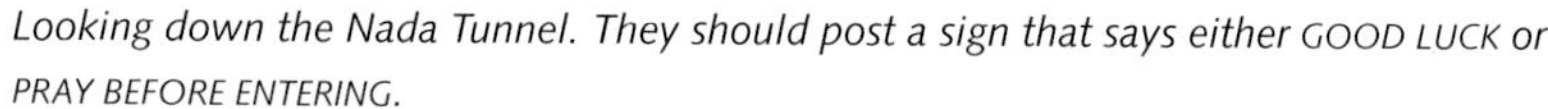

*Looking down the Nada Tunnel. They should post a sign that says either GOOD LUCK or PRAY BEFORE ENTERING.*

*Count on us to take you to the finest places here at Motorcycle Journeys.*

overlooks. Red River Gorge is unique for its array of natural arches. Most of the arches can been seen from the trails that run throughout the area, so if you're getting a little stiff, this is a good chance to stretch your legs. One of the easiest arches to get to is Sky Bridge. This also means it will be pretty popular. But if you like what you see, there are dozens of other less-traveled trails in the gorge you can follow to find other arches. As you navigate along 715, you'll cross the Red River. At this point, the right turn for Sky Bridge Road is about 1.2 miles ahead on the right. Sky Bridge Road is less than a mile long and leads to a picnic area and parking. From this point it is a short walk to the arch.

As the road departs the gorge, it scales the ridges, which means good twisty riding. Route 715 eventually intersects again with Route 11. Make the left turn. Once again you'll follow 11 for a distance, now heading south on the way back to Hazard. This section of 11 is straight and fast. In Beatyville, abandon Route 11 in favor of Route 52 east for a return to a more relaxed touring posture. Route 52 concludes at the intersection with Route 30 in Elkatawa. Turn left on 30 to rejoin Route 15 in Jackson. The right turn on 15 will deliver you back to Hazard and complete your return. Then you can safely say that you've made it back from Rock Bottom.

# Trip 28 Chicken Run

**Distance** *271 miles*
**Terrain** *An equal mix of modest hills and agricultural areas*
**Highlights** *Sanders Cafe, Kentucky River moonbows, Cumberland Gap*

Have you ever gotten an idea for a destination fixed in your mind and nothing would satisfy you until you'd achieved that destination? Truth be told, that was part of my motivation for mapping out this tour. I'd gotten wind that Corbin, Kentucky, was home to Colonel Sanders's original cafe and from the first, I knew I had to seek it out. I've made trips for lesser reasons; I'm sure you have, too. As riding buddy Red Fehrle jokes, "Running out of milk is a good thing. I hear they sell milk in West Virginia." So let's make a chicken run.

This run begins following Route 451 west out of Hazard at the junction with the KY 15 bypass. As noted before, Route 451 is a rough but passable road. At the junction with Route 80, turn left to follow 80 south. On this

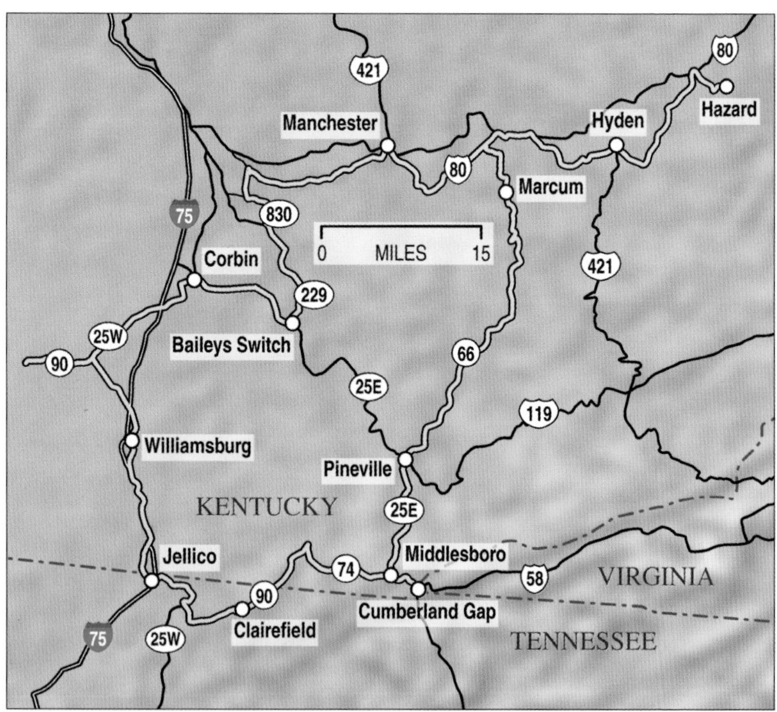

**THE ROUTE FROM HAZARD**

| | |
|---|---|
| 0 | Depart Hazard on KY 451 west |
| 4.0 | Left on KY 80 |
| 17.8 | Right on US 421 (421 joins KY 80) in Hyden |
| 48.3 | Left on KY 80 in Manchester |
| 64.2 | Left on KY 830 (Rough Creek Road) |
| 71.1 | Left on KY 229 (Barbourville Road) |
| 82.0 | Right on US 25E north |
| 93.3 | Left on KY 312 (East Master Street) |
| 94.7 | Left on US 25W south |
| 106.0 | Right on KY 90 to Cumberland Falls |
| 114.5 | Arrive Cumberland Falls, then turn around |
| 123.0 | Right on US 25W south |
| 152.8 | Left on TN 90 |
| 182.5 | Right on US 25E south |
| 184.1 | Arrive Cumberland Gap National Park |
| 184.7 | Join US 25E north |
| 197.8 | Right on KY 66 |
| 237.2 | Right on KY 80/US 421 |
| 253.3 | Left on KY 80 at KY 80/US 421 split |
| 267.1 | Right on KY 451 toward Hazard |
| 271.1 | Arrive Hazard on KY 451 |

side of Hazard, Route 80 is a good route west. Most of the route features good pavement and plenty of curves. Route 80 joins US 421 at Hyden. Make the right turn onto US 421/KY 80. US 421 completes the journey out of high country and into the low hills that mark the transition from coal country to the farming region. Route 80 departs from US 421 in Manchester and we'll follow it to the left. Now, Route 80 runs through open country.

You'll begin to see housing developments that mirror familiar suburban growth in other parts of the country. Before you get too entrenched in suburbia, make the left turn on KY 830, also known as Rough Creek Road. KY 830 winds through a series of well-tended farms and is a nice ride. At the intersection with KY 229, turn left and work your way west down to US 25E. This is a busy route that will soon bring us to our first destination. In Corbin, turn left at the light on KY 312. This leads to downtown

Corbin. Turn right on US 25W and head north for just a few tenths of a mile. Just ahead on the left you'll see a familiar sign for Kentucky Fried Chicken. On most tours, I'd pass by a fast-food franchise, but in this case, the franchise is the story. This is no ordinary KFC. This is where it all started.

The Sanders Cafe is part contemporary KFC restaurant and half museum. While you wait on your order, you can browse memorabilia associated with Sanders' early business ventures. When your order arrives, carry it over to the museum, which doubles as a dining hall. There you'll see the original Sanders kitchen setup and other artifacts from the early years.

The evolution of the KFC franchise is an interesting story, and an inspirational one. Harland Sanders held a variety of jobs in his early days including farmhand, streetcar conductor, private soldier, railroad fireman, insurance salesman, steamboat operator, tire salesman, and service station operator. At age 40, Sanders began cooking for hungry travelers who stopped at his service station, serving them in the living quarters at the station. Over the next decade or so, he perfected his cooking technique, which included a process of pressure frying.

This, in combination with the Colonel's "secret recipe of 11 herbs and spices" became known as Kentucky Fried Chicken. Sanders was named a Kentucky Colonel in 1935 by Gov. Ruby Laffoon to recognize his contribution to state's cuisine. His fame was growing, but business was not. In the 1950s, Sanders sold off his station, motel court, and restaurant when he learned an interstate highway would bypass Corbin and likely kill his business. Think the Colonel was finished? *Pffff.* He was just getting wound up.

At age 65, Colonel Sanders began traveling across the country by car, living off his Social Security check. He visited restaurants, cooking up batches of chicken for the owner and employees. If they liked his recipe, a handshake agreement was struck to pay the Colonel a nickel for each chicken sold, and thus a franchise was born.

Ever wondered how Colonel Sanders became a colonel? I've heard about "Kentucky Colonels" and have met a few, but it took a little digging to uncover the story. The title Kentucky Colonel (kycolonels.org) is the highest honor awarded by the Commonwealth of Kentucky. The tradition started when first Governor Isaac Shelby bestowed the title upon his son-in-law, Charles Todd. Later, Shelby extended the commission to everyone who served in his regiment during the War of 1812. Today, a colonel's commission is granted by the governor to recognize special achievement or outstanding community service. You don't have to be a citizen of Kentucky to qualify—

*At Sanders Cafe, birthplace of the Kentucky Friend Chicken franchise, there is a collection of memorabilia and a working KFC restaurant.*

English Prime Minister Winston Churchill was made a colonel. Muhammad Ali is, too. Senator John Glenn was named a colonel while in orbit.

Out of Corbin, follow US 25W south out of the downtown area. At the end of downtown, US 25W makes a right and heads west out of town. This path leads us to KY 90 and Cumberland Falls State Resort (parks.ky.gov/findparks/resortparks/cf). On nights with a full moon and clear skies, something unusual happens at Cumberland Falls. Tiny forest inhabitants—pixies and wood nymphs—come out and dance over the falls in a celebration of the full moon. What? Don't buy that? Actually, as the falls pound the rocks below, the resulting waterspray produces a moonbow in the soft lunar light. The effect is so mesmerizing, you'll never notice the dancing pixies and wood nymphs.

After visiting the falls, return to 25W and continue south. Stick with this route riding parallel to the interstate. It has a few good sweepers and some whoop de doos along the straights, then crosses the border into Tennessee at Jellico. A mile or two out of Jellico, turn left on TN 90. This is another great section of road. You'll start off with a rapid mountain ascent then spend the next thirty or so miles heading up, down, and around. On weekdays you'll catch up to a few trucks, but as I have found elsewhere in the region, they'll either turn off just a little way up the road or they'll slow down and let you pass. Somewhere along the route, you'll cross the state line and the road becomes KY 74. This leads directly into Middlesboro. When you reach the intersection with US 25E, turn right and you're right at the entrance to Cumberland Gap National Historic Park (nps.gov/cuga).

Cumberland Gap occupies an important place in colonial American history. It hadn't been much more than about fifty years since Europeans began arriving in force on the shores of the New World and already things were getting a bit tight. All the good farming land along the Shenandoah Valley had been claimed and new arrivals, notably the Scots-Irish, were being pushed further south and west into the less desirable hill country.

In the years following the French and Indian War (1754–1763), serious exploration began along a buffalo trace and Indian trail documented in 1750 by Dr. Thomas Walker. This gap, worn through the mountains, provided frontiersmen with the break they needed to enter the rich hunting lands of Kentucky (originally pronounced ken-tuh-KAY by Native Americans). The success of these early expeditions attracted folks like Daniel Boone, who in 1769 began his first trek through the Gap. Six years later, he was commissioned to open a road through the gap. Through the early 1800s, thousands of settlers poured through, settling Kentucky and opening up the midwest. As railroads came online in the 1830s and 1840s, the importance of the Cumberland Gap diminished.

*At Cumberland Gap, the author executes the ol' standing-in-two-states-at-one-time cliché photo. Nice shoes ya got there, pal.*

Be sure to check out the visitor center. It features Appalachian artisans practicing their craft, an excellent timeline display that takes you through the early history, discovery, boom, and bust of the region, and a film that documents Daniel Boone's exploration of the area. You'll also want to check out the road to the pinnacle of Cumberland Gap. It's a crazy, curve-filled, four miles up to the top. Low-hanging parts are guaranteed to drag on this short blast of a run. The pinnacle view lets you look down on the Gap and the point where Virginia, Tennessee, and Kentucky come together.

Departing Cumberland Gap, follow US 25W north to Pineville and turn right on KY 66. Great road. Route 66 (no relation to the famous Route 66 "Mother Road") is an isolated and mostly uninhabited stretch of 40 miles between Pineville and its terminus on US 421. Great pavement, great curves, and zero traffic (tinyurl.com/motojourneys18). I remember this vividly, because I made the mistake of turning onto 66 with the gas gauge tending toward empty. By the time I did encounter a gas station—thirty-five miles later at Marcum—the bike was stumbling badly. So take heed from my ill-considered decision. If you're running below a half tank, fill up in Pineville. Marcum is just six miles from US 421/KY 80 where we passed earlier in the day. At the junction, turn right to follow KY 80 back to Hazard.

As I made my way back, I rounded a bend to find a volunteer fireman standing at the entrance to a tight corner on 421, waving a flag to stop traffic. I was first in line, so I sidled up to his location and stopped. The axle had dropped out of a truck and it was stuck, literally, in the middle of the road. Had this been the old days, I suppose dynamite would have been liberally applied to the situation and the road cleared in a matter of minutes. Today's approach was to be somewhat more conservative; a tow truck was summoned.

It appeared we were all going to be here a while, so I cut off the bike and popped off the helmet which—to the fireman—was a sign he'd been looking for. "Nice bike," he said, "Where you from?" I told him where I was from. "I came down to the area to explore the roads," I replied. "Well, how in the world did you get down here?" he wondered aloud. Who should think to come to this part of Kentucky to ride? Why, us, of course. We had to make a chicken run.

# Trip 29 Them's The Breaks

**Distance** *255 miles*
**Terrain** *Hills and hollows of Coal Country*
**Highlights** *Breaks Interstate Park, Natural Tunnel, Trail of the Lonesome Pine, Kentucky Coal Mining Museum*

My first touring introduction to coal country was along Route 160, a road that originates in Appalachia, Virginia, and runs the mining region in eastern Kentucky. It is a road of vast contrasts—vistas of beauty and landscapes of destruction, perfectly illustrating the conflicting personalities of the area. Route 160 is featured in this tour along with some other great roads. If you've set out to discover what this mythical region is about and you have time for just one tour, this is it. There's a lot to see and do and tell, so let's get started.

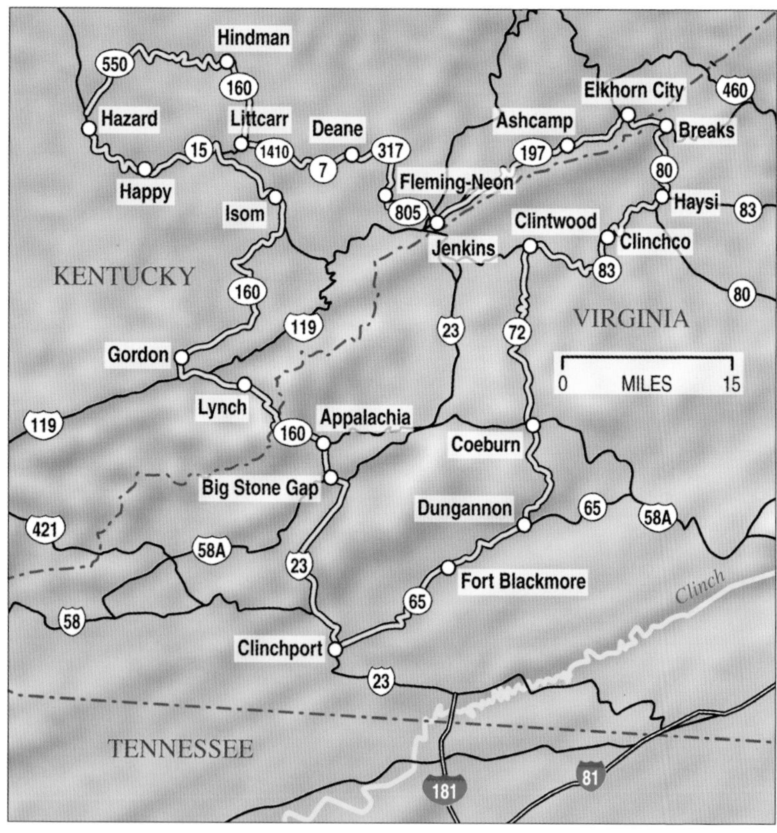

**THE ROUTE FROM HAZARD**

| | |
|---|---|
| 0 | Depart KY 550 in Hazard at junction with KY 476 |
| 18.4 | Right on KY 160 in Hindman |
| 26.7 | Left on SR 1410 at Littcarr |
| 32.8 | Left on KY 7 at Colson |
| 38.4 | Right on KY 317 at Deane |
| 47.0 | Right on KY 805 |
| 53.1 | KY 805 joins US 119/KY 197 |
| 58.9 | Right on KY 197 at US 119/KY 197 split |
| 75.4 | Right on KY 80 in Elkhorn City |
| 89.6 | Left on VA 80/VA 83 in Haysi |
| 90.0 | Right on VA 83 at VA 80/VA 83 split |
| 109.0 | Left on VA 72 at Clintwood |
| 146.9 | Right on VA 65 at Ft. Blackmore |
| 161.5 | Right on US 23 north at Clinchport |
| 162.7 | Right on VA 871 (Follow signs for Natural Tunnel) |
| 164.2 | Arrive Natural Tunnel State Park |
| 165.7 | Right on US 23 north |
| 182.0 | Right on exit at Big Stone Gap (US 58A/US 23 Business north) |
| 186.2 | Stay on US 23 Business north thru Big Stone Gap, then left on VA 160 |
| 206.8 | Right on KY 160 at KY 160/KY 463 split |
| 229.7 | Left on KY 15 north |
| 255.3 | Arrive Hazard via KY 15 north |

The first few segments of the route move east out of Hazard and deep into the center of the active mining region. The first section along Route 550 is not an unpleasant motoring experience. Most of the route cuts through small valleys and is a decent little road. The right turn on the northern end of Route 160 takes you through Hindman which is fairly active, but after a mile or two out of town, you're back to riding alone. In fact, this was very often the case. I'd find that if I did pick up a car or two along a route, they usually turned off soon. After a while it dawned on me that none of these roads are through-routes, so you wouldn't expect to follow someone for more than a mile or two.

The left on Route 1410 is an equally nice stretch bordering on the Carr

*Tail of the Dragon? Mere child's play. The posted speed limit on VA 160 is 55 mph. No guardrails. Have at it.*

Creek Wildlife Management Area. Route 1410 ends on Route 7, where you'll make the left turn at Colson. At Deane, pick up the right turn on KY 317 and follow that through Fleming-Neon. This section of the route portrays the current state of the economy in the region.

You can tell that, at one time, Fleming-Neon boasted an active retail district. But as you ride down Main Street now it looks nearly like a ghost town. Both sides of the street are lined with boarded-up buildings and shuttered businesses. You have to wonder, will prosperity ever return to this region? Will downtown Fleming-Neon flourish as it once did? For now, the answer seems to be no (tinyurl.com/motojourneys22). Route 317 ends on Route 805. Turn left and follow Route 805 as it joins US 23 Business and US 119 along Elkhorn Creek. Eventually, Route 23 splits off to the north and you'll bear right to continue toward Elkhorn City on KY 197. This, again, is another section of decent road. But things get really exciting just outside of Elkhorn City.

In town, turn right on KY 80. This leads directly east out of town and into Breaks Interstate Park on the Kentucky-Virginia border. This is a great section of road. Fantastic curves on a smooth ribbon of pavement. I stopped along a wide shoulder to take a break and review my route. For the entire 15 minutes I was stopped, not a single car passed by. Route 80 is some great riding!

Just a few miles over the border, the entrance to Breaks Interstate Park (breakspark.com) appears on the right. The canyon here at the park is the deepest gorge east of the Mississippi River with some areas as deep as 1,600 feet. Breaks is well worth considering as a base camp for exploring this region. There are dozens of hiking trails to enjoy, fishing, boating, horseback riding, rafting, and more. Whether you prefer a room at the lodge, a cottage, or a campsite, Breaks offers inexpensive accommodations in a beautiful setting. Even if you're not of a mind to settle in, you'll still want to visit for the views of the gorge.

Back on Route 80, continue east by turning right when you leave the Park. VA 83 joins your route in Haysi. When the two routes split, make the right onto VA 83 and follow it through Clinchco. In Clintwood, pick up Route 72 south and follow it through Coeburn down to Dungannon. At this point, VA 65 joins Route 72. When these routes split at Fort Blackmore, follow Route 65 west.

Fort Blackmore was a wooden fort erected here on the frontier in the late 1700s. It mostly served as a waystation for folks passing through on the way through Cumberland Gap. For a period of time there was a small town built here along the banks of the Clinch River. That all changed in 1973 when Hurricane Camille caused the Clinch River to take away the town. After that, the area was declared a flood plain and no further building was allowed.

Route 65 ends in Clinchport on US 23. This is a good time to crank up the tunes if you're equipped. I recommend Dwight Yoakam's *Hillbilly Deluxe,* featuring the song "Readin', Rightin', Route 23." Yoakam's song showcases the plight of people who left Appalachia along this road, headed for northern cities seeking "the good life they had never seen." But as the story later reveals, their measure of success was misguided and "they didn't know that old highway could lead them to a world of misery."

*Breaks Interstate Park is a base camp worthy of consideration for riding in the Appalachians.*

*The old Appalachia City Hall reflects both the charm and the state of affairs in Appalachia, Virginia.*

Just a couple of miles up Route 23, you'll see the sign for Natural Tunnel State Park (dcr.state.va.us/parks/naturalt.htm). Make the right on VA 871 and head up the road about two miles. Natural Tunnel evolved as acid-laden groundwater dissolved softer rock compounds. Later in its evolution, Stock Creek was diverted and began its process of carving out the tunnel as it is seen today. Railroad track was laid through the tunnel in the late 1800s and this route is still in use today for hauling coal out of the region. For a couple of bucks, a chairlift will carry you to the bottom of the gorge and bring you back to the top.

Returning to Route 23, head north to Big Stone Gap. Route 23 is a four-lane highway, but typically not very busy, at least not by metropolitan standards. When you arrive at Big Stone Gap, take the exit for the downtown area. That's US 23 Business north/US 58A.

Big Stone Gap is home to the outdoor drama depiction of the *Trail of the Lonesome Pine*. The original novel by John Fox, Jr. from which the play was adapted, tells of the romance between a young Appalachian girl and an engineer from the East who arrives during the coal boom of the early '20s. The story is as much about the effects of the sudden influx of wealth on clannish mountain families and customs as it is about the lovers. Although the book is a fictional account, many of the characters such as Devil Judd Tolliver and Bad Rufe Tolliver bore striking resemblance to some of the better known (or notorious) real life clansmen who lived on both sides of the Kentucky-Virginia border.

Ready for a seriously hot stretch of road? Follow US 23 Business north out of Big Stone Gap to Appalachia. On the south end of town, you'll see the left turn for VA 160. Route 160 starts out somewhat inauspiciously through an industrial section, but that soon gives way to long straights. A couple of miles later, you'll look up to the side of the mountain and see a couple of clearings. You'll be riding along those clearings in just a few minutes. At the base of the mountain, Route 160 begins to ascend the mountain with an unending series of sweepers and switchbacks (tinyurl.com/motojourneys19). Some of the curves remind me of Deal's Gap—sweep, sweep, sweep, turn! Sweep, sweep, turn! This glorious pattern continues for a good ten miles over Black Mountain and the state border, depositing you in Lynch, Kentucky.

Like a lot of other towns, Lynch was a company town. This means that the mining company literally owned the town. It shipped in all the building materials and supplies and built the town from scratch. The houses were owned by the company and employees were often paid in "scrip" instead of cash. Scrip could only be used at the company store. Tennessee Ernie Ford sang about this system in "Sixteen Tons." "You load sixteen tons, what do you get? Another day older and deeper in debt. St. Peter don't you call me, 'cause I can't go. I owe my soul to the company store."

Lynch and the next town, Benham, have preserved their coal heritage with museums. In Lynch, you can now tour Portal #31 (kingdomcome.org/portal), what was one of the largest coal loading operations in the country. In Benham, the Kentucky Coal Mining Museum (kingdomcome.org/museum) provides an in-depth examination of the mining era and its people. The basement features a mock mine exhibit and the third floor is dedicated to Loretta Lynn.

The remaining section of Route 160 passes through Cumberland then makes a sharp, uphill turn right out of town. It's along this section, from Cumberland to Isom where you're likely to run upon trucks. If you happen to tour this route on a weekend, you probably won't see any at all. Route 160 intersects with Route 15 at Isom. Turn left on 15 to make the return to Hazard.

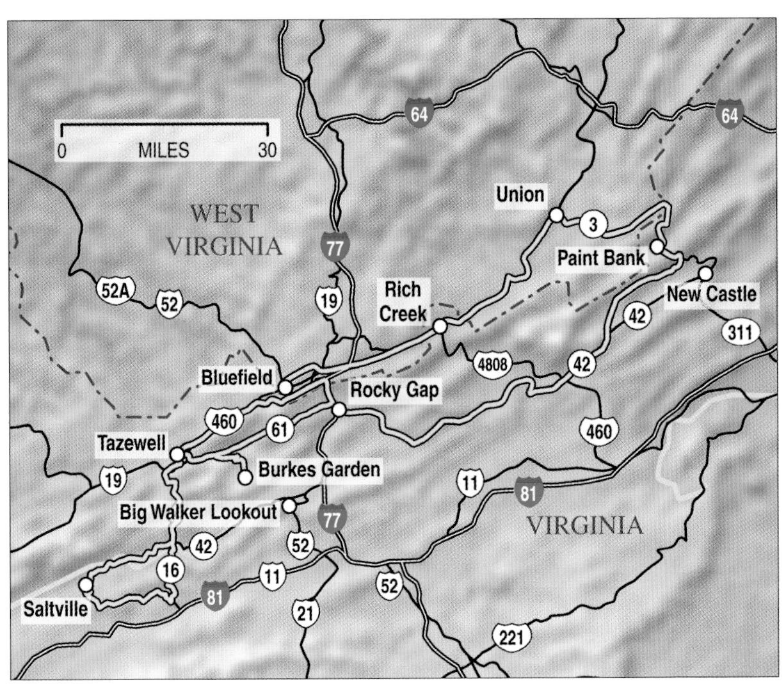
0 MILES 30
WEST VIRGINIA
VIRGINIA
Union
Paint Bank
New Castle
Rich Creek
Bluefield
Rocky Gap
Tazewell
Burkes Garden
Big Walker Lookout
Saltville
64
64
77
77
81
81
3
19
19
52A
52
52
52
42
42
42
311
4808
460
460
61
11
11
16
21
221

# High in the Hills

## *Bluefield, West Virginia*

The height of the riding season, July and August, coincides with the hottest months on the calendar here in the eastern mountains. It can get downright oppressive at times, especially in the valleys between mountain peaks. However, if you are committed to a midsummer tour, there are spots you can reach here in the Appalachians that avoid much of the misery.

One such place is Bluefield, West Virginia, billed as Nature's Air Conditioned City. Doesn't that title just make you feel a little cooler when you hear it? Bluefield is a great place to launch an assault on the central Appalachians, especially during the "Lemonade Days" of summer. More on that in a minute.

Bluefield is spread out along the border between Virginia and West Virginia along I-77 toward the southern end of the Greenbrier Valley. Some folks say that Bluefield took its name from the blue chicory plants that line

*The roads in the two-state area around Bluefield are largely empty, and always beautiful.*

*A rider takes advantage of a warm November day along scenic Virginia 42.*

roadways and fields while others believe the name is derived from a reference to the Bluestone coal fields.

However its name came about, "coal" is certainly the most important word in the history of the town. Even in Thomas Jefferson's day, it was known that a vast deposit of soft bituminous coal lay beneath the valley floor. Active mining began in the 1890s. From the beginning of that period, Bluefield's growth exploded. The coal boom, which lasted until the 1960s, flooded Bluefield with wealth to a degree that rivaled New York and Chicago. Bluefield had a skyline comparable to those cities, a nearby town boasted the most millionaires per capita, and Bluefield had more automobiles per capita than any other city. Bluefielders were probably the first folks to experience "rush hour."

After a heady half-century, Bluefield's prospects began to dim as the coal boom turned to bust and the Interstate Highway System bypassed the town. It's a story repeated over and over, not just in the Appalachians, but everywhere a town is founded on one or two key economic drivers.

While coal played the lead role in the rise and decline of Bluefield, it is also contributing to its return. In 1996, Congress created the National Coal Heritage Area (www.coalheritage.org), encompassing 13 counties in southern West Virginia. That act provides funds that are helping communities like Bluefield develop tourism programs for folks like you and me to enjoy.

As a result, Bluefield is on the rebound and is remaking itself into an attractive place to visit. Tourism is a growing emphasis, so visitors will find a warm welcome. Saying that it's on the rebound is another way of also saying that you'll find most of the region's travel services in the surrounding area, not necessarily downtown.

Cottages and modern rental cabins are plentiful ("modern" meaning electricity, heat, and most importantly, indoor plumbing). Hidden Path Cabins offers rentals built in 2008 with fully-equipped kitchens. Bluefield is also close by two outstanding West Virginia State Parks: Pipestem (www.pipestemresort.com) and Bluestone (www.bluestonesp.com). Pipestem's accommodations include a lodge with 113 guest rooms and suites, 26 rental cottages and plenty of camping. It also features a 30-room lodge that is accessible only by a 3,600-foot tramway. Bluestone's facilities also include modern cabins and dozens of campsites.

One very successful program developed over the last decade or so has been the Hatfield-McCoy trail system (www.trailsheaven.com). There are over 500 miles of off-road trails for ATVs, mountain bikes, horses, and dirt bikes. When it's done, the entire system will have over 2,000 miles of trails. The newest trail in the system begins in Ashland, West Virginia, just 18 miles from Bluefield. You probably won't be trailering an ATV behind your bike, but you can still enjoy these trails. There are ATV rentals and guided tours available. Paths are graded from easy to difficult, clearly marked, and professionally maintained, so even the least experienced off-road rider can have a great time.

If you get back early one afternoon and need to fill in some time, head north on US 52 to Pinnacle Rock State Park (pinnaclerockstatepark.com). From an elevation of 3,100 feet, you'll have a commanding view of the region including downtown Bluefield. Just a little farther north is the town of Bramwell (bramwellwv.com). Bramwell is worth an afternoon's visit, too. It was here the coal barons built their opulent mansions, putting their enormous wealth on conspicuous display. Unheard of for a town (really, a village) its size, Bramwell had a water department and telephone service. Some of the mansions featured indoor pools and showers, and one home even had a speaking tube that ran from the front door of the home to the town doctor's bedroom.

*Rising 100 feet above the ridgeline of Big Walker Mountain, this lookout gives you a five-state, 360-degree view.*

The most spectacular view in all the Appalachians awaits you about thirty miles south of town at Big Walker Lookout (scenicbeauty-va.com). When you're in the Bluefield area, make a special point to take a trip down to Big Walker. There, on top of the 3,400-foot mountain ridge is a 100-foot tower. I'm not afraid of heights, but I have to tell you, it made me just a little queasy climbing to the top. It's that high. The unobstructed view is worth the effort. On a clear day, it's said you can see the peaks of mountains in five states. (That would be Kentucky, West Virginia, Virginia, North Carolina, and Tennessee. Given Big Walker's centralized location and proximity to the surrounding state borders, I don't doubt the claim.) The view at Mount Mitchell in North Carolina is reputed to have the finest view, and Roan Mountain in Tennessee is nice, too. But neither offer a complete 360-degree panorama like Big Walker. Check it out. You will not be disappointed.

Summer evenings in the Bluefield area are filled with the sounds of baseball because the region hosts two minor league affiliate teams. Venture out to visit the Bluefield Orioles (appalachianleague.com) at Bowen Field, a historic ballpark built in 1939, or check out the Princeton Rays at Hunnicutt Field. Both teams are members of the Appalachian League and affiliates of major league franchises, so there's a good chance one or more of the players you see on the field will end up in "the bigs." When you look through the list of past players on both teams, more than a few recognizable names pop off the list, including Don Baylor, Armando Benetiz, Larry Bigbee, Carl Crawford, Eddie Murray, Boog Powell, and some kid named Cal Ripken, Jr. He was pretty good.

The climate in Bluefield is consistently cooler due to its overall elevation. At an average height of 2,655 feet above sea level, Bluefield is the highest town in West Virginia. Plan to have an extra layer with you, just in case. If a Canadian high-pressure weather system blows through town, it'll feel chilly compared to the rest of the area. On those rare occasions when the temperature exceeds 90 degrees, Bluefield has a plan. Since 1939, the Bluefield Chamber of Commerce has served free lemonade any time the temperature tops that mark at the Bluefield airport. When a hot day is imminent, the chamber will declare a Lemonade Day, offering free lemonade at its headquarters downtown and a few other places around the city.

Like our trips through Hazard, Kentucky, the roads you'll traverse in this section of the country will lead you through what most people think of when they hear "Appalachia." This is the heart of the Appalachians. Stark contrasts between the haves and have-nots can be seen, not just in Bramwell, but throughout the region. For every area that seems to be prospering, you'll find others where the effects wrought by long-term economic neglect and poverty are all too obvious. Despite these apparent disparities, I think you'll find that after spending just one day here, the overwhelming majesty of the mountains and the genuine likeability of the people who live here will immediately win you over.

It must be time for a run to Bluefield. I'm starting to get thirsty.

# Trip 30 Heartland Loop

**Distance:** *169 miles*
**Terrain:** *Pastoral byways threaded among rolling hills and mountains*
**Highlights:** *Paint Bank, Potts Mountain, Craig Healing Springs*

This loop, in my opinion, is a testament to the simple but stunning pleasures that await riders who venture down these Appalachian byways. Other rides offer more history or more curves. When you ride this route and enjoy the viewscapes this route has to offer, I think you'll come to understand why those who are born here feel there's no reason to live anywhere else. Sometimes less is more. Speaking of less, how about less talk and more action? Let's get to the ride.

This route begins out of the Bluefield area on Route 112 along the East River. Route 112 meanders frequently through a quiet hollow and frequently parallels the main line of rail tracks running out of Bluefield. Often, you are just a few feet from a rumbling train. The road repeatedly turns on a dime to cross under the tracks, switching sides several times throughout its length.

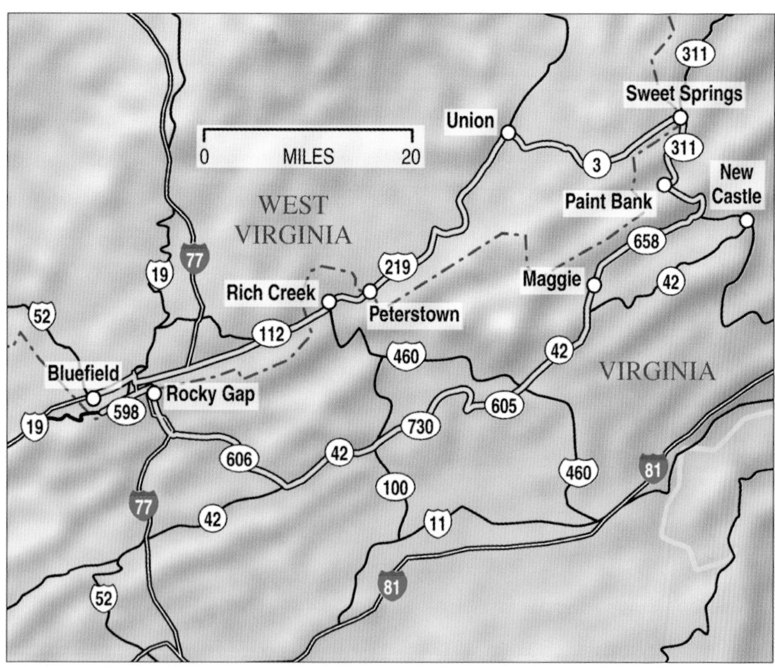

**THE ROUTE FROM BLUEFIELD**

| | |
|---|---|
| 0 | Leave Bluefield on WV 112 |
| 14 | Turn right on US 460 |
| 23 | Left on US 219 at Rich Creek |
| 49 | Right on WV 3 at Union |
| 68 | Right on WV 311 at Sweet Springs |
| 85 | Right on VA 658 |
| 103.5 | Right on VA 42 |
| 113.2 | Cross US 460, continue on Spruce Run Road (VA 605) |
| 119.5 | Right on VA 625 |
| 121.7 | Left on VA 682 |
| 122.5 | Becomes VA 730 Eggleston Road, continue straight |
| 130.7 | Left on VA 100 |
| 134 | Right on VA 42 |
| 144.3 | Right on VA 606 |
| 157.2 | Right on US 52 |
| 162.6 | Left on VA 598 |
| 168.8 | Arrive Bluefield |

I was not long out of bed as I began this ride, and had this gone on long enough, the pleasing rhythm and the easy pace would have lulled me to sleep. That was about to change.

As I traced the route, I caught up to a plodding, mile-long freight train pulling an endless line of chemical cars. I began to pull ahead of the lead engine as I neared Oakvale, when just ahead I could see we'd soon meet at an at-grade crossing. Did I have enough time to cross safely? Was I being stupid even thinking about outrunning a train to save a few minutes?

I dialed up a little more throttle, promising myself that if the gates began to close at the crossing, I wouldn't try to beat them; I would stop. As I neared the crossing, I heard the engineer lean on the horn, wondering what curses and incantations he might be reciting as he saw me surge ahead and angle for the crossing. I popped across the tracks just as the bells began to ring and the gates descend. I wasn't sleepy anymore.

It was probably just as well that the route ended on US 460 at this point, lest I be tempted to try that again. I sat at the intersection before turning onto the highway, not because I was waiting for an opening. I was waiting to

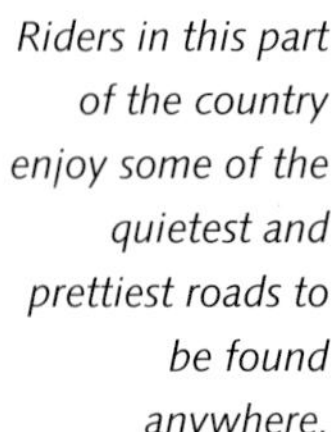

*Riders in this part of the country enjoy some of the quietest and prettiest roads to be found anywhere.*

see how long it would be before I saw a car at all. On a Saturday morning, this road is so wide open it's effectively deserted.

In Rich Creek, make the turn left on Island Street and pick up US 219. If you were to ride Route 219 to its other end, you'd reach West Seneca, New York, some 535 miles to the north. There've been on-and-off proposals over the years to convert US 219 into a divided highway and extend it an extra 1,000 miles to spur trade between Canada, the U.S., and the Caribbean. I hope that doesn't happen. As north-south routes go, US 219 is one of my favorites. I like 219 because the route offers a variety of fast sweepers, long straights with great views, and an occasional mountain pass. Here out of Rich Creek, the road is mostly straight and a little built up, but still not heavily traveled.

Monroe County, West Virginia, is the perfect exemplar of the less-is-more philosophy. Monroe County features hundreds of miles of country lanes with no divided highways, no traffic lights, and not one fast-food restaurant. Speaking of food, if you planned to ride a few miles before you got breakfast, you made a good decision. In Peterstown, stop in at the Hometown Restaurant (304-753-4788 ) right along 219. In Union, check out the Kalico Kitchen (304-772-3104 ).

Union, West Virginia, is the county seat of Monroe. Union takes its name from its days as a town on the frontier where it served as a meeting place for cavalry regiments who used it as a rendezvous point for campaigns against warring Indian tribes. Today the only shooting you'll hear is during hunting season. As I stopped from time to time, I could hear the sharp report of high-powered rifles firing off in the deep woods. If you do happen to wander along the roads during fall hunting season, keep a keen watch for spooked deer making a fast getaway.

Bearing right on WV 3, I began riding toward Sweet Springs. The path through eastern Monroe County is dotted with farms and pastureland. As you near the intersection of 3 and 311, Peters Mountain rises on the right. We'll be headed that way shortly.

When you look at maps of Sweet Springs, an odd notation may catch your eye. I found a spot marked "Government Floyd Monument" on both my Street Atlas maps and on Google maps. Doing a quick search revealed nothing about the monument. I couldn't imagine what exactly a "Government Floyd" was. Could it mean a "flood" monument? As I pulled into the intersection, I could see a marker just ahead. Oh. Somewhere, somebody goofed. The monument is to "Governor Floyd," as in John Floyd.

*Virginia governor and one-time presidential candidate John Floyd's memorial marks the intersection of WV 3 and 311.*

*Paint Bank General Store, Restaurant, and Lodge offers a one-stop shop for riders. Dedicated bike parking, too.*

Floyd played a vocal role in many of the nation's early debates including slavery, national expansion, and the role of the state militias. He served first as a U.S. Representative and later as Virginia's governor. He also ran for president in the late 1820s. Floyd died here in Sweet Springs and was buried in an unmarked grave.

Although it's not on our route, you might care to venture just around the corner to check out the Sweet Springs Resort (oldsweetsprings.com). Like many others in the area, Sweet Springs prospered as a getaway destination beginning as early as the late 1700s. Many attribute the stately designs of the main resort to Thomas Jefferson. Like most other resorts, its fortunes declined with the rise of the automobile. By the 1940s the resort was converted to an elderly-care facility, closed in the 1990s, and repurchased in 2005. There are new plans to rebuild and restore the springs to their original prominence. It's an interesting story to follow to see how these old facilities might be reinvented.

On the other hand, how about some more great riding? In fact, the best riding of the day lies just ahead. Turn east on Route 311 and begin the ascent over Peters Mountain into Virginia. This lightly traveled road features a steep ascent up the mountain to the border. Unlike many descents, this one is far gentler with graceful sweepers, allowing you to keep more speed as you descend into Paint Bank.

Paint Bank is a great place to stop for lunch. In fact, it's a great potential place to hole up for a couple days of great riding. You'll find the Swinging Bridge Restaurant inside the General Store (www.paintbankgeneralstore.com). If you've never had buffalo before, this is the place to try it. The Great White Buffalo Sandwich is tender and tasty.

Want to hang out for an overnighter? Stop by the Depot Lodge for accommodations. You can stay in the converted train depot, the caboose, or one of two separate properties including a cabin situated along Potts Creek. The cabin sleeps six and is fully equipped for housekeeping, making it a perfect spot to stop over if you're traveling with a group of friends.

Before you leave, top off your gas tank at the store. There aren't many opportunities for gas in the next 30 to 40 miles.

Paint Bank marks the halfway point of this loop. To begin your return, continue following Route 311 east over Potts Mountain. This begins a remarkable, 70-mile run back to Bluefield that encompasses some of the most scenic riding in the region. That's saying something.

On the other side of Potts Mountain pick up Route 658. It begins as a narrow path, threatening to turn to gravel. It quickly opens up. Route 658 follows one creek after another, passing through Craig Healing Springs, yet another former resort. Fortunately the facilities here have found a new purpose as a private retreat operated by the Disciples of Christ Church.

In Maggie, Route 658 joins Route 632. Turn right and continue until Route 658 splits off to the left again. This takes you over another mountain pass and joins Route 42. Turn right, following Route 42 to its intersection with US 460. At the intersection, cross over 460 and continue on Spruce Run Road. This narrow, twisty lane will nearly tie you in knots as you try to keep up with the curves. When this road ends on VA 625, turn right and follow Goodwinds Ferry Road until it joins Eggleston. Hang a left to continue west and get set for more laughs on Eggleston! This road picks up right where Spruce Run left off. Narrow, twisty, and great fun.

Even when you come to a major road like Route 100, the good times continue to roll. Turn left on 100 and continue south for just a few miles to pick up the last segment of VA 42. Turn right and head west on this stunning section of road.

On my last trip through the area, I pulled over at one particular point along the road, a long straightaway set against a backdrop of mountains (tinyurl.com/motojourneys01). I had no particular agenda in mind. I just wanted to stop and enjoy my surroundings. No rushing wind. No speed. No sound. Just stillness, enhanced by the sight of this beautiful landscape.

Like I said, some times, less is more.

# Trip 31 Frog Level Loop

**Distance** *139 miles*
**Terrain** *Numerous mountain ascents into Burke's Garden and along VA 16, a valley run along 617 through Saltville, then a return over the mountains*
**Highlights** *Burke's Garden, Hungry Mother State Park, Frog Level Yacht Club*

Maybe I shouldn't publish this route. Despite the fact that VA 16 is one of the great motorcycling roads in the whole of the Appalachians, it remains relatively unknown. I'm not sure why that is. It's easy to find along Interstate 81 at Marion, Virginia. It runs through some of the prettiest rural country in southwestern Virginia. Selfishly, I'd like to keep it to myself, but it's just too good not to share.

The tour begins on Route 61 west off of US 52 near Bluefield, Virginia. Route 61 is a two-lane primary route threading though a valley between the Buckhorn Mountains to the north and Garden Mountains on the left. The

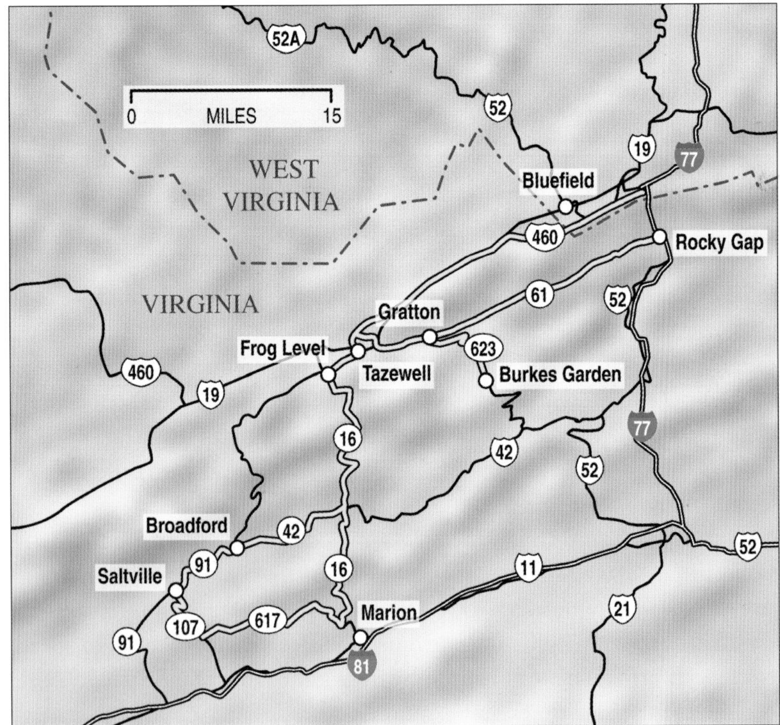

**THE ROUTE FROM BLUEFIELD**

| | |
|---|---|
| 0 | Depart VA 61 west at VA 61/US 52/I-77 intersection in Bluefield |
| 19.2 | Left on VA 623 (Burke's Garden Road) |
| 26.6 | Arrive Burke's Garden, then turn around |
| 34.0 | Left on VA 61 |
| 41.0 | Left on VA 16 in North Tazewell |
| 42.3 | Left on VA 16/US 19 south in Tazewell |
| 45.3 | Left on VA 16 south at Frog Level |
| 72.1 | Right on VA 617 (Walker Creek Road) |
| 84.6 | Right on VA 107 |
| 89.2 | Right on VA 91 in Saltville |
| 96.0 | Continue straight on VA 42 at Broadford |
| 105.4 | Left on VA 16 north |
| 121.4 | Right on US 19/VA 16 at Frog Level |
| 124.4 | Left on VA 16 in Tazewell |
| 125.2 | Right on US 460 east |
| 139.4 | Arrive Bluefield via US 460 east |

Garden Mountains rise steeply from the valley floor as if they are guarding something from discovery. That something is Burke's Garden. There is only one paved road in and out of the valley and you'll find it at Gratton. Turn left on VA 623 to enjoy several miles of twisty pavement over the gap and enter the pastoral beauty that is Burke's Garden (tinyurl.com/motojourneys20).

At an elevation of 3,000 feet, Burke's Garden is the highest valley in Virginia. James Burke discovered the valley on a hunting expedition in 1740 although the first permanent white settlement did not occur here until the 1800s. The valley is surrounded by mountains on all sides, and owing to its fertility and beauty, its nickname is "God's Thumbprint."

Once you get settled in, it's hard to leave a place like this. Maybe that's why many of the families that remain here are descendants of the original settlers. It's said that George Vanderbilt made Burke's Garden his first choice for a large country estate, but no one would sell him any land. He went to his backup choice, Asheville, North Carolina, where he constructed the Biltmore Mansion.

*Burke's Garden General Store and Post Office is open for your convenience Monday through Thursday, 9 a.m. to 11 a.m.*

A brief thunderstorm drove me off the bike and into the Burke's Garden General Store. I picked up a snack and then went back to the covered front porch where I drifted lazily on the porch swing waiting for the rain to let up. In ten minutes, the showers had passed and I resumed my exploration of the valley. I suppose if you had a dual purpose bike you could attempt to exit 623 on the south end of the valley. It's not a route you'd want to attempt on a regular street bike.

I had a hard time turning the bike around to leave the garden, but managed to break free and follow Route 61 west into Tazewell. In North

Tazewell, turn left on VA 16 and follow it through town, over Route 460 and through Tazewell. A few miles outside of town, VA 16 turns to the left and the ride of a lifetime begins.

Route 16 runs through Thompson Valley before tackling Clinch Mountain. Several pullouts along the road encourage you to stop and snap some shots of the panoramic vistas. There are few roads I can honestly compare to western North Carolina's array of great riding roads, but this is one of them. Route 16 takes Clinch Mountain straight on like a feisty bantam weight boxer, ducking, bobbing, and weaving, landing a great left hook here, a roundhouse right-hander there, and a series of left-right combinations that leave you punch drunk with delight. Twenty-five sweet miles pass before you run out of the good stuff.

As you come down off your curve induced high, Hungry Mother State Park (dcr.state.va.us/parks/hungrymo.htm) appears on your left. Hungry Mother derives its name from a sad tale. According to legend, a number of settlements along the New River, which runs south of the park, were destroyed by Native Americans. Some survivors were carried by the raiders into the mountains north of the park, including Molly Marley and her small child. They managed to escape and wandered through the wilderness, following a small creek and eating what berries they could find. Molly collapsed and her small child continued on, eventually finding help. All the

*There's only one paved road in and out of Burke's Garden. And it's a fun one, too! Photo by Dan Bard*

child could say was "hungry mother." When help returned, Molly was found dead.

Despite its heritage, the park and its 108-acre lake sparkle against a backdrop of Walker Mountain. Hungry Mother is about five miles north of Interstate 81. If you happen to be traveling the I-81 corridor, this is a spot worth considering as a base camp for riding in the area. Cabins are available for weekly rental. Camping is also available.

About a mile and a half below the park, turn right on VA 617, labeled Old Lake Road. The road splits in just a few tenths and you'll want to stick to the right. The route remains VA 617 and becomes Walker Creek Road. Route 617 cuts across the valley north of Marion and ends on VA 107 just south of Saltville (saltville.com). Turn right on VA 107 and follow it into town. Salt and gypsum deposits formed in this area as a vast inland sea receded. Over time the salt deposits attracted Ice Age animals such as mastodons and woolly mammoths. More recently, salt mined from this area made it an important natural resource for the Confederate Army during the Civil War.

The return to Bluefield begins here on VA 91. Your map and mine clearly depict Route 91 notching its way gracefully across Clinch Mountain before arriving back at Frog Level. Boy, I wish that were the case. From the turnoff at Bradford, the pavement skirts Little Mountain and ends 5.8 miles later without warning just after you've completed a great pass. For the second time in the same day I found myself wishing I was astride a TransAlp

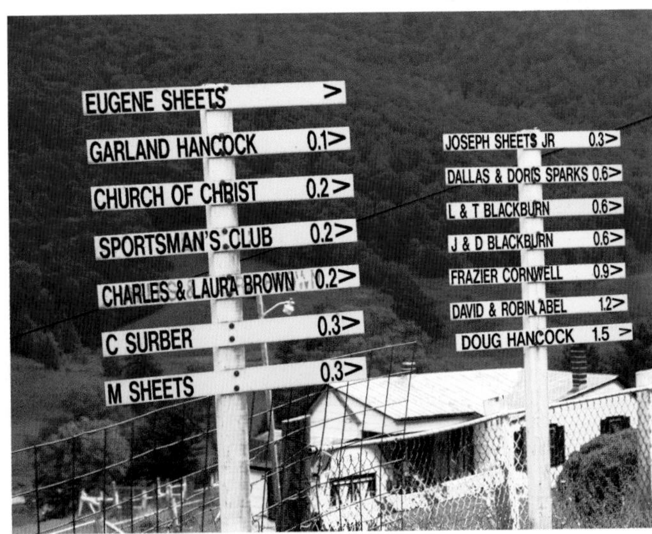


*Directions are pretty straightforward in Burke's Garden, Virginia.*

*The setting sun closes out a fun ride over VA 16 near Tazewell, Virginia.*

instead of a Gold Wing. I was faced with little choice but to return over the pass and then follow VA 42 up to its intersection with VA 16 and ride that great section back over Cheat Mountain.

On your way in and out of the loop you'll pass through Frog Level (craborchardmuseum.com). Local storyteller and humorist Jack Witten was out frog hunting with a friend one night along the banks of Plum Creek. A thick blanket of fog rose upon the valley. Nothing could be heard but the sound of frogs. Witten dubbed this combination of fog flattened landscape and amphibious concert "frog level" and soon after began using the phrase as his dateline for a column in the local paper. Today the Frog Level Yacht Club at the corner of VA 16 and US 19 is known locally as the place to gather for storytelling and music.

From Frog Level, head east on VA 16 into Tazewell and pick up US 460 for the return to Bluefield.

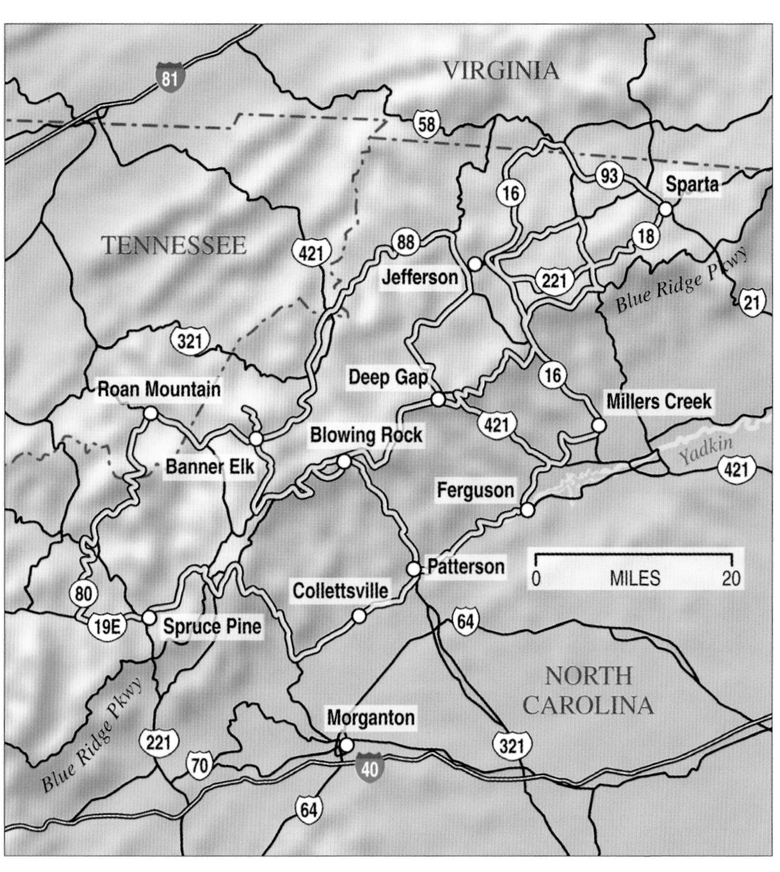
VIRGINIA
81
58
93
Sparta
16
18
TENNESSEE
421
88
Jefferson
221
Blue Ridge Pkwy
21
321
16
Deep Gap
Roan Mountain
Millers Creek
421
Blowing Rock
Banner Elk
Yadkin
421
Ferguson
Patterson
0
MILES
20
80
Collettsville
19E
Spruce Pine
64
NORTH
CAROLINA
Blue Ridge Pkwy
Morganton
221
321
70
40
64

# Lost in the Mountains

## *Blowing Rock, North Carolina*

There are two distinct base camps for tours in Blowing Rock, depending on whether you prefer to camp or motel it during your stay. In either case, you'll fall in love with this area of the country. The pace of life really is slower here, and the folks you meet aren't as concerned about getting ahead or making it big as they are about doing what it takes to get by and enjoying life while they're at it.

*The Linn Cove Viaduct around Grandfather Mountain may be one of the most recognizable road structures in the world. Photo by Jimmy McLean*

For motorcycle campers, Ferguson is your destination. It's a dot on the map about 20 miles southeast of Blowing Rock and home to a motorcycles-only campground called Rider's Roost (ridersroost.com). If you look at a detailed map, another spot labeled Elkville indicates the precise location of the campground. The Roost is run by brothers Bruce Colburn and Roy Yelverton, "one hundred percent scooter people" who are serious about their riding. Both are Harley fans with a garage area where they do custom work on their bikes and will also allow campers to do some wrenching. Try finding that at a Kampground of America.

The campground, along the banks of Elk Creek, features a large, open, grassy area with newly planted ornamental cherries. It is perfect for setting up either tent or camper. Rates are a bargain compared to some larger campgrounds: ten dollars will fetch you a level, grassy camping spot by the river. You can also rent a cabin (reserved in advance) for 30 dollars per night. Hot showers, laundry facilities, and a game room are located at the campground.

If you're not into camping, Blowing Rock (blowingrock.com) is a great place to stay. It's a small town that takes its name from a rock formation where a constant wind sweeps up under the rock and returns small items that you throw over the edge. If that sounds kind of insignificant compared to Niagara Falls or Yosemite, well, it is—but that's not the real attraction here. The real draw for me is the town itself.

Main Street is lined with rows of shops and restaurants. You can walk from one end to the other in 15 minutes and have a grand time sitting in front of the courthouse watching others walk by. It's even better in the evening when a cool breeze sets in and the traffic subsides. At night under the

*The Homestead Inn offers quiet rooms just a couple blocks off the main drag in Blowing Rock.*

*Blowing Rock Cafe not only serves good food, it's also owned by a Harley enthusiast as evidenced by the H.O.G. banner out front.*

streetlights, Blowing Rock becomes the setting for a Norman Rockwell painting—and you're part of the picture.

There are many places to stay in Blowing Rock, but if you're arriving in town during the peak summer travel season, you should reserve a room if you want one in the walking district. One that fit the bill is the Homestead Inn (homestead-inn.com), about a block off the Main Street. Just on the outside of town, Cliff Dwellers Inn (cliffdwellers.com) is another good spot to find lodging. Cliff Dwellers, true to the name, is situated on the side of a hill overlooking Blowing Rock. A wraparound deck offers you a chance to sit outside and enjoy the sunset in the evenings.

You can eat well in Blowing Rock, as well as any place I've visited. Earlier in the day, I passed through town and spied a clutch of Gold Wings parked outside Cheeseburgers in Paradise (828-295-4858). Go figure. This place does serve great cheeseburgers that are huge, and cooked to order. Another special place to eat is the Speckled Trout Cafe (speckledtroutcafe.com) right next door. They serve the tastiest mountain trout I've ever had. Out on the Route 321 bypass is Woodlands Barbeque and Picking Parlor (woodlandsbbq.com) The picking parlor is for bluegrass music, not a special room for after-dinner toothpick users.

The only other town of any size in the immediate area is Boone, due north of Blowing Rock and easily reachable on Route 321. Boone is home to Appalachian State University which houses the Appalachian Cultural Center. A visit to Boone is a good idea for a lazy afternoon when you aren't up to riding too far.

# Trip 32 The Lost Provinces

**Distance** *162 miles*
**Terrain** *Two mountain passes, low hills, and valleys*
**Highlights** *Hiking on the Parkway, paddling the New River, exploring small towns and villages*

The hills and valleys of the Appalachians have an influence that goes beyond the manmade boundary lines that separate one state from another. Many of the roads throughout the region follow the river valleys that provide the most natural way of getting from one ridge to another. Trading routes in

**THE ROUTE FROM FERGUSON**

| | |
|---|---|
| 0 | Begin SR 1135 (Mount Pleasant/Champion Road) |
| 7.0 | Right on US 421 east |
| 8.2 | Left on Boiling Springs Road |
| 10.6 | Right on Old US 421 (Boone Trail) |
| 15.5 | Left on NC 16 |
| 38.3 | Right on US 221 north/NC 16 |
| 39.6 | Left on NC 16 at US 221/NC 16 split |
| 55.6 | Right on US 58 east at Mouth of Wilson |
| 57.0 | Right on VA 93 |
| 67.7 | Left on US 221 north |
| 68.5 | Straight on US 21 south |
| 71.3 | Right on NC 18 south |
| 82.8 | Right on NC 113 north |
| 87.6 | Left on US 221 south |
| 99.1 | Left on US 221 south/NC 16 |
| 100.4 | Left on NC 16 south |
| 103.5 | Straight on NC 88 at Index |
| 113.5 | Right on NC 18 south |
| 115.5 | Right on Blue Ridge Parkway south |
| 143.3 | Left on US 421 east/south |
| 155.2 | Right on Mount Pleasant/Champion Road |
| 162.2 | Arrive Ferguson via Champion Road |

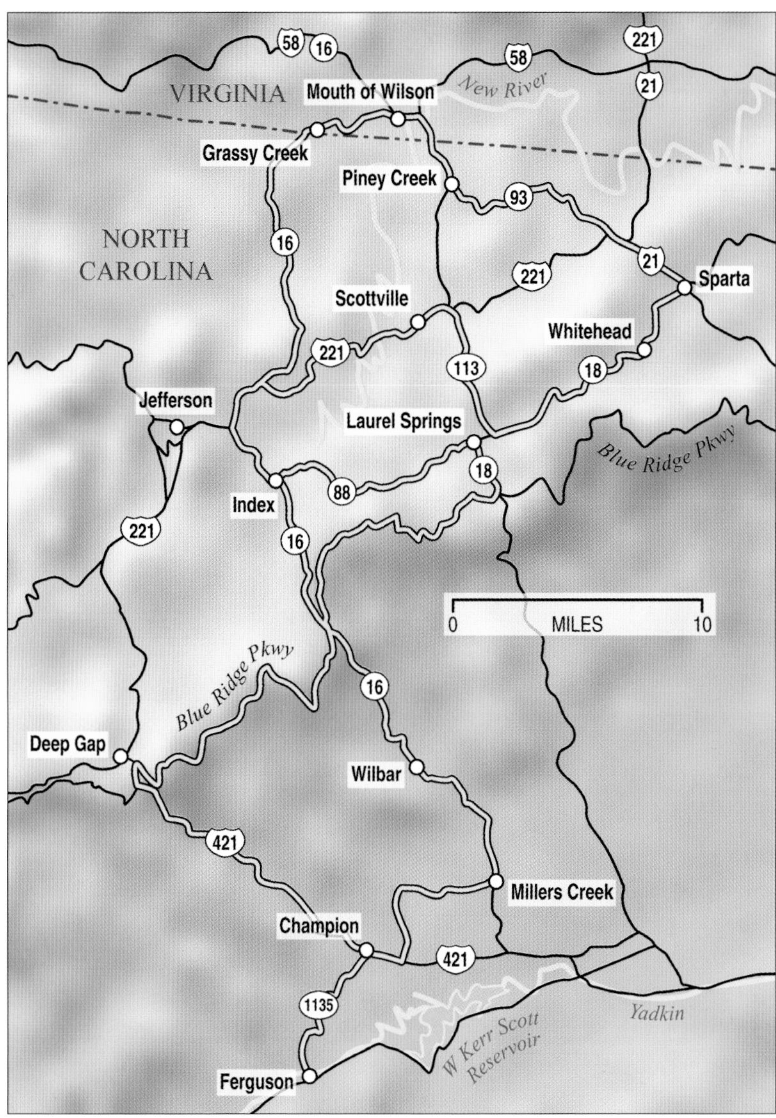


this area ran southeast to northwest, and settlers found it most convenient to build commerce with their neighbors in Tennessee and Virginia. In fact, it used to be said that the only way to get to Boone was to be born there. Being isolated from the rest of the state, this area became known as the Lost Provinces.

Begin your search by following Champion Road out of Ferguson to Route 421. At 421, turn right and head east just a few tenths to Boiling

Springs Road. A left onto Boiling Springs will bring you to Boone Trail, an old section of US 421. I like these older sections of road because they are far less traveled and more varied than the newer section. Old 421 passes through farm country and development is scarce.

Old 421 meets Route 16 in Millers Creek. Turn left to head north on Route 16. Looking at my maps a few weeks after running this route, I discovered that I had been tricked. I somehow missed an older alignment of Route 16 that departs from the main road a few miles north of Millers Creek and continues to the Blue Ridge Parkway at Glendale Springs. Judging from the alignment, it is probably no longer maintained and may not be paved. It looks like a good dual sport option to the top.

Today's Route 16 makes a direct assault on the Blue Ridge and, after seven or eight miles of relatively straight road, begins to weave across the eastern face of the mountains. Occasionally there is some traffic on this route, but by metropolitan standards the volume is low. The view improves with height but the co-rider benefits the most. There aren't any real places to pull over and stop, so reserve your sightseeing for the Parkway, which will come up soon.

It can be cool anywhere in the highlands and mountains, the Parkway included. My last visit to this area in June was a chilly one, with morning temps on the Parkway in the 40s. On the good side, that brisk Canadian air sweeps away the haze, providing spectacular vistas of the mountains.

While you're at the Parkway, there's a nice short trail you can hike to get the blood pumping on one of those chilly mornings. Turn north on the parkway and in about a mile you'll find the Jumping Off Rock Trail. It's a short, easy half-mile hike out to an overlook of the eastern slopes of the Blue Ridge and the North Carolina Piedmont.

They say you learn something every day and my lesson on this particular day was about wildlife. As I made my way down the trail, I stepped through some low brush along the trail. Without warning, the brush came alive, and the silence of the forest was shattered by a storm of shrieks, fluttering, and floundering. To be honest, I was scared witless. Turns out I had stepped on the tail feathers of a turkey hen protecting a half-dozen newly hatched chicks. They were pretty darn cute, but each time I stopped to take a peek, she would come after me. The best course of action quickly became apparent—exit stage right.

Route 16 runs across the northwestern corner of the state and ventures briefly into Virginia. This section of the route is mostly wide and straight, with lots of hills to make the scenery interesting. On a clear day along this road, the sky looks like a reflection of the Caribbean. It's so fresh it sparkles.

*Thousands of riders enjoy the Blue Ridge Parkway every year. Many experience perfect riding moments like this.*

In fact, I got off my bike several times just to marvel at the sky. Now I know what Carolina Blue looks like.

Route 16 intersects Route 58 at Mouth of Wilson. Turn right and follow 58 east for a short distance to pick up Route 93 south. Scattered among the signage along the state border is a telling one: MOTORCYCLES MUST BURN HEADLIGHTS. Taken literally, this could cause serious damage to your motorcycle.

Route 93 is like a gentle roller-coaster ride, rising up small hills, banked turns and twists, and rolling gently down the other side. Photo opportunities abound along this route, with scenic vistas, old barns, green pastures, and those blue skies. Wildflowers in season carpet the roadside and the hills with brilliant yellows, purples, and blues.

Route 93 ends on US 221. Turn left and follow Route 221 to Route 21, then turn right and follow the road to Sparta. There isn't much that's fancy about Sparta. It's just a small, clean town that could easily have been the inspiration for *The Andy Griffith Show.* You can find a good lunch at Sparta Restaurant (336-372-8016) on Main Street across from the courthouse. The specialty there is chicken livers. That may suit you, but for those like me who turn green at the thought, try the fried chicken and homemade pies. After lunch you can stroll the streets to settle your lunch or just hang out in front of the courthouse for a little while and watch the cars go by.

Head west out of town on Route 18, where you'll find more rolling

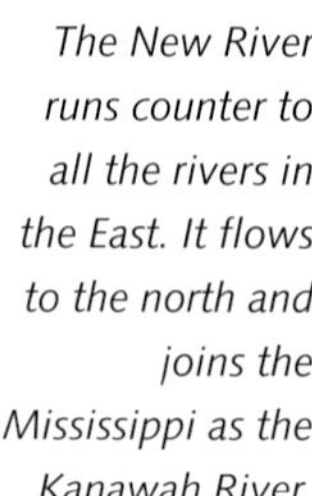

*The New River runs counter to all the rivers in the East. It flows to the north and joins the Mississippi as the Kanawah River.*

countryside and fast sweepers bounded by the Blue Ridge on your left and Peach Bottom Mountain on your right. You'll probably see a lot of space being given to Christmas tree production through this region. The Fraser fir grows well in this climate and has become an important export.

Hang a right on Route 113, which makes an end run on Peach Bottom Mountain, climbing a few hundred feet in the air. This gives you a great view of the mountains in western Ashe County. Turn left on Route 221 to follow this road to the New River. US 221 is a study in contrasts. One section is smooth and seamless pavement with nary a ripple to unsettle your suspension, while other sections are rideable but rough and noisy. In this section, the pavement narrows down to a two-lane country road.

You'll come upon the south fork of the New River just a few miles ahead. On the other side of the bridge is the New River General Store. Out front is a long porch just made for relaxing with a cold soda. Mosey down to the bridge and watch the water pass by. The store is also the headquarters of New River Outfitters (canoethenew.com) where you can rent a canoe and equipment for runs as short as an hour or as long as a day.

You can also enjoy the river from the banks with a picnic lunch. Pick up the fixings at the store, then ride a few tenths of a mile west to New River State Park (ncparks.gov). In addition to a boat launching site, there are trails, a few primitive campsites, and picnic tables with grills. I visited the park in the early afternoon and was alone except for two deer and a park ranger. The ranger said that despite appearances, the parking lot is usually full on weekends, but during the week you have the full run of the place.

From its beginnings here in western North Carolina, the New River runs a course predated only by the Nile. The New is the only river on the North American continent that runs from southeast to northwest. Most rivers east of the Appalachians drain into the Atlantic, but not the New. It has maintained a path that cuts directly through the mountains against the usual flow. It was once the headwaters of the prehistoric Teays River which flowed across most of the continent. The Ice Age disrupted the flow and the only original part that remains is the New. North Carolina has declared a 26-mile portion of the New to be protected from development so it remains free-flowing and unspoiled as it has for thousands of years.

After leaving the park, continue west on 221 to Route 16. If this area looks familiar to you, it should. Our route made a big figure eight and we are near closing the final loop. Follow Route 16 till it picks up Route 88. Turn left at Index to stay on Route 88. Follow Route 18 a few tenths of a mile to the Blue Ridge Parkway south. The timing of this route should bring you to the Parkway near time for sunset. Sunsets on the Parkway are a magical experience you never tire of watching. Incurable romantics will be drawn to an overlook to watch in awe as the sun sinks over the infinite ridges to the west. Just remember to ride below posted speeds near dusk and after dark to reduce your chances of an encounter with whitetail deer. You wouldn't fare nearly so well hitting one of those as stepping on a turkey's tail feathers.

If you're headquartered out of Blowing Rock, stay on the Parkway to US 321. To return to Rider's Roost at Ferguson, follow the Parkway to US 421. Follow US 421 east to Champion Road and Champion south to Ferguson.

*There are dozens of easy hikes right off the Parkway.*

# Trip 33 Roan Mountain Mystery

**Distance** *149 miles*
**Terrain** *Foothills and lowlands to begin, followed by a mountain ascent to Blue Ridge, a section of wild backwoods twisties, then a long, high, twisty pass over Roan Mountain and a valley ride to finish off the day*
**Highlights** *Brown Mountain "lights," Linnville Gorge and Falls, Loafer's Glory, Roan Mountain, the Linn Cove Viaduct*

Western North Carolina is filled with legends of ghostly figures, strange events, and unexplained phenomena. The strange things which happen in this area aren't as widely known as sightings of the Loch Ness monster or those unexplained crop circles in England, but they remain well documented events which defy scientific explanation.

Our search to uncover these mountain mysteries begins westbound on Route 268 toward Happy Valley. Here the road hugs one side of the Valley in places, perhaps to maximize the amount of land available for farming. This makes the road follow a drunken path with an occasional straight followed by a series of curves. It's a good warmup exercise. It's also part of the

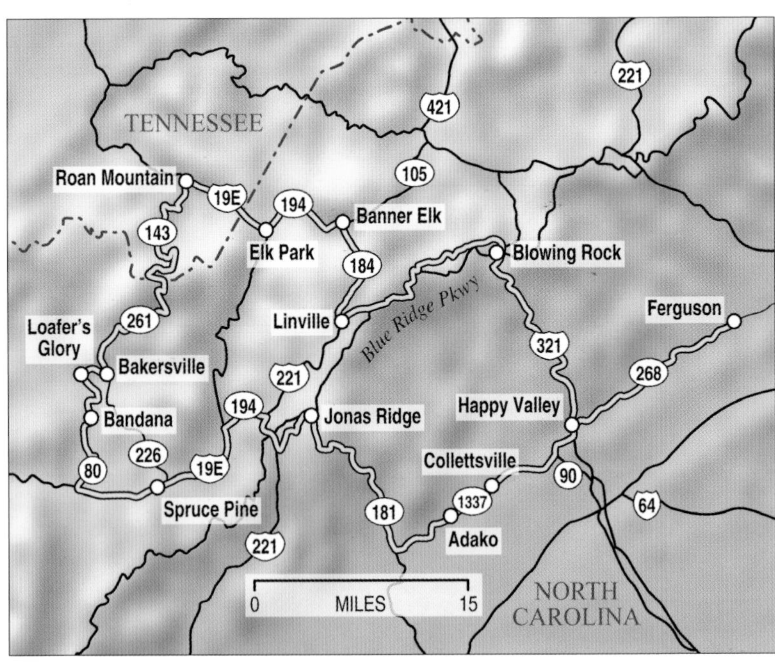

**THE ROUTE FROM BLOWING ROCK**

| | |
|---|---|
| 0 | Begin NC 268 out of Ferguson |
| 15.4 | Right on Warrior Road |
| 16.0 | Right on SR 1353 (Setzers Creek Road) |
| 18.3 | Right on NC 90 (Collettsville Road) |
| 23.5 | Left on SR 1337 (Adako Road) |
| 31.8 | Right on NC 181 north |
| 45.3 | Left on NC 183 |
| 49.3 | Right on Old NC 105 |
| 49.8 | Right on US 221 |
| 51.7 | Left on NC 194 |
| 55.7 | Left on US 19E north |
| 69.7 | Right on NC 80 north |
| 82.0 | Right on NC 226 |
| 84.4 | Left on NC 261 (Roan Mountain Road) |
| 97.0 | Arrive Roan Mountain Summit, continue on TN 143 |
| 109.4 | Right on US 19E south at Roan Mountain, Tennessee |
| 116.1 | Left on NC 194 |
| 122.5 | Right on NC 184 |
| 127.0 | Right on NC 105 |
| 131.0 | Left on US 221 north |
| 134.0 | Left on Blue Ridge Parkway north |
| 147.3 | Right on US 321 at Blowing Rock |
| 148.8 | Arrive Blowing Rock via Blue Ridge Parkway |

Overmountain Victory Trail, marking the route that a band of mountaineers marched to fight the British in the battle of King's Mountain, South Carolina. It was a decisive victory for the patriots and a turning point in the Revolutionary War.

Route 268 ends on Route 321. Cross the road and you will be on Warriors Road, a dinky little footpath that could be called paved in the loose sense of the word. This leads through the woods to Setzers Creek Road, a right turn. Setzers Creek Road then ends on Route 90. For a state route, 90 isn't much bigger. The road has stood up well to the beating it has taken from lumber trucks. This area is well suited to dual purpose bikes. There are dozens of side roads to follow, some leading deep into the hollows that see few outsiders. Route 90 turns northward at Collettsville and passes through some beautiful, remote backcountry, bounded by the Johns River on one side and sheer rock walls vibrant green with native ferns and mosses on the other. Suddenly the road becomes dirt. *Huh?* I thought state primary routes were supposed to be paved, but this one isn't. I made a note to myself: "Get knobbies for Wing." Like General MacArthur, I shall return. Retracing my path to Collettsville, I found the turn I had planned to make. Adako Road crosses the Johns and continues to follow the narrow valley around Brown Mountain. It becomes Brown Mountain Beach Road before intersecting with Route 181.

Brown Mountain (brownmountainlights.com) has a long history as a source of mysterious lights, reported by Indians well before the first settlers reached the eastern shore. They are seen at night and are reported to roam around the mountain. Dozens of studies and expeditions have been conducted to discover the source of the lights, including some done by departments of the federal gub'ment. Explanations include trains (there are no tracks on the mountain), car headlights (there are no roads on the mountain), swamp gas (no swamps) and a slave searching for his lost master. That one can't be so easily disproved.

Make the right turn on Route 181 to return to the mountains. Soon the road becomes one long, well-banked sweeper after another—a pleasant, fast ride. A left turn on Route 183 will bring you to a parking area for the Lin-

*Rider's Roost is situated along the Yadkin River in Ferguson, North Carolina. Owners Uncle Roy and BC have a great moto-only facility.*

ville Gorge and Falls (linvillegorge.net). You can easily spend an hour or two here hiking the paths that lead to different views of the waterfalls of the Linn River. The gorge, about 2,000 feet deep, was formed when twisting and shearing forces that built up the mountains caused a weak seam to split, kind of like popping a kernel of corn. (Well, that's how my mind pictures it, a geologist would no doubt take issue with that.) You don't have to walk far to see the falls, just a few tenths of a mile for the upper section, another few tenths for the lower.

You can find a good lunch at Famous Louise's Rockhouse Restaurant (828-765-2702). Follow Route 183 to Old Route 105, then right on Old 105 to Route 221. You'll find Louise's at the intersection. What's so famous about Famous Louise's? All you have to do is walk inside and look at the ceiling. The restaurant sits on the exact intersection of Avery, Burke and McDowell counties, and signs along the ceiling indicate which county you are in. Your food is prepared in Avery, eaten in Burke, and paid for in McDowell!

Return to Route 221 and follow it east to the point where Route 194 enters from your left. Turn on Route 194 to cut across to Route 19E, a busy corridor through the upper northwest. Some areas around Spruce Pine are ragged from mining operations. People have been digging holes in the ground around here for a thousand years for minerals. There is a spot somewhere in the hills called Sink Hole Mines, a place where Spanish conquistadors reportedly found silver in great quantities.

Past Spruce Pine is a nice little road, Route 80. The road surface is good in most places, if not smooth—though a few gravel hazards exist at some entrances. The road twists in and out of the North Toe River Valley, making three turns where seemingly one would do. Suits me fine. You'll often find a few other riders out here, as this is a popular spot among locals. About halfway along your route you pass through Bandana, which got its name when a railroad worker tied a bandana to a tree to indicate where a stop was to be made (tinyurl.com/motojourneys21). When route 80 arrives at a T intersection, make a left turn. Route 80 ends in Loafer's Glory on Route 226. There was once a store here which was a popular gathering place for the local men folk to hang around during the day, playing checkers, taking an afternoon snooze, and generally being stinking lazy. Eventually it became known as a "loafer's glory" among the wives of the community and the name stuck.

Enter the town of Bakersville and make the left on Route 261. This section of road is reminiscent of Route 181 in its sweeping curves and great sightlines. It takes its good ol' time winding up the mountains, eventually reaching Roan Mountain State Park on the Tennessee-North Carolina border.

Roan Mountain is the typical southern Appalachian bald. A bald is a treeless area, usually filled with large rhododendron gardens like Roan, although it can be a large grassy area. Except for a few peaks up in New England, none of the Appalachians rise above the treeline. There isn't anything inherently different about the soil. So why haven't they been covered with trees like other areas? No one knows. Another unusual feature of Roan Mountain is occasional strange humming or buzzing noises, as though bees are swarming. Sometimes the sound is described as crackling, like high-tension electrical wires. The most likely source, we are told, is the passing of opposing electrical charges between clouds and the ground. Again, no one knows why.

The view from Roan is nothing short of spectacular. The Blue Ridge fills the southern and eastern horizon while the Great Smokies lie to the north and west. You can almost ride right into the gardens. Across from the visitor center is a trail leading to the peak of Roan, a lofty 6,285 feet.

Route 216 becomes Route 143 in Tennessee, making a graceful descent through Cherokee National Forest and Roan Mountain State Park (state.tn.us/environment/parks/roanmtn). The state park would make a nice night's layover. They have cabins and a lodge, trails, and a swimming pool, but most of all they are in a beautiful location with a relaxing atmosphere. The road through the park gets twisty and narrow in places. Look well through your curves before picking an aggressive line. You will encounter an occasional recreational vehicle on its way to the camping area and you don't want to be so fully committed to a line that you can't make an adjustment.

Route 143 ends on Route 19E. We've caught up to the same road we followed west to get to Spruce Pine, now we'll follow it south to return to Route 194. I found myself checking and rechecking my map at each intersection on routes throughout this area. The confused folds and tucks of the Appalachians have made a mess out of the usual north-south, east-west corridors. A global positioning receiver would be more useful than a map.

You'll find Route 194 at Elk Park. (No elk, no park. Hmmm . . . ) This brings you back to the Banner Elk area. (No banner, no elk. What's going on here?) A right on 184 and another on Route 105 puts you in Linville. This is the fastest way to return to the Parkway. Turn left and follow Route 221 to the Parkway. Just a little way ahead is the Linn Cove Information Center (blueridgeparkway.org/linncove.htm) at the head of the Linn Cove Viaduct. Since its completion in 1987, the viaduct is probably the most photographed spot on the Parkway.

*The actual rock of Blowing Rock is a mother's nightmare—a kid on a rock, and no safety fence!*

The Blue Ridge Parkway had been built from both ends until reaching a difficult area at Grandfather Mountain. The roadway had to be built without attachment to the mountain, and to preserve the delicate ecosystem, no heavy equipment or traditional techniques could be used. In fact, the means to construct the viaduct had to be invented as there was no precedent anywhere in the world. The resulting bridge uses pre-cast concrete and steel beam construction. The pieces were cast to such tight tolerances there was never more than a one-hundredth-inch variance from the specified fit. No piece of the bridge is perfectly straight except for the southernmost link. It's a blast to ride—you feel like you're just hanging in the air as you glide across the face of Grandfather. For an up-close look, there is a 300-yard paved trail from the information center to the underside of the bridge. Your path home can be traced down the Parkway to Blowing Rock. Here you can follow Route 321 south to Route 268 to return to Ferguson.

# Trip 34 Old as the Hills

**Distance** *170 miles*
**Terrain** *Slow-paced rural roads with moderately good pavement, some sections with incredibly tight switchbacks, with the section of US 221 between Linville and Blowing Rock among best in its class*
**Highlights** *Two unique general stores, Grandfather Mountain, Cone Manor House*

Some areas of the country still evoke a feeling of the glory years of motorcycling. Western North Carolina is one of them. Open country roads are lined with small farms set against a backdrop of low hills. Old road alignments pass buildings that once served as filling stations and country stores that are now converted to another purpose or stand empty and fallen into

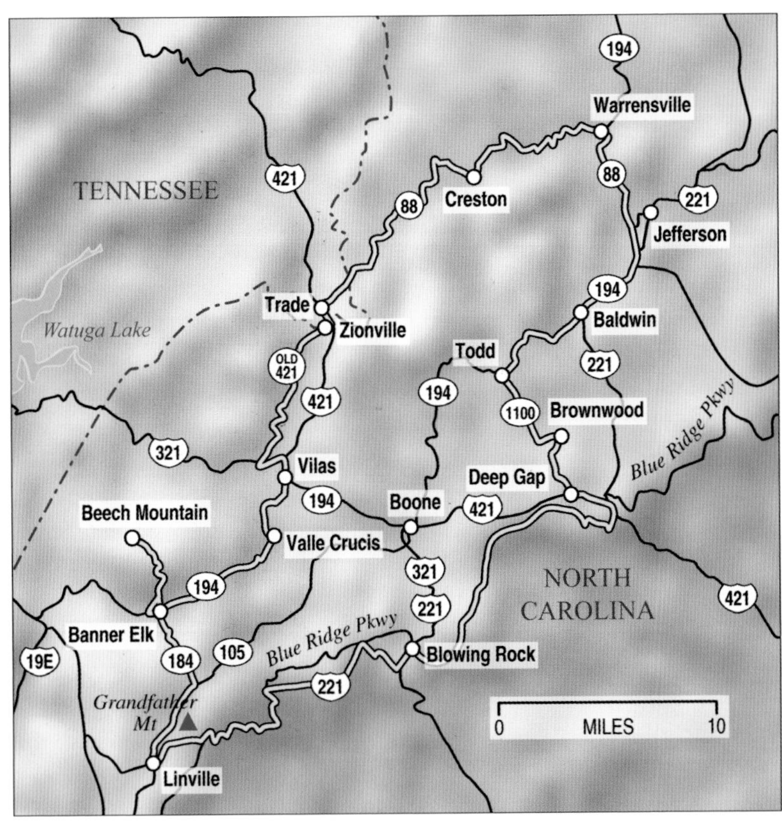

**THE ROUTE FROM BLOWING ROCK**

| | |
|---|---|
| 0 | Begin Blue Ridge Parkway north out of Blowing Rock |
| 15.2 | Left on US 421 north |
| 17.7 | Right on SR 1359 (Brownwood Road) |
| 20.4 | Left on SR 1100 (Cranberry Springs/Todd Railroad Grade Road) |
| 25.1 | Right on NC 194 at Todd |
| 32.0 | Left on US 221 north/NC 194 at Baldwin |
| 35.5 | Left on US 221 Business north/NC 194 at West Jefferson |
| 38.7 | Left on NC 88 at Jefferson |
| 64.4 | Left on US 421 south at Trade, Tennessee |
| 65.2 | Right on SR 1233 (Old US 421) |
| 73.2 | Left on US 321 south |
| 74.9 | Right on NC 194 |
| 85.6 | Straight on NC 184 in Banner Elk |
| 89.9 | Arrive Beech Mountain, then turn around and follow NC 184 |
| 98.3 | Right on NC 105 |
| 102.3 | Left on US 221 in Linville |
| 119.7 | Arrive Blowing Rock via US 221 north |

disrepair, mute testimony to the changing times. Surely the next bike you meet will be a '27 Harley or a Henderson.

Our tour begins following the Blue Ridge Parkway north out of Blowing Rock. At the junction with US 421 at Deep Gap, exit the parkway and follow US 421 west. At Brownwood Road, turn right and follow the sign for the Todd General Store. Where Brownwood Road meets Railroad Grade Road, turn left and follow Railroad Grade. True to its name, this section of road follows an old railroad line. There is at least one bone-jarring dip on this road soon after you make the turn from Brownwood. It just comes out of nowhere and could be a real spring-buster if you hit it at speed. Where are those DIP signs when you need them?

Todd was a bustling timber center in its earlier days. As with many towns, it diminished when the timber ran out and many stores closed. Todd General Store, built in 1914, continues to serve the community as a tourist draw, museum, and functioning store. You can buy various items such as brass tacks, beeswax, and Double Yellow Line brand sun-dried, canned possum. A fellow riding friend says they make great sandwiches here, too. Just be sure you count the cans of possum on the counter before and after they make your sandwich. Besides the general store, there are a few craft houses and emporiums to knock around in. You just might find an abandoned vintage machine hidden in the back of one of them.

When you arrive at the crossroad with Route 194, you'll need to make a difficult turn uphill and back to the right to get on track. It's a hard trick to do on big bikes and it's easier to take as a left turn, so you might want to follow Railroad Grade across 194, turn around in a flat spot, and return to the intersection to make your turn. Part of Route 194 is known as the Old Buffalo Trail, a route that herds of bison used to follow through the mountains. Biologists tell us that the great beasts would migrate east to spend winters on the coast where temperatures were milder, then return over the mountains during the summers. Some of the trails they left were used by early settlers and eventually incorporated into roads we still use. Nearby is a small village with the gruesome name of Meat Camp. That answers the question of what happened to the buffalo.

NC 194 north is freshly paved and good riding. After leaving Todd it crests a hill and settles down into a small valley dotted with a few small farms. Route 194 intersects with Route 221 at Baldwin and heads north to West Jefferson. You'll also find an older alignment of the road here that parallels the route into town. Follow the old road for less traffic and more curves.

West Jefferson is home to the Ashe County Cheese Factory, the lone survivor of a state sponsored program from the early 1900s to promote cheese making as a way for dairy farmers to earn extra cash. Soon after the program started, cheese factories popped up all over. Making cheese was easy enough. Getting it to market over tall hills and bad roads was another matter though, and soon put most would-be cheese kings out of business. One industry that did thrive during that time was moonshining. And the practice of 'shine-running actually formed another industry: stock-car racing. The ridge runners who drove souped-up cars with special tanks to hold the whiskey were the forerunners of today's racers. The better drivers among the early members of the National Association of Stock Car Auto Racing (NASCAR) often started out running corn liquor along the narrow, dark roads of the Lost Provinces.

Mount Jefferson State Park is a good place for a picnic. It's just east of the town on Route 221. A short drive to the top rewards you with a nice view of the Stone Mountains to the west, the Blue Ridge to the east.

Follow Route 88 west out of West Jefferson along the north fork of the New. A few small villages are strung out along the banks of the river, interrupted by farms that manage to squeeze a few acres of crops in the narrow

*Two riders navigate a lonely North Carolina byway.*

river valley. Eventually Route 88 meanders into Tennessee and becomes Route 67. A small sign announces your arrival into the Volunteer State in a matter-of-fact way. At the junction of Route 67 and 421, turn left, following Route 421 east. Just as you return into North Carolina, look for Old US 421 on your right and follow it.

Along Old 421, buildings that once served the traveling public abound, evoking a nostalgic feeling as you meander along. Around one corner you'll pass an old filling station, now vine-covered and returning to nature, while around the next an old store has been rescued from the same fate, now serving as a craft shop or home. Most of the activity around these buildings is gone, but the shadows they cast in the early morning light are unchanged. If you look into those shadows, you can see and hear images of the past—a towheaded boy with a white cap putting "50 cents worth" in a '49 Ford coupe or Joe the mechanic applying incessant banging and verbal torque to a stubborn bolt on a shiny Hudson. As you pass the station, your visions of the past vanish as quickly as they appeared, and the only sound that remains is the throbbing in your engine. If you still hear a banging noise now, it only means your tailbag has gotten caught in your rear wheel. Then again, it might be your stomach clanging the lunch bell.

The old route ends on Route 321 just a few miles west of Vilas. Make a right and continue on Route 321 until you reach Vilas where Route 194 joins. Turn right to follow 194 west. You'll see a sign of things to come: WARNING: STEEP WINDING ROAD . . . NOT RECOMMENDED FOR VEHICLES OVER 35 FEET IN LENGTH. They aren't kidding either. Wing drivers with trailers might want to make sure their rigs don't exceed the recommended length! This is more of a paved goatpath than a road, but it is always fun. There are some incredibly tight switchbacks here that have you looking fully back over your shoulder while you are still negotiating the cur-

*You'd think picking through a bucket of rocks would get tiresome after a while, but it's actually a lot of fun. And you do find some quality gemstones.*

rent turn. If you aren't comfortable with looking fully through a turn and countersteering, stay on the Interstate and off of this road.

The big twisty stuff lasts for a few miles, then you are deposited into Valle Crucis. Stop at the Mast General Store (mastgeneralstore.com), established in 1883 and the oldest continuously operating general store in the country. The heavy wooden front door displays a plaque indicating the store is on the National Register of Historic Places. The front room is where the groceries and hardware are kept. The center of the room is dominated by a huge pot-bellied stove that looks big enough to burn a cord of wood at a time. Other rooms are filled to the ceiling with crafts and a lot of outdoor gear.

The post office has finally settled at the Mast store. In earlier times, you might have picked up your mail here or down the road at the Farthing's place, depending on whether the local politburo was Republican or Democrat. It moved to the Mast store when a Democrat was elected or to Farthing's Republican stronghold when the GOP won a local election. It went on this way until H.W. Mast married Mary Hazel Farthing near the turn of the century. After that the post office stayed at the Mast store, since it was now in the family.

More twisty road awaits your ride to Banner Elk. Another section of nearly 180-degree switchbacks, then another valley ride. Pavement markings along the way click off the distance in kilometers, remnants of the Tour DuPont bicycle race. Some of the steep uphill climbs on this section will make you rejoice in the fact that your two wheels aren't powered by your two legs alone! In Banner Elk, follow the signs for Beech Mountain (skibeech.com) to complete your ride to the top. Beech Mountain is a popular ski resort and at 5,506 feet it's also eastern America's highest town.

When you start rolling back down the hill, just imagine what it would be like to blast down this mountain on a bicycle, with contact patches the width of your pinkie finger, wearing no more protective gear than a half-helmet and skin-tight spandex clothing, wheeling through a crowd of others hell-bent on getting down ahead of you. And people think motorcyclists are crazy?

Route 184 south out of Banner Elk has a moderate amount of traffic, mostly the Florida set. It ends on Route 105. Turn right and follow 105 into Linville. In town, turn left on Route 221. You'll find the entrance to Grandfather Mountain (grandfather.com) just a few miles up the road. Grandfather Mountain got its name from Indians who thought the mountain looked like the face of an old man. Unlike some other natural attractions where you have to stretch your imagination to see a familiar shape, this one really does look like the profile of an old man outlined in the rock. Grandfather Mountain is unique in two other respects. It is formed of some of the oldest exposed rock found in the Blue Ridge chain and is the highest summit in the chain. Grandfather Mountain is privately owned and there is an admission charge. At the top there are 25 miles of hiking trails, a nature museum, and the famous mile-high swinging bridge. If you cross it, you can climb a moderately difficult trail to get to Linville Peak and 360-degree views of the area.

The route is finished off with a 19-mile dash into Blowing Rock along Route 221. The stretch between Grandfather Mountain and Blowing Rock is pristine motorcycling road, mostly flat and very curvy. This section parallels the Blue Ridge Parkway and was used as a connection during the years when the Linn Cove Viaduct (the last link in the Parkway) was being built. The viaduct was finished in 1987 and Route 221 was abandoned by the touring set. Great! It's like having your own personal section of the Parkway, but with more and tighter curves, and no 45 mph limit!

The last stop of the day is the Moses H. Cone Flat Top Manor House where the Parkway and US 221 meet near Blowing Rock. Built by textile magnate Cone as a summer home, the manor house is now home to the Parkway Craft Center and features a wealth of finely crafted Appalachian goods. These are several notches above the roadside craft stands. If you carry a National Parks Passport, you can get a Blue Ridge Parkway Passport stamp here. Outside, you can enjoy the cool breeze on the front porch while you pass the time in a straight-back rocker. Can't you just picture yourself living here, glass of lemonade in hand, admiring your vast estate?

If you're staying in Blowing Rock you have only to travel a few miles down Route 221 to reach your destination. If you're returning to camp at Ferguson, follow Route 321 south and then Route 268 east.

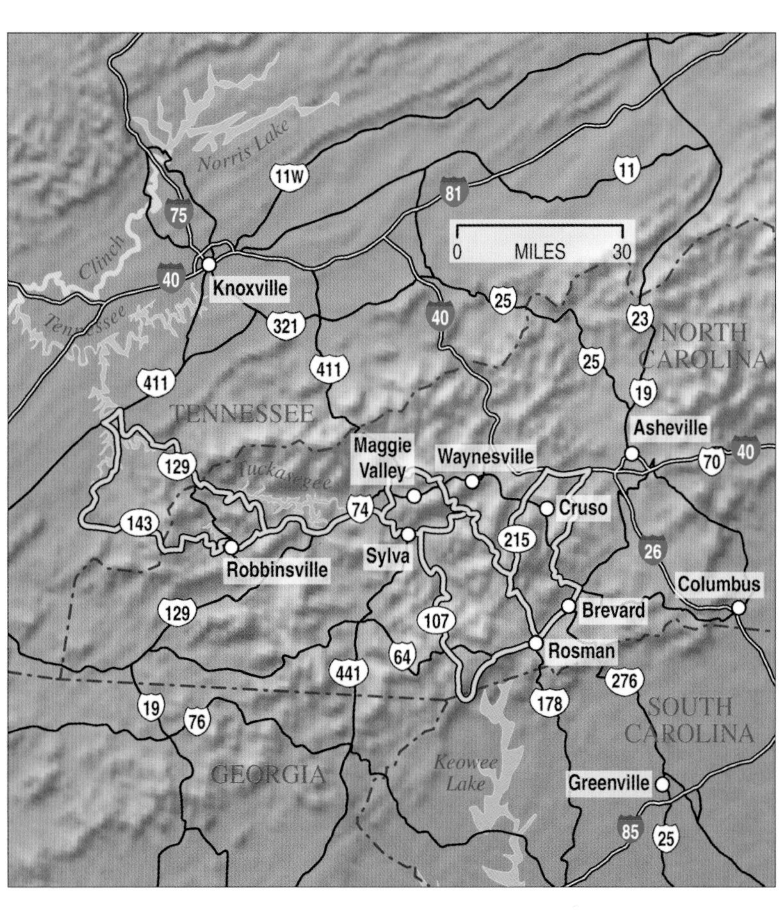
Norris Lake
11W
81
11
75
Clinch
0 MILES 30
40
Knoxville
25
Tennessee
321
40
23
NORTH CAROLINA
411
25
411
19
TENNESSEE
Asheville
Maggie Valley
Waynesville
40
129
70
Tuckasegee
74
Cruso
143
215
26
Sylva
Robbinsville
Columbus
Brevard
129
107
Rosman
64
441
276
19
178
SOUTH CAROLINA
76
Keowee Lake
GEORGIA
Greenville
85
25

# The Southern Slopes

## *Brevard, North Carolina*

Brevard (brevardnc.com) is an art-rich town at the southern entrance of Pisgah National Forest. Make sure you build in time to spare, as downtown Brevard is a comfortable place to park the rig and stroll. The Brevard Music Center (brevardmusic.org) is open from late June to early August with performances scheduled nearly every evening. You can also have a good time dropping by the softball diamond at Brevard College, where a game is being played most days of the week during the summer.

Camping is plentiful down here. The Davidson River Campground in Brevard is a popular and clean location. During summer vacation season, reservations are a must. However, motorcyclists are particularly fortunate to have an outstanding motorcycles-only option. Riders coming to this area needn't look any further than the Blue Ridge Motorcycle Campground (blueridgemotorcyclecamp.com) operated by Phil and Leslie Johnson near Cruso, North Carolina. The campground is situated along US 276, a whale of a touring road. Campsites are on level ground right next to the Pigeon River. The Johnsons also offer cabins for folks who prefer sleeping in a bed with a fixed roof.

*Keep your eyes looking through the turns to avoid drivers who can't read NO TRUCKS signs. Photo courtesy of Killboy.com*

The Key Falls Inn (keyfallsinn.com) south of Brevard is a quaint country bed and breakfast owned by Clark and Patricia Grosvenor. Their daughter, Janet Fogelman, runs the front desk and manages the inn. I happened to meet Clark, a personable fellow who is pleased to entertain riders in his home. He tells me he has owned bikes at different times in his life and looks forward to having another one someday. True to their name, there is a small waterfall at the back of the property that you can walk to. The stream runs down by the house under a huge shade tree, making this spot a favorite place to hide from the summer heat. I put the Key Falls at the top of my list for my next visit to the area.

In case you run out of things to do, Asheville is just 30 minutes away. One place I urge you to visit is Biltmore Estate (biltmore.com), the home of George Vanderbilt. Its scale and elegance are staggering. When it was finished in 1892 after five years of construction, Biltmore was the largest private residence in America—and it still is. Marble, stained glass, gigantic works of art, a gymnasium, bowling alley, pool, the list keeps going. The grounds were designed by the landscape architect Frederick Law Olmsted, whose credits include Central Park in New York. After a tour, you can stroll around and pretend that you are Vanderbilt himself. You could easily spend the better part of a day here—and once you get a taste of the good life, you'll want to stay a lot longer than a day. The estate will validate your ticket for a complimentary second day if you wish to return.

*A rider picks his line carefully on US 129 at Deal's Gap. Be sure to stop by Crossroads of Time to pick up your "I Survived the Dragon" T-shirt.*

*Wheels Through Time bills itself as "the museum that runs." Everything on display is operated regularly. Photo courtesy of Wheels Through Time*

There are hundreds of miles of trails through the national forests in this area, and you can hike for days in the backcountry. There are dozens of waterfalls, many of which can only be seen by getting off your bike and hiking to them. The ranger station at Pisgah offers detailed information about the hiking trails. Fishing is a certified Big Deal down here because of the hundreds of clear running streams that are stocked.

While you're in Brevard, you have to visit the Wheels Through Time American Transportation Museum in Maggie Valley (wheelsthroughtime.com). It's about a 90-minute ride from Brevard by way of the Parkway. Why didn't I include Wheels in a tour? Frankly, the museum offers so much to see an do, it merits a multi-day visit on its own.

Wheels is easily the most unique motorcycle museum in existence. I'm sure you've seen dozens of vintage bike collections, but how many owners are willing to pull out a 60-year-old machine, fire it up, and do donuts with it? How many would assemble a collection of vintage 1935 bikes to ride the length of the Blue Ridge Parkway to celebrate it's 75th anniversary? This is a working museum where the past isn't just remembered, it continues to live.

Y'all have a good time, ya hear?

# Trip 35 Enter The Dragon

**Distance** *199 miles*
**Terrain** *Several high mountain passes, valley rides, and the "curviest" road in America at Deal's Gap*
**Highlights** *Cherohala Skyway, Cherokee and Nantahala National Forests, The Dragon, Fontana Dam*

Over the years, I've had a hard time getting worked up about the section of US 129 near Deal's Gap that riders refer to as "The Dragon." I've ridden it a few times and it is a great stretch of road, no doubt about that. But it seemed like a lot of hype and a pretty far distance to go just to bag an eleven-mile ride. The opening of the Cherohala Skyway changed all that.

A trip to The Dragon was once an out-and-back proposition; ride, ride, ride, hit The Dragon, ride back, and you're done. Now with the opening of the Cherohala, it's the fitting end to a fantastic motorcycle journey of just under 200 miles, originating from Sylva, North Carolina.

The route begins on US 74 heading west out of Sylva. For an expressway, Route 74 is not a bad ride. It's big, open, and virtually empty. Graceful sweepers are accented by high mountain ridges in the background and towns and villages in the valley below. Before you know it, you've arrived at Almond and you follow Route 28 west. The first few miles of Route 28 is

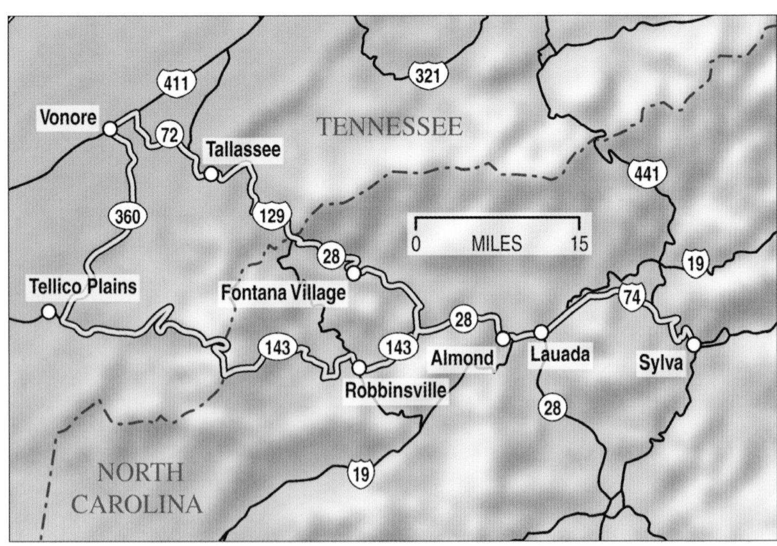

*A large group negotiates the tight turns of The Dragon at the peak of the fall color.*

**THE ROUTE FROM SYLVA**

| | |
|---|---|
| 0 | Begin on US 74 west out of Sylva |
| 22.8 | Right on NC 28 |
| 34.3 | Left on NC 143 |
| 43.0 | Right on US 129 north in Robbinsville |
| 44.5 | Left on NC 143 (signs say TO CHEROHALA SKYWAY) |
| 90.7 | Right on TN 360 (Ballplay Road) |
| 112.1 | Right on US 411 north/east |
| 114.8 | Right on TN 72 |
| 123.6 | Right on US 129 south |
| 144.4 | Left on NC 28 |
| 176.0 | Left on US 74 east |
| 198.8 | Arrive Sylva via US 74 east |

being converted from a fun, frolicksome road into a blasé four-laner. I don't know how far construction is planned, but it would be a shame to lose any more of this road's unique character.

About twelve miles up Route 28, hang a left on NC 143. This is not a preview of what the rest of Route 143 will look like. This section of road from Route 28 to Robbinsville lacks charm, but it does have a few decent curves. In Robbinsville, turn right on US 129 north and follow it through town for about one and a half miles, then turn left on NC 143. You'll probably see a sign for the Cherohala Skyway.

Without a doubt, the Cherohala Skyway is the best long stretch of touring road in the Appalachians, excepting only the Blue Ridge Parkway. It doesn't connect any substantial population centers, nor is it developed in any way. That, of course, is what makes it such a special treat for motorcyclists. For nearly 50 blissful miles, I was by myself. I never caught up to a car and met three on the whole segment. I don't know anywhere else on the East Coast where you can say that. I know western riders are laughing up their sleeve right now; three cars in fifty miles would be a brisk flow in some places.

The skyway was officially opened in 1996 and connects Robbinsville, North Carolina, with Tellico Plains, Tennessee. It would have been better, environmentally speaking, if the Cherohala was never built. The road cuts through the nearly roadless Cherokee and Nantahala Forests of western North Carolina and eastern Tennessee. Judging from its history, I get the impression that this road was one of those pork-barrel projects built to enhance local political reputations as opposed to providing real taxpayer value.

*The dam at Fontana Lake was the setting for Harrison Ford's escape scene in the movie* The Fugitive. *Photo by Henry Winokur*

*It's easy to find a riding partner along the Parkway. Marc Bell of Fairhope, Alabama, and I hooked up for a spirited ride to the motorcycle campground at Cruso, North Carolina.*

But it's there now and it won't be going away, so you had just as well enjoy it as I did.

The ride on the Skyway starts at an elevation of about 2,600 feet at Santeetlah Gap. It ascends to an elevation of about 5,400 feet around mile marker 11. Ahead and to your right is the Joyce Kilmer National Memorial Forest. Kilmer, author of the famous poem that begins, "I think that I shall never see a poem as lovely as a tree," was an avid outdoorsman with a deep love for the forest. In his memorial forest is a stand of virgin timber, including a yellow poplar tree eight feet wide, the second largest of its kind in the United States.

Weather along the Skyway is highly variable. At times I found myself riding in brilliant sunshine; two miles later I was riding just under a ceiling of thick gray clouds. After around 17 miles you begin a slow descent into Tennessee and many smiles later you'll find yourself following the Tellico River.

Just before entering Tellico Plains, hang a right on TN 360. This is not a bad country road in its own right. It cuts across the low hills of eastern

*Traffic Census #2: Miles on Skyway: about 50. Vehicles met: 3. Vehicles caught: 0. Riding experience: priceless.*

Tennessee ending on US 411 in Vonore. Make the right on US 411, then another right on TN 72 just three miles up the road. Route 72 offers you a good look at the mountains you're about to tackle again, this time via US 129. Local riders warn of a blind sharp curve on TN 72. It's about 2.75 miles along Route 72 from the turn on US 411. I wasn't riding at warp speed and I was looking for the sharp curve, thanks to their warnings, so I found it easy to manage. Just take it easy for the first few miles and you'll be fine.

Deal's Gap lies just a few miles farther east. Like many people, I first heard about Deal's Gap a few years ago when the motorcycle magazines began hyping the "curviest road in America," a sure-fire attention getter if I've ever heard one. According to everything that has been printed, there are 318 mountain curves in 11 miles. Hmmmmm. It's just eleven miles? Is it really 318 curves? Who counted them? I started thinking that all this hype must be the East Coast rider's way of compensating for not having a few thousand miles of curves in his backyard as do some of our West Coast friends. Sounded like a case of pavement envy to me. Still, as I rolled through the first few curves on US 129, I could feel my stomach tighten a little and my palms sweat at the prospect of riding what local riders call The Dragon.

I've ridden the gap from east to west and vice versa more than a few times. I prefer this approach from west to east. It could just be my imagination, but it feels like the route spends more time gaining elevation in this direction and I much prefer to ride aggressively uphill than down.

What were the engineers thinking when they laid out the roadbed for US 129 at Deal's Gap? We can only be thankful that they didn't use today's blast-and-level road building techniques which make for fast roads and boring rides. After a couple miles of straight road, the ride takes off with a quick set of ascending switchbacks at mile marker 11 and from there, never lets up. If you're like me, you'll find the road a bit daunting at first, but soon you'll be drawn into the rhythm and find that you're attacking each corner a little harder, hitting each apex with a bit more precision, until soon you are weaving, leaning, braking, accelerating like a pro. Now that you've made the trip into North Carolina, you can legitimately claim your "I Survived US 129 at Deal's Gap" T-shirt at the Deal's Gap Motorcycle Resort (dealsgap.com). Just because you've survived The Dragon, that doesn't mean the curves have come to an end.

NC 28 heading east from Deal's Gap is just as much fun as US 129 in my opinion. It doesn't have the same cambered switchbacks as 129, but it has a multitude of high-speed flat sweepers that are a blast to ride. This return will take you by Fontana Dam, the largest on the East Coast, at 480 feet high and 376 feet wide. This Tennessee Valley Authority (TVA) project was commissioned after the bombing of Pearl Harbor to provide hydroelectric power to aid in the production of atomic energy. Now devoted to a more peaceful purpose—recreation—the 29-mile Fontana Lake seems like a perfect environment for a restful vacation. And unlike other lake resorts I've visited, it doesn't seem overly crowded or busy. Nearby is Fontana Village Resort (fontanavillage.com), a good place to make a stopover for the evening, or just a convenient place for lunch. They have a big cafeteria and good food. There's also an ice cream store located next to the cafeteria. Fontana Dam is probably better known as the dam that Harrison Ford "jumped" from in the movie *The Fugitive*. Route 28 returns to US 74 and the return to Sylva is about 20 miles east.

With the addition of the Cherohala Skyway to this route, my assessment has changed. I used to think of running The Dragon as something nice to do, but now this qualifies as the best loop route in the Appalachians. This is a route now worthy of the special effort it takes to seek it out. I hope you'll enjoy it as much as I did. I'm smiling again just thinking about it!

# Trip 36 Cradle of Forestry Loop

**Distance** *91 miles*
**Terrain** *Two lengthy roads through mountain passes and a small section of the Blue Ridge Parkway*
**Highlights** *Abundant hiking opportunities around Mount Pisgah, Sliding Rock, Cradle of Forestry, Looking Glass Falls*

The route we're following on this tour constitutes the National Forest Scenic Loop run in reverse. This would be a good day to pack a lunch, because most time is spent within the boundaries of the national forest, and while you might find a stash of wild blueberries to feast on, you might have to share them with a black bear.

Follow Route 64 west out of Brevard to Rosman, then turn north on Route 215 to get the show underway. Within the first mile the forest swallows you up and teases you with a few sweepers that make you hungry for more. Any straggling traffic can be dispensed with a flick of the wrist in some of the straighter stretches. Somewhere within the first few miles, you round a corner and—*look out!* Something huge flashes over your head. Instinct forces you to duck. Scanning your rearview mirror you'll discover you've just been bitten by Alligator Rock. There isn't any danger that you'll actually run into it, but the effect is startling.

The route through Pisgah on 215 is a beautiful trek, and the closer you get to the Parkway the more fabulous the view becomes. And the more twisty. (You were just waiting for me to say that, weren't you?) Somewhere within 20 miles of the Parkway the road begins a steep climb up Tanasee Ridge with switchbacks galore. Suddenly you break out of the trees and the

**THE ROUTE FROM BREVARD**

| | |
|---|---|
| 0 | Depart Brevard on US 64 west |
| 9.7 | Right on NC 215 |
| 49.7 | Right on US 19 (Main Street) |
| 58.7 | Right on NC 151 (Pisgah Highway) |
| 70.5 | Right on Blue Ridge Parkway south |
| 76.8 | Left on US 276 south |
| 91.2 | Arrive Brevard on US 276 |

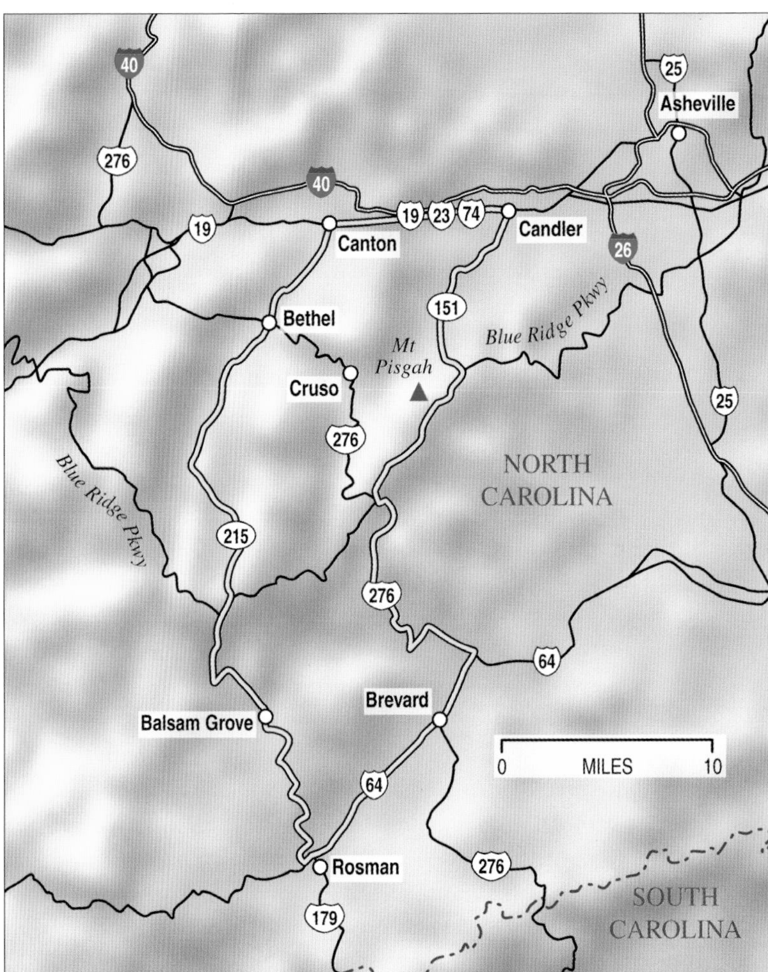


entirety of Pisgah National Forest (www.cs.unca.edu/nfsnc) unfolds below. There are several places to pull over for a mile-high photo opportunity; some have no guardrail or stone retaining wall. You can walk right to the edge of a sheer cliff and look down a thousand feet. Having nearly launched myself off one of them with an untimely slip of the clutch hand, take my advice: get off the bike and walk to the cliff!

On the other side of the Blue Ridge Parkway, the road continues to pass in and out of the trees, allowing you to steal glimpses of the valley below. It also intermingles with the Pigeon River which graces your view with waterfalls at regular intervals. Popular swimming holes are marked by cars parked along the road.

Route 215 intersects Route 276 at Bethel. Time to make a decision. If you want to spend a little more time hiking, turn right here and follow Route 276 back to the Parkway. If you need to ride a little more, turn right on US 276, then continue on Route 215 when it turns off to the right. This area of the country has a lived-in look and there is some traffic to contend with. I guess you get a little spoiled after spending time with nothing but trees and twisties, eh? Route 215 brings you directly into the town of Canton, a nice enough place to visit if the wind is blowing in the right direction. A paper mill in the middle of town makes this a fifty-fifty proposition. In Canton, turn right and follow Route 23/74 toward Asheville to Route 151 in New Candler. This section of road is straight and heavily traveled.

The reward for your toils is Route 151 as it approaches the Parkway. The pavement along this road is of an older vintage and broken in places, but it's good enough, and I just love the way the curves are stacked together one on top of the other. Part way up the mountain, a waterfall right on the road had attracted the attention of a carload of vacationers who were standing in the middle of the road taking pictures as I rounded the curve. When they saw me they scattered like bowling pins, except for two confused members of the party who stood stock still in the middle of the road like a seven-ten split. I flashed between them before they had a chance to move and picked up the spare.

Upon reaching the Blue Ridge Parkway, follow it south. Mount Pisgah is on your right. Reverend James Hall gave the mountain its name because he thought it resembled the mountain Moses stood upon as he viewed the Promised Land. There is a parking area and a one and a half mile trail that leads to the summit of the mountain. It's a moderate hike with a bit of scrambling involved in places, but a good opportunity to let your legs do some work and let the mind rest from curve chasing. Just down the road from the trailhead is a nice picnic area with large stone tables and grills, plus restroom facilities. Many of the tables rest among the tower oaks and massive rhododendrons, making it the perfect place for a quiet lunch.

As you stand at the overlooks along the Parkway and other scenic backroads, it's amazing to think that at one time all the forest in this area was clear-cut. What looks like a mature forest (climax forest, in forestry lingo) is young by comparison to what once stood here. Giant hemlocks, poplars, and other trees hundreds of years old covered these mountains so thickly that you could have probably jumped one branch to another from the eastern seashore to the Mississippi River. All that changed, though, with the landing of the Europeans and the tools they brought with them.

Forestry management was unknown in America until the late 1800s.

One tree after another fell for palisades, homesteads, fences, and fire to ward off the wintry chill. Within 200 years, what had once seemed an endless supply of wood was nearly exhausted. Higher and higher the railroads climbed until some peaks had been cleared entirely, while the steepest ones looked as though they'd been given a bad haircut by a nearsighted barber.

*An unsuspecting traveler narrowly escapes the jaws of Alligator Rock on North Carolina Route 215.*

*Looking Glass Falls is a popular stop along US 276 near Brevard, North Carolina.*

You can thank George Vanderbilt for the lovely view you have today. Vanderbilt became concerned that the destruction of the forest to the west would soon eliminate the vistas from his Asheville estate, Biltmore. He hired Gifford Pinchot to manage the forest around his home. Soon after he added another 100,000 acres, which today approximates the boundaries of Pisgah National Forest. Some people have a knack for making money; Vanderbilt was one of them. When it was discovered that his forest management policy generated greenery in big denominations, interest in managing forests spread across the nation. Pinchot went on to serve as the head of the U.S. Forestry Service and his replacement, Dr. Carl Schenck, established the first forestry school in the United States in Biltmore's forest.

When you've had enough hiking and picnicking, pack up and follow the Parkway south to Wagon Road Gap, where you'll head south on Route 276. The first few miles feature good riding with a few big switchbacks. You will come up quickly on the next stop. Schenck's forestry school is the setting for the Cradle of Forestry in America (cradleofforestry.com), an interpretive association dedicated to continuing the work that Schenck did and to educate folks like you and me in the ways of forestry management.

People lived in this area before Vanderbilt bought it, and their empty buildings served as the campus for Schenck's school. Evidently, some of the accommodations were less than luxurious. Students named some of their quarters "Hell Hole," "Little Hell Hole," and "Rest for the Wicked." The route continues to cascade down Pisgah Ridge, eventually hooking up with Looking Glass River. Route 276 and Route 215 are both old logging trails that were constructed before Vanderbilt bought this land. You can't mistake the parking area for Sliding Rock. On a hot day it's jammed with cars as everyone seeks an escape from the summer heat. Being on a two-wheeler, you shouldn't have any trouble squeezing your scoot into a small spot. Sliding Rock is a natural waterslide—a gigantic, smooth rock face, 150 feet in length. About 11,000 gallons of water between 50 and 60 degrees flow over the rock each minute. A lifeguard is on duty during the summer season.

Just a little farther down the road and near the end of the loop is Looking Glass Falls, another popular stop. A boardwalk lets you climb down to the river for a closer look and better camera angle without tearing up the riverbank. This is one of the most photographed falls in the area.

From here it is just a few miles to Brevard on an easy stretch of road.

# Trip 37 Whitewater Falls

**Distance** *119 miles*
**Terrain** *Lightly traveled roads between small towns afford a comfortable touring pace. Higher elevations toward end of tour, including a short section of the Blue Ridge Parkway*
**Highlights** *Highest waterfall in eastern U.S., Mountain Heritage Center, Jackson County Courthouse, highest point of the Parkway*

The first part of the route is wide open, dual-laned road following Route 64 west, but somewhere around Rosman things get tight and kinky. I turned right and tried Route 281, finding gravel after a few miles. A side road off of

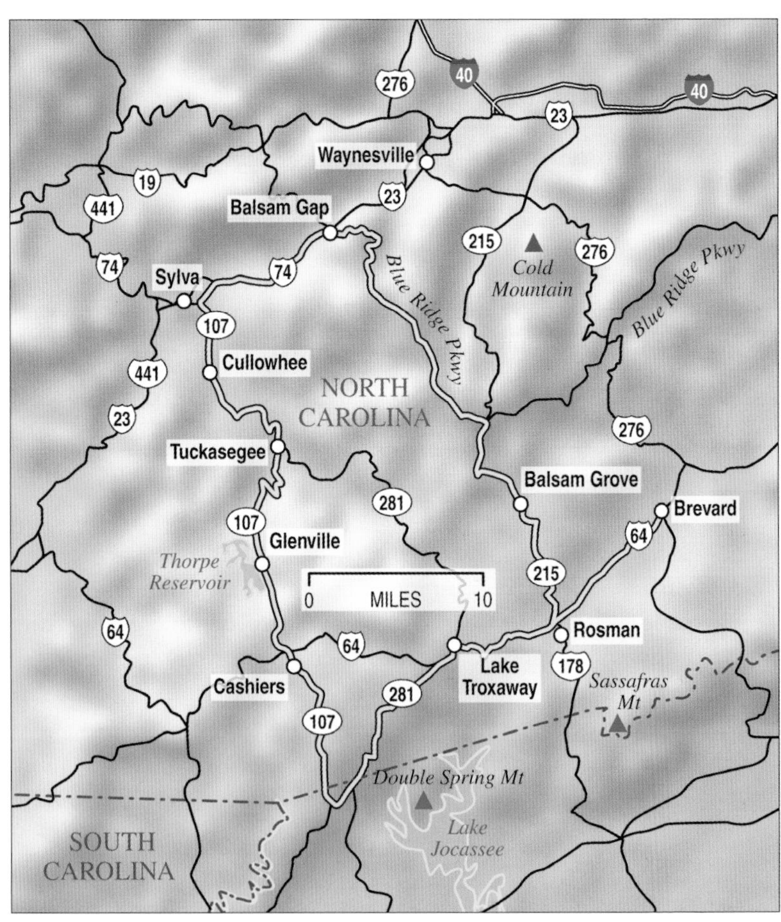

**THE ROUTE FROM BREVARD**

| | |
|---|---|
| 0 | Begin on US 64 west out of Brevard |
| 17.8 | Left on NC 281 |
| 27.5 | Right on SC 413 (Wiginton Road) |
| 29.7 | Right on SC 107 (becomes NC 107) |
| 65.5 | Right on US 74 west |
| 74.0 | Right onto Blue Ridge Parkway north |
| 93.4 | Right on NC 215 south |
| 110.0 | Left on US 64 east |
| 118.8 | Arrive Brevard on US 64 east |

that, Slick Fisher, promised to shortcut across the gravel section, but when it ended, Route 281 remained unpaved. Good for dual sports and smaller bikes you can hold up with your feet. Bad for my full-dress touring couch. I turned around to remain on sure footing and as I retraced my path, I began mentally rearranging my garage, trying to visualize space for a dual sport bike.

The day was growing remarkably hot. The increase in humidity made even my well-ventilated Aerostich riding suit feel like I was wearing a wet plastic bag. As I returned to Route 64, I determined it was time to shed the suffocating suit and find some relief. Private enterprise is alive and well along Route 64, guaranteeing that if it is quick refreshment you seek, you will rarely have to travel far to find it. The Toxaway Falls Stand (pantherridgecampground.com) is everything you'd want in a roadside stand, and more. Plunk down just a dollar for a cup of cold cider and you'll get a hundred dollars worth of conversation and travel advice in return. I mean that in a good way. Having found my first potential route thwarted by unexpected road conditions, I asked the stand operator, a kind country woman in her mid-fifties, what she would recommend I see in the area. She pointed west. "Follow 281 south and you'll find Whitewater Falls. It's the biggest on the East Coast," she said. Who says a dollar won't get you anything these days?

Follow the combined routes 64 and 281 west until they split, then continue to follow Route 281 south. I'll pass along a bit of advice she forgot: bring a bucket. The entire nine miles of the route is covered with blackberry vines, and it didn't look like a single one had been picked. I couldn't help myself, I had to stop a couple of times along the way, whenever a particularly inviting patch came into view, and enjoy one handful after another. I felt like Rutherford B. Hayes and his "great, armed blackberry party." That was the slowest nine miles I've logged on any bike I've owned!

Whitewater Falls is situated on the border between North and South Carolina. At 411 feet, these falls are twice as high as Niagara. Of course, not nearly as much water passes over them, but they are beautiful, nonetheless. There is a parking area and a short walk to see the falls from a high and distant view. If you would rather have a closer look, the hike is substantially longer, but there are picnic facilities near the base of the gorge. If you had in mind to ride only a short distance and take a picnic lunch, this would be a great destination.

Out of the lot and a mile later you'll find yourself in the state of South Carolina. Just a mile or two after the South Carolina border, turn right to follow Route 413 (Wiginton Road) through Sumter National Forest. At the end, turn right and you'll pick up Route 107, our return route north. This route passes through Cashiers (pronounced CASH-ers, rhymes with flashers), a quaint town and another popular summer haunt of the wealthy lowland planters. From the state border to about Glenville, the road is two-lane, a little twisty, and mostly empty. There's a flurry of activity around Cashiers, but north of town you're by yourself. Once you pass the Thorpe Reservoir, the road snuggles up to the west fork of the Tuckasegee River and that means we've got work to do!

Roughly halfway along this section of the route is a rather large and unusual marker, a monument to a woman known locally as Aunt Sally. The monument was placed alongside the road by Dr. John Brinkley to honor the memory of a woman who served the community with her knowledge of folk medicine in the days before trained physicians were readily available. Her example inspired Dr. Brinkley to follow in her footsteps and become a doctor himself, returning to the same area to continue her work.

Route 107 continues its trek through the river valley, and begins ascending into the higher elevations, which rewards you with cooler temperatures. Gradually the route straightens as you approach Cullowhee, home of Western Carolina University. The school is located in one of the prettiest natural settings I can recall. Situated in a natural bowl, the Grand Balsam Mountains rise behind it with dramatic effect. On campus is the Mountain Heritage Center, a museum which tells the story of the Scots-Irish. It's an interesting story because it demonstrates how the social engineering that takes place on one side of the pond can affect the other.

From the time King James I of Scotland ascended to the throne of the British Empire, his single greatest desire was to unite the kingdom by bring-

*Near Cashiers, there's an unusual roadside memorial to a woman known only as "Aunt Sally."*

ing the unruly and predominantly Catholic Irish into the Protestant English fold. His idea for accomplishing this was to transplant a colony of loyal Scottish subjects into Ulster, Ireland, and hope that they would have some calming effect on the population. It didn't work. Ultimately the Ulster Scots or Scots-Irish had enough, and decided it was time to get out of town while the getting was good. Most of them fled to ports like Philadelphia where they had trade ties, moved to the interior of Pennsylvania, and slowly worked their way down the Great Valley of Virginia, settling in the hills and hollows of the Appalachians.

The Scots-Irish continue to follow many of the traditions of their former life; you can see and hear them today in the strains of bluegrass, the annual Gathering of the Scottish Clans at Grandfather Mountain, and the Mountain Heritage Day sponsored each year by the university.

The best place to find a good meal is a few miles north of the museum in Sylva. For a small town, Sylva has a good selection of places to eat. Stop by the Jackson County Travel Authority (mountainlovers.com) for maps, fliers, and more information. After consulting with local gustatory expert Dean Cloer, I followed his recommendation to try LuLu's Cafe (lulusonmain.com). Located along Main Street in the heart of downtown, it's an excellent restaurant featuring a wide selection of healthfully prepared dishes with an "impressive presentation" (that's the only snooty dining term I know, so I use it sparingly). I can heartily recommend the chicken served on a bed of wild rice, and the excellent gazpacho.

Before you depart Sylva, you might want to take a picture or two of the Jackson County Courthouse, which dominates the landscape. An impressive rotunda crowns the building and the 108 steps which lead to the top make for good photo opportunities.

Follow combined Routes 23 and 74 east out of Sylva toward Waynesville. This is a great stretch of road for its huge sweepers and fantastic view of the mountains. This is one of the prettiest sections of road off the Parkway I've seen. The road through the valley is high enough to get you above the treetops and your view of the Balsam Mountains on either side is unparalleled. You'll find yourself holding the throttle open wider than normal on

*Even if it's not raining or snowing, flowing water can still freeze on the region's higher roads. Photo by Brooks Avery*

*A sign like this portends good riding. Route 215 does not fail to deliver the goods.*

those big gentle curves, feeling the cool mountain air rush over your body, and buddy—you'll be loving life.

Our route rejoins the Blue Ridge Parkway at Balsam Gap. Along the way you'll reach 6,053 feet, the highest elevation on the Parkway and just a few hundred feet shy of the highest elevation in the eastern U.S. In areas above 5,500 feet where the climate remains cool enough throughout the year, flora and fauna of the Canadian forest zone dominate the landscape. Here are the big red spruce and towering fir, making it look for all the world as though you had been transported a thousand miles north.

This section of the Parkway contains some of the most dramatic scenery along its entire length. Most of the mountains you see have summits above 5,000 feet, and on a clear day views can exceed 80 miles. When you reach the vicinity of mile marker 425, look for Route 215 and exit following it south. Don't worry, the fun's not over just yet, because Route 215 is one of the finest riding roads in the area. It passes through Pisgah National Forest and in higher elevations it has pullovers with commanding views of its own. About halfway down the mountain, it turns up the heat with switchbacks bunching up together, causing you to reach for the throttle and drop a gear or two. There's a breather, followed by more quick turns, and then Alligator Rock. All too soon you've arrived at the intersection with Route 64 to make the left turn for home base.

# Trip 38 Trail of Tears

**Distance** *50 miles*
**Terrain** *Mountain expressway to Cherokee then the final miles of the Blue Ridge Parkway*
**Highlights** *Cherokee Indian Reservation*

I have conflicting opinions about my visits to Cherokee. On the one hand, it's overrun with tourists during the prime riding season and commercial development compromises the experience. On the other hand, the Cherokee have an interesting, if tragic story to tell, and Cherokee is the gateway to both the Blue Ridge Parkway and the Great Smoky Mountains Parkway. You can't say you've ridden the whole length of the parkway without going through Cherokee. Weighing both sides, I'd say a trip to Cherokee is worthwhile.

This is a simple route departing from Sylva heading west on US 74, the Great Smoky Mountain Expressway. The expressway is not the most glamorous piece of road, but unless you are riding a pack mule, it's the only way into Cherokee from this direction. At least you can travel at the posted speeds on this expressway, unlike others in the northeast that are "express" in name only. The signs indicating the turn to Cherokee, are only seven

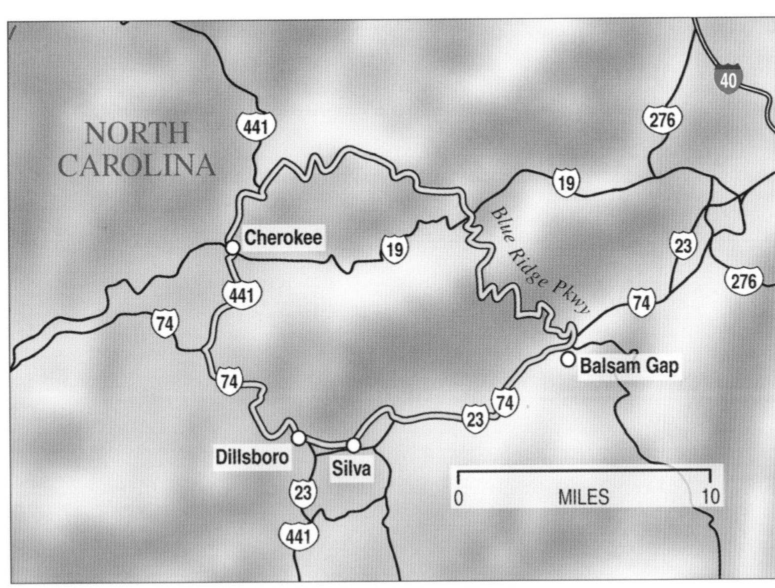

**THE ROUTE FROM SYLVA**

| | |
|---|---|
| 0 | Begin on US 74 heading west out of Sylva |
| 7.0 | Right on US 441 toward Cherokee |
| 11.1 | Right onto US 441 Business to downtown Cherokee |
| 11.7 | Left on US 19/US 441 |
| 14.9 | Right onto Blue Ridge Parkway |
| 40.0 | Right onto US 74 west toward Sylva |
| 50.2 | Arrive Sylva via US 74 west |

miles up the road from the departure point. Another four miles along US 441 will bring you into Cherokee proper.

You can't miss the new face of Cherokee as you wait to turn on US 19. At 15 stories, the landscape is dominated by the brand new Harrah's Casino. The Harrah's in Cherokee is mostly a video gaming facility with video slots, poker, and other games, all in electronic format. The evolution of Indian gaming is an interesting story. Indian reservations are sovereign territory

*Aviator Aaron Miller stands by his flying machine for tours over Cherokee.*

*Dale Walksler exercises his 1915 Harley at the Wheels Through Time museum, a short side trip to Maggie Valley, North Carolina. Photo courtesy of Wheels Through Time*

and very broadly speaking, they have a similar stature with the federal government as states, meaning that laws in a particular state are not always applicable on a reservation unless Congress specifically makes it so. Criminal law is one example where state laws have been extended to apply to reservations by an act of Congress. Indian nations have the power to levy and collect taxes, but that's always been a problem. Since many tribal areas are economically underdeveloped, there has been no economic base to tax. In the 1980s some tribes found success in gaming and that success quickly spread. After kicking around the courts for a while, the U.S. Supreme Court ruled that if a state allowed any form of gaming for any purpose (such as for fundraising), then tribes in that state could operate a casino for profit. Later, Congress enacted the Indian Gaming Regulatory Act which imposed some limits on Indian gaming and stipulated that the revenues generated could only be used for purposes such as funding tribal government.

Taking a left on US441/US 19 will bring you into the old downtown area of Cherokee and the more familiar sight of shops designed to appeal to only the most discriminating consumers of rubber tomahawks and bow-and-arrow sets. There's a better than average chance you'll see Chief Henry

Lambert out having his picture taken with some visitors. Chief Henry is known as the most photographed Indian in the world and is one of the few remaining "roadside chiefs." The practice of roadside chiefing originated with the rise of the automobile. Roadside chiefs aren't really chiefs, they just capitalize on tourist's desires to have their picture taken with a "real" Indian. Chief Henry has been at it for more than 50 years.

The real reason to visit Cherokee is to gain a better understanding of, and appreciation for, the tribe's history. The best place for that is the Museum of the Cherokee Indian (cherokeemuseum.org). The museum depicts the early life of the Cherokee, contact with Europeans, colonization by the new government, and ultimately the forced relocation of thousands of Cherokee along the route called the Trail of Tears. While the museum gives you a good grounding, I think it's fun to see some of the Cherokee's practices in action. The Oconaluftee Indian Village (cherokee-nc.com/index.php?page=17) is a model village as it would have appeared 225 years ago.

The Blue Ridge Parkway is just on the other side of Cherokee. Follow US 441 north out of town. From the point where US 441 separates from US 19, the entrance to the Parkway is just under three miles. This is the southern terminus of the Blue Ridge Parkway. Riding its full length will cover a distance of 469 miles, bringing you to Afton, Virginia. It's then another 105 miles along Skyline Drive to reach Front Royal, Virginia, one of our base camps. Along this section of the Parkway you'll ride through some of highest points on the parkway, around 6,000 feet in elevation.

I stopped to take a few pictures at an overlook when a fellow on a snazzy new Honda ST1300 pulled up. I had considered an ST when I bought my Wing, so I went over to check out his bike. He introduced himself as Marc Bell from Alabama and he was out for a vaction ride. We swapped a few riding stories and route ideas, then hopped on our bikes and rode together for a good distance up the Parkway. Even though we soon went our separate ways, it felt good riding with someone else for a while. That's how it is up here on the parkway. Everyone seems at ease up here and it's easy to fall in with another rider or group if you so desire. Hop off the Parkway at the junction with US 23/US 74 and head west back to Sylva.

On my last trip through the area, I visited Dillsboro (visitdillsboro.org), Sylva's next door neighbor. Dillsboro's Haywood Street (US 23 Business) is suitable for walking, browsing, and finding a bite to eat. I can particularly recommend the Dillsboro Smokehouse (828-586-9556) for lunch or dinner. I had a great pulled pork sandwich and enjoyed browsing the walls, covered with signed menus and testimonials of famous folks who have visited the restaurant.

# Through-Routes and Favorites

As often as I have spoken with fellow riders about riding through the Appalachians, it isn't long into the conversation before someone asks "What's your favorite ______ (road, town, camping spot, point of interest, etc.)?" I am more than happy to answer those questions because it gives me a chance to relive some of my favorite times and trips. Asking about a favorite road is an especially delicious question because there are so many possible answers.

Many ask about preferred methods for getting from Point A to Point B without using the Interstate Highway System. That, too, is a question with many possible satisfactory answers.

In the past, the only way I felt comfortable getting from one point to another was to head toward Interstate 81 and blast down the road for a few hundred miles. I understand that thinking; the interstate is a known quantity and you can usually approximate your travel distances and times with great accuracy. Now, however, thanks to good mapping software, I think you can do much the same with local roads and US highways you might have previously avoided. If you'll allow, I'd like to explain why you'll want to do that.

These are the "blue highways," so named by William Least Heat Moon in his book of the same name, because they were often colored blue on highway maps. Blue highways have weathered good times and bad. Early federal highways prospered as they were the only means of moving people and cargo across the land. The rise of railroads caused the highways to decline, but the advent of the automobile revived the highways' fortune once again, raising some roads like US Route 66 to permanent cultural icon status. The Interstate System marked the next downturn in the old federal highways by routing traffic around towns and clustering development at interchanges, the effect of which can still be seen in the many abandoned businesses along shoulders of many federal highways. However, it appears to me that the prospects of these roads are on the rise once again as people like you and me search for alternatives to the interstate experience.

Blue highways afford unique touring opportunities you will never see on the interstate. For one thing, blue highways in the Appalachians offer the best combination of smooth pavement and great curves for hundreds of miles over dozens of mountain ranges. Many of these roads were built by following previously existing paths or traces, fitted to the natural contours of the land before it became the accepted practice to blast off the faces of mountains to make straight, but sterile, roadways.

The pace of riding on most blue highways is noticeably relaxed compared to their interstate counterparts. The lower speed limit is a factor, true, but other things contribute to the slower pace as well. On a blue highway, you won't be run off the road if you slow a little to watch a farmer bailing hay or enjoy a waterfall as it tumbles off a cliff. I like to think of it this way: on the interstate, the countryside looks like a lovely painting; on a blue highway, you are riding in the painting.

Blue highways are the main street of most towns small or large. For some, this is a distraction, a nuisance to be avoided. But for the touring rider, it is part of the reward. You won't discover the unique architecture of a town or find its best restaurants off an interstate exit ramp. You won't find that rider-friendly B&B near the superslab, nor have a conversation with someone

*The Appalachians make a perfect destination for a group of riders seeking quiet country lanes. Photo by Dan Bard*

*Discovering covered bridges, such as this one in Landisburg, Pennsylvania,, is one of the joys of traveling on the blue highways.*

about your tour at a stoplight. You'll only discover these pleasures on blue highways.

## NORTH-SOUTH ROUTES

These routes will move you up and down the region. Many folks plot north-south routes as their primary riding experience. This is good if you want to cover a lot of territory and visit a lot of places. With a few exceptions, these routes will not yield your best riding opportunities. Look to the east-west routes for that distinction.

### *US 29*

I have mixed opinions of US 29. This route is now a full four-lane highway with some areas converted to limited access, but it is just about your only option if you want to make a fast getaway out of the Washington D.C. metro area and into the countryside. This is a major commuter route, so if you're heading south, avoid doing so in the late afternoon. Likewise, if heading north, avoid mornings. South of Culpeper, the pace relaxes a bit, and once through Charlottesville, it becomes a fairly pleasant means of making good time into south-central Virginia (the area through Lynchburg is congested at peak travel times as well). Route 29 passes through the heart of Virginia wine country and the Charlottesville area abounds with things to see and do. Route 29 also connects with many of the great east-west routes including US 33 at Ruckersville, US 250 in Charlottesville, US 60 at Amherst, and US 460 at Lynchburg. Beyond the North Carolina border, US 29 transforms into a fully limited access highway and loses all appeal.

*US 15*

I don't much care if I ever travel US 15 north of Gettysburg again. *Phew.* South of Gettysburg, this route has a few pleasant stretches. It is a heavily traveled route for nearly its entire length through the territory covered in this book. The most scenic stretch is between Frederick, Maryland, and Leesburg, Virginia, as the route crosses over the Potomac at Point of Rocks and into the Virginia countryside. I guess I should say it's still better than interstate, but it just doesn't have as much to recommend it as other north-south routes.

*US 522*

This is a little known north-south route that crosses through three different regions we ride through. We first cross paths with Route 522 as it departs Culpeper, Virginia, for a scenic ride across the Blue Ridge into Winchester, Virginia, where it passes the gravesite of Patsy Cline. Out of Winchester, Route 522 cuts through Berkeley Springs, West Virginia, before crossing the Potomac at Hancock, Maryland, home of the Wing rider's home away from home, the Park-n-Dine. From Hancock, Route 522 heads into Pennsylvania's farm country, through Burnt Cabins and into Orbisonia where we stop off at the East Broad Top Railroad. If you're coming into the area from central Pennsylvania, I can certainly recommend US 522 over the combination US 22/US 15.

*US 340*

You could do worse than following US 340 from its origin in Frederick, Maryland, to its end at Greenville, Virginia. It's a pretty pleasant, scenic ride for its entire 165-mile length. US 340 takes you directly past several fun stops including Harpers Ferry, the entrance to Skyline Drive in Front Royal, Skyline Caverns, and Luray Caverns. Although it starts out as a four-lane road in Frederick, much of the traffic peels off at the US 15 exit a few miles south. The section through Harpers Ferry, West Virginia, is backed up on summer and fall weekends. Once south of Charleston, West Virginia, you're back to a sedate touring pace. US 340 makes stops in pleasant small towns, including Berryville, Front Royal, Luray, Shenandoah, Elkton, Waynesboro, and Stuarts Draft before ending on US 11 at Greenville. This is a great way to get to the best part of US 11 and probably takes less time than if you took all interstate between the same two points.

*US 11*

The history of US 11 through the Appalachians goes back to nearly the beginning of European history on the North American continent. What began as a buffalo path through the Great Valley (now referred to as the Shenandoah Valley) became an Indian trace, then a settlers path, a turnpike (hence the name Valley Pike), and finally, part of the road system that comprises US Route 11. For all of its run through our territory, US 11 parallels Interstate 81. It is not a particularly fast route. It passes through the many towns that sprang up along its path as the Valley was settled. However, for the touring rider, it is a far more interesting route than the superhighway alternative. You'll pass through Winchester, Virginia, a prize swapped often between opposing armies during the Civil War. Strasburg and New Market are attractive towns for getting off the bike and exploring. One of my favorite restaurants, the Southern Kitchen in New Market, is found along US 11. Beautiful Lexington, Virginia, is located along this route. So, too, is one of my favorite curvy roads, VA 16 north of Marion.

*US 220*

We touch on US 220 in several places during the course of our Appalachians journeys. From Bedford, Pennsylvania, to Cumberland, Maryland, US 220 is an accommodating route through rural farmlands. The stretch from Cumberland into West Virginia, at a spot called Junction, is a bit worn and gritty—not my favorite section, but what comes later makes it worthwhile. Once you get below Junction, traffic begins to thin and travel conditions improve. After Franklin, West Virginia, Route 220 becomes a pure riding joy. High-speed sweeping turns with little traffic are to be found for the next 70-plus miles, through the motorcycle friendly town of Monterey, the historic Warm Springs, and into Covington, Virginia, at US 64. The section of US 220 from Clifton Forge to Roanoke has some scenic moments such as the passage through Eagle Rock, but it is a significant through-route for trucks shortcutting from I-64 to I-81. Below Roanoke, US 220 is a busy dual-lane highway through Martinsville and into North Carolina.

*Chances are, the only thing you'll be able to see from the observation tower is your hand in front of your face—if that. Photo by Kim Ross*

*US 219*

I've ridden most of this route from the New York-Pennsylvania border down to Lewisburg, West Virginia. In Pennsylvania, the route has been converted to standard four-lane highway. Matters improve when the road enters Maryland, reverting back to the old two-lane design. In western Maryland from Keysers Ridge to Oakland, traffic picks up as the route passes through the Deep Creek Lake area. South of Oakland, US 219 enters its prime. From here to Lewisburg, this ribbon of asphalt is the finest north-south route through West Virginia. Along the way you'll pass Fairfax Stone, Droop Mountain, Watoga, and Beartown—all West Virginia State Parks. You're within a short distance of Cass Scenic Railroad, Snowshoe Resort, and the Highland Scenic Highway. The towns of Marlinton and Lewisburg are attractive for cruising through or walking and contain a number of family owned eateries. All things considered, this is my favorite north-south route through the Appalachians outside of the Blue Ridge Parkway.

*Skyline Drive and the Blue Ridge Parkway*

Each year, many riders find themselves at one end or the other of this fabled road for the first time and wonder what lies ahead. Beauty? Certainly. Peril? Yes, at any time of the year. Riding? Among the best the region has to offer. Many, many good books have been written about the Parkway, so I'll skip that part and just talk about the route from a rider's perspective.

*At the higher elevations of the Blue Ridge Parkway, the wildflowers bloom later than in the valleys*

*Distance.* First of all, it's a long ride. Taken together, Skyline and the Parkway are 574 miles of the prettiest roadways in the eastern U.S. Don't try to do it in one day. It can be managed in two days if you're in a hurry and with good weather, but three or four days are best if you want to savor the ride and enjoy some of the unique features these parks offer along the way.

I've found that the route lends itself to being ridden in three distinct segments. Front Royal to Roanoke covers Skyline Drive and the first hundred or so miles of the Blue Ridge Parkway. Skyline Drive is part of Shenandoah National Park and offers hundreds of miles of hiking trails. At mile marker 105, the road leaves Shenandoah National Park and becomes the Blue Ridge Parkway. Mile marker zero is at Afton Mountain, just east of Waynesboro, Virginia. The first hundred or so miles of the Parkway seem a bit more wide-open and less restrictive than Skyline. Perhaps that's due to the higher speed limit, or maybe because there are fewer travelers. In any case, it's probably the fastest section of the Parkway to travel. Not fast in a literal sense, of course. A stopover in Roanoake gives you access to a plethora of travel services.

The second segment is one that some might dub the loneliest stretch of the Parkway, running for about 180 miles between Roanoke, Virginia, and Blowing Rock, North Carolina. After departing Roanoke's urban cluster, you quickly escape to Virginia's grassy highlands. Intersecting roads and travel services are few and you're following a route far from interstate. Perhaps that's why I like this section of the Parkway best. At the end of this segment is Blowing Rock, a bustling town atop the ridge and a few miles east of Boone, North Carolina. I vastly prefer Blowing Rock over Boone because it exists for the sole purpose of catering to travelers. Nearly every hotel, shop, and restaurant is independently owned and the main street is just the right length for an evening stretch.

The last 180-mile segment of the Blue Ridge Parkway features the most dramatic vistas and highest elevations. Out of Blowing Rock, the route soon crosses the Linn Cove Viaduct, the last section of the Parkway which was only completed in 1987. The Viaduct was constructed especially to convey travelers past Grandfather Mountain without resorting to the usual blast-and-level road-building techniques. Before entering Asheville the Parkway passes Mount Mitchell, which at 6,684 feet is the highest ground in the eastern U.S. West of Asheville, you'll pass through the Pisgah Mountains and the highest elevation on the Parkway at 6,053 feet. The Parkway comes to an end on the southeastern cusp of the Great Smoky Mountains at Cherokee, North Carolina, home to the Eastern Band of the Cherokee Indians. Visiting Cherokee is a bit like slipping back half a century to vacations of the 1950s. Dozens of "actual Indian" souvenir shops line the streets, but the Museum of the Cherokee Indian gives you an authentic portrayal of the Cherokee story.

It's a long road. Take the time to enjoy it properly.

*Weather.* The second thing I'd like to tell you about the Parkway is . . . the weather. No doubt you've already heard or read that the weather can change rapidly on the Parkway and you think to yourself, "Well, hello. I know that." I knew that too when I turned north on the Parkway out of Asheville in early October, 2002.

It was a spectacular day and pleasantly warm when I started toward my destination, Roanoke, Virginia, some 270 miles to the north. (The alert reader will note that I violated one of my suggestions outlined above regarding recommended daily mileage.) A few miles above Asheville, I ran straight into a cloud bank.

What I failed to realize was that I was heading straight into a cold front that was penned up against the western slopes of the Blue Ridge, attempting to push its way over the ridge and into the Piedmont. With my visor open, I kept my eyes glued to a centerline visible no more than ten yards ahead. It was the only point of reference I could make out. Miss a turn of the line to the right or left and I could easily have been riding off the side of a cliff.

I was doing well to average 20 mile markers in an hour's time. Above Blowing Rock, the fog was compounded by a significant drop in temperature, followed by rain, then subsequent patches of sleet. I was thankful for the electric vest I'd brought along. In short order, I had it cranked to the max.

There were a couple of points where I could have bailed out and joined the interstate, but the route between Blowing Rock and Roanoke cuts a diagonal across the region and doesn't really run close to the big roads. So once you commit to the Parkway, you have to go well out of your way to get down off the mountain. When I passed the exit for US 52 to head into Hillsville, I had made my final decision to stick to my original plan. A few miles later, even the combination of the suit and vest weren't enough to keep me warm. I was getting cold. The last 90 miles to Roanoke were miserable.

More than ten hours from my starting point, I finally crawled off the Parkway at US 221, wet, stiff with cold, exhausted from tracing a centerline for hundreds of miles, and altogether shaken by the experience. Returning to Interstate 81, temps quickly zoomed back up to the mid-sixties even as the sun was descending. Scattered clouds ahead suggested rain, but the route remained dry the rest of the way home.

*Motorcycle camping is a popular option in the Appalachians. There are more than a handful of rider-only campgrounds in the region.*

I made a serious mistake that day by not consulting weather maps before leaving and clinging to a badly placed faith that if I just kept going, conditions would improve. I then compounded the error by passing up the few chances I had to escape the bad weather. Later at home, I found a hotspot in my vest had left a quarter-sized burn. I felt lucky. I could have easily acquired a more serious and lasting souvenir.

Because the Parkway is subject to severe weather, and because it doesn't offer as many safeguards or travel services, it isn't unusual for the Park Service to close stretches of it. You will also find sections closed days after heavy weather systems move through. Sections of the road may be impassable due to large numbers of fallen trees.

I don't want to paint an overly bleak picture of the Blue Ridge Parkway for you, just a realistic one. Remember that any weather event you ride through will be magnified several times over when you're a couple thousand feet above the valley. Check the Weather Channel before you head out, and if you hit bad weather, head off the Parkway at your next opportunity rather than riding through it to see if it will improve.

No doubt we'll pass each other up there some time. But not if it's foggy.

*Time of Year.* In terms of days of the week, I like riding Skyline Drive best mid-week. That's when you'll find fewer slow-moving vehicles and people stopping in the middle of the road to catch a glimpse of a deer. (True story: I once came around a curve on Skyline to find a dozen cars stopped in my lane and the same number in the oncoming lane. Thinking an accident must have taken place, I waited patiently for a few minutes. Then I noticed folks getting out of their cars. Must be a bear in a tree, I thought. I could see no one was going anywhere soon, so I swung into the opposite lane to pass the traffic. When I got to the head of the line, I found a couple dozen folks gawking over three does.) You'll find fewer issues with the Blue Ridge Parkway. It carries less traffic than Skyline and I haven't found any particular time when one might call it "crowded."

Time of year is an important consideration. Bad weather will frequently cause the Park Service to close sections of Skyline or the Parkway during the winter. Spring comes late to the higher elevations, as you might expect. The surrounding valleys will be near full bloom in mid-May. On the Parkway, the buds are just beginning to swell. Your best times for touring will be from April to October. The most comfortable in terms of temperatures will be May, June, September, and October.

Bad weather is not the only thing that can close sections of the Parkway. Before you plan to ride end-to-end, be aware that some sections of the Parkway may be closed for reconstruction. These closures can last for years and involve detours of dozens of miles. For updates, contact the Parkway office or visit the Park website (www.nps.gov/blri/planyourvisit/roadclosures.htm)

## EAST-WEST ROUTE

North-south routes are fun, but the better riding action can be found on east-west routes. These roads cut across dozens of Appalachian mountain ranges while north-south routes typically follow the valleys between ridges. With a couple of exceptions, the east-west routes retain much of their original curvy charm.

### *US 30*

Route 30 runs along the northernmost boundary of our territory. Thanks to improvements made between Lancaster and York, this road is no longer the horror story it once was; however, no one would regard it as a "gentle country road." Many segments of US 30 have been upgraded to four-lane highway. The pace seems to relax a bit once you get out of Gettysburg. The lower hills of the region mean that many portions of the road run straight over and through the ridges. For me, it's an acceptable alternative to the Pennsylvania Turnpike, but there are better east-west routes in the region, such as US 40.

### *US 40*

It takes a bit of exploration and patience to follow US 40 out of Frederick, Maryland, into southern Pennsylvania, but I like it. US 40 was once known as the National Road and was the first federally funded highway to the West. It's best to begin with US 40 Alternate out of Frederick. This takes you through Boonsboro and past Washington Monument State Park. After Hagerstown, Maryland, US 40 is aligned with I-70 and you have no choice but to follow the interstate for a few miles to Hancock. At this point, you can rejoin the old alignment of US 40, now labeled Maryland 144. You'll rejoin US 40 over Sideling Hill, then have the option to follow US 40 Scenic over Town Hill, then back to MD 144. In Cumberland, you have the option to pick up US 40 Alternate again. This alignment will take you through Frostburg and then into Pennsylvania past the tollhouse at Addison. Like I said, you'll want to study your maps a bit to take full advantage of this route. I should add that at Hancock, you might want to consider following I-68 west until crossing over Sideling Hill. That's because the Sideling Hill exhibit and visitor's center is an interesting stop you would

*The Bluegrass Valley in Highland County, Virginia, is picture perfect.*

otherwise miss. After departing Sideling Hill, you can then pick up US 40 Scenic on the other side of the mountain for the run to Town Hill.

*US 50*

One of my favorite routes through the region is US 50. The segments you'll find most interesting begin after US 50 crosses US 15 in northern Virginia. Here, the route traverses the region known as Mosby's Confederacy and passes through the history-rich towns of Aldie, Middleburg, Upperville, and Winchester. Out of Winchester, a brief stretch of four-lane highway gives way to smooth, curvy pavement as the road enters West Virginia. It retains this wonderful character through much of the ride across the state. Shortly after you pass Aurora State Forest, home to centuries-old hemlocks, you'll cross the Cheat Mountain Pass, a great stretch of motorcycling road. Some days you'll catch up to traffic that can be easily passed in the valley before you reach the next fun-filled ridge. Other days I've encountered virtually no one.

*US 211*

This route is well known among area riders and you'll find plenty of riders out on weekends. Even though US 211 is a divided highway for most of its length, it makes up for that with a low traffic volume and scenic views of the Blue Ridge as you approach from the east via Warrenton, Virginia. After

Sperryville, the curves come fast and tight over the Blue Ridge, then again for a few miles over Massanutten Mountain. US 211 effectively ends in New Market, Virginia, where you can either pick up US 11 or hop on the interstate. Along the way you should stop to enjoy the mountain town shopping bazaar that is the Sperryville Emporium.

*US 33*

This is another sweet route filled with lots of curves and great scenery. You can follow US 33 all the way out of Richmond, Virginia,, but the better touring begins north of the US 29 junction at Ruckersville. Here the road offers nice views of the coming mountains along with a few good curves thrown in. In the Shenandoah Valley, US 33 passes through Harrisonburg, but the slow pace there is rewarded with the first in a series of fantastic runs over the Shenandoah Mountains west of town. After Franklin, West Virginia, the road tackles a half-dozen or so additional ridges before landing in Elkins, West Virginia. Route 33 continues to please, all the way into Ohio. It's a great road to follow across the region.

*US 250*

West of Staunton, Virginia,, US 250 is a great touring road. For the next 60 miles, the road seemingly looks for ridges to cross, resulting in one pass after another filled with tight turns. On a family road trip, my young son Carl dubbed it a "swibble-swabble road," and that seems a fitting description. US 250 passes through my favorite motorcycling town, Monterey, Virginia,, where you'll find hospitable people, a relaxed pace, and good food and lodging. Beyond Monterey, many more miles of curves are to be found through Bluegrass Valley and into West Virginia. Like US 33, US 250 runs the entire length of West Virginia and into Ohio.

*US 60*

Similar to its counterpart to the north (US 40), Route 60 is also an old road that is fun to follow when you can. On the eastern side of the Blue Ridge, it is mostly straight, but on crossing the Blue Ridge, it offers some challenging curves. Route 60 passes through Buena Vista, then Lexington, Virginia,. On the west side of town, US 60's official alignment is with I-64, but a little map sleuthing reveals an old alignment of the highway is now renamed as State Route 850. Beyond Clifton Forge, I couldn't find any old segments of US 60 until arriving in White Sulphur Springs, West Virginia. At Sam Black Church, US 60 shakes loose its entanglement with I-64 and heads for more interesting territory across the Mountaineer State. The most rewarding section of US 60 is found between Sam Black Church and Chimney

Corner. At this point, it picks up the gorge carved by the New River and follows the river into Charleston.

*US 460*

Route 460 is a hit-or-miss experience. It's a pretty miserable ride heading east out of Kentucky. Maybe the 100-degree temperatures, construction, and heavy traffic colored my perceptions somewhat, but even on a better day, it isn't a particularly engaging ride. At least until you get to Pikeville. At this point, matters improve as a large portion of traffic splits off to follow US 23 south. By the time you get to Mouthcard, the road resumes a more sedate pace. Beyond Grundy, Virginia,, the landscape opens up considerably as the mountains retreat and Route 460 becomes a pleasant, four-lane motoring road.

## SEEDS FOR PLANTING

Sometimes one little notion becomes the central mission in a motorcycle journey. Before we part, I'd like to offer a few last thoughts. I hope one of them becomes the seed that blossoms into your next motorcycle journey. We'd love to have you come visit us in the Appalachians.

*Best overall touring*

If you're looking for the highest number of curves per mile, then best overall touring honors would fall to western North Carolina. It also comes closest

*Rod and Sharon Oberholzer pause for a popular photographic memento—a picture at Mabry Mill along the Blue Ridge Parkway. Photo courtesy of Sharon Oberholzer*

*Tuggles Gap Restaurant, situated near the Parkway, is one of the few eateries you'll find close by the Parkway. Great pies!*

to what one might call the "eastern wilderness" as this region features tracts of national forests measured in hundreds of square miles. For those interested less in how many curves they log but prefer interesting towns and lesser-known tourist destinations, look to western Virginia's Bath and Highland Counties and Pocahontas County in West Virginia. You'll find the full range of accommodations here, intimate B&B's, historic country inns, and two of the region's remaining grand resorts. You'll also find plenty of wide open spaces and great motorcycling roads.

*Coolest road*

WV 72, Canaan Valley to Parsons. I like the fact that what appears to be a "major" road on a West Virginia map is, in fact, barely wide enough to accommodate two-way traffic. WV 72 is about 20 miles of sharp switchbacks and hairpins on asphalt last laid down during the Eisenhower administration. It's not a road you travel for speed, it's just an accomplishment to finish it. This road feels every bit like a moonshiner's shortcut, twisting back and forth as though trying to shake a pesky sheriff.

*Most surprising*

You'd think after two decades of riding around here, I'd have shaken most of my preconceptions about the Appalachians. That notion was once again tested with my time spent in southeastern Ohio. The Buckeye State isn't even a blip on most riders' radar screens. It should be. The tri-state area between Ohio, West Virginia, and Pennsylvania offers some of the most outright fun-to-ride roads on the East Coast.

*Loneliest road*

I don't think it was a fluke that I encountered practically no one on my journey along Kentucky 66 between Pineville and US 421. I expect you could have the same experience nearly any time. Had I been smart enough to fill up my tank before leaving US 23, I could have enjoyed Route 66's playful course through the Kentucky hills. KY 66 is a route I'll definitely seek out on my next trip through the area.

*Most rider-friendly town*

Monterey, Virginia,. There are a lot of folks around town who like motorcycles and the people who ride them. It doesn't hurt that Monterey sits at the intersection of two great motorcycling roads. And if you're nice to the locals, they might take you on a ride and show you some of the roads they prefer to keep to themselves or if you're really lucky, the Shrine of the Weeping Norton.

*Rider-friendly B&B*

Cherry Hill Bed and Breakfast, Monterey, Virginia,. Might as well add here that fellow riders Rich and Linda Holman are a big part of the reason you'll feel so at home in Monterey. They'll treat you right at Cherry Hill.

*Nicest tourist town*

Blowing Rock, North Carolina. Don't get me wrong when I say "tourist" town; I mean that as a compliment. Blowing Rock's proximity to the Blue Ridge Parkway, comfortable temperatures, and attractive downtown have created an atmosphere where you begin to feel rested and relaxed the minute you put down the sidestand.

*Best diner*

Baby's Burgers and Shakes, State College, Pennsylvania. It's been through several transformations since this diner rolled into town in 1950, but in its current iteration, Baby's delivers on all the things a diner should. The food and service are great while the atmosphere makes you feel like you just stepped into the set of *Happy Days.*

*Place most likely to offer you a ticket*

Fayetteville, West Virginia. Several folks have told me the friendly officers in Fayetteville have awarded them with notices of deficient riding techniques though I've never experienced this myself. Maybe I've just been lucky. In any case, consider yourself duly warned.

*Prettiest town*

Lexington, Virginia,. This is just one rider's opinion, but Lexington is the most attractive town I've visited in the region. Its historic downtown area is filled with one-of-a-kind venues: centuries-old inns, attractive shops, a viable downtown cinema, and good restaurants. The picture perfect campuses of Washington and Lee University and Virginia Military Institute bolster the town's collegial atmosphere. Two great motorcycle friendly B&Bs, Riders Rest and Llewellyn Lodge, make it the region's most attractive riding destination.

*Best restaurant name*

Chat 'n Chew, McCoole, Maryland. Actually it's the Chat 'n Chew Restaurant and Gazebo Room. I was attracted by the name, but didn't find the food equal to my expectations. Of course, I don't know what one should expect from a place that includes "chew" in its name. In fairness, it appears the action was really going on in the Gazebo Room.

*Place I'll miss most*

Hinton Hot Dog Stand, Hinton, West Virginia. It's just too dang bad that the Hot Dog Stand had to close up. I picked up some of my best stories from that place. Then I discovered the Path Valley Restaurant in Spring Run, Pennsylvania, and knew I had found a new best place for picking up on the local goings-on.

*Prettiest view*

Big Walker Lookout offers a stunning 360-degree panorama of five states. I took some panoramic photos from atop the 100-foot tower. They weren't wide enough. Even if you're just passing through the area on your way to another spot in the Appalachians, look up Big Walker and make a plan to visit. It's worth seeking out.

*Favorite camping spot*

Brandywine Recreation Area, Brandywine, West Virginia. Tucked behind Brandywine's recreation area is an unassuming little campground that has been a favorite of mine for years. It lies at the end of a great run from Harrisonburg over Shenandoah Mountain on US 33. There are a couple of restaurants in the village and the gas station doubles as a market with everything you'd need if you elect to cook while camping. Inexpensive, quiet, surrounded by great riding roads. Who could ask for anything more?

*Funniest question*

New River Gorge, West Virginia. I once signed up to take a plane ride over the New River Gorge Bridge with a local flyer everyone knew as "Five Dollar Frank." As I waited for Frank to land and take on his next load of victims, the fellow working the concession looked me up and down, paused and spat, then asked, "Boy, how much do you weigh?"

*Easiest place to get lost*

Southeastern Kentucky. I usually have a pretty good sense of direction, but down here, things get turned around a bit. There are so many hills and the roads a tangled web, it's hard to remember which direction you're going at any one moment. Be sure to take a detailed map. It's fun exploring the side roads, but you'll dang sure want some assurance you can find your way back.

*Best museum*

Wheels Through Time, Maggie Valley, North Carolina. Wheels is known as "The Museum That Runs," and for good reason. Wheels isn't just a collection of dusty vintage machines. These bikes are run and enjoyed the way they were meant to be. Looking at old bikes is interesting. Hearing them run and seeing them operate is endlessly fascinating.

*Most interesting point of interest*

Fairfax Stone, boundary of Maryland and West Virginia. Fairfax Stone is one of those obscure historic spots that makes a great excuse for a ride. There isn't much when you get there, just a marker and the spring (still active) that was dubbed the headwaters of the Potomac, thus marking the northwestern most point of Lord Fairfax's claim in the New World. I like sitting at the spring and imagining a troop of early colonials trudging up through the woods following a tiny creek. I wonder if someone shouted "Aha!" or perhaps "Behold!"

*Most peaceful place*

Burke's Garden, Virginia,. Also referred to as "God's Thumbprint," Burke's Garden is remarkable for its geological uniqueness as well as its sense of time. When you enter this high valley encircled completely by mountains, it's almost as if you've passed through a veil in time. You'll get this unmistakable sense that life's events unfold at a pace more in keeping with nature's rhythm, not the artificially fast pace we endure elsewhere.

# Google Maps

Mapping technology has changed incredibly over the last decade, bringing us detailed information about backroads and byways that just didn't exist. Perhaps no change has been more striking than the development of Google's Street View feature, part of Google's online mapping service.

If you're not already familiar with Street View, check it out. It will rock your motorcycle touring world. Street View photographically documents roads, using nine cameras mounted atop a vehicle, creating a 360-degree panoramic view. From the comfort of your lounge chair, you can literally ride the world, at least, wherever Street View cameras have gone. Of course, it's no substitute for being on those roads yourself, but it's an awesome tool to preview what an area or a road might be like.

As I began preparations for this edition of *Motorcycle Journeys Through the Appalachians,* I began revisiting old routes and mapping new ones with Google Maps. I soon realized that virtually every road I've traveled throughout the Appalachians has been photographed in Street View.

I decided to add links to Street View scenes that add something unique, owing to their 360-degree perspective. A regular picture is nice, but the ability to look all around gives you an even stronger sense of place. These links were also useful to take you places where I couldn't safely get off the bike—the middle of Nada Tunnel comes to mind.

If you find a special place in the Appalachians on Street View you'd like to share, please send it to me. I'd love to post it on my website for others to enjoy. Thank you, and many happy journeys!

# Index

# About the Author

Dale Coyner's journeys through the Appalachians began out of a curiosity for what was "around the next bend." He came to riding later than some, purchasing his first motorcycle, a Yamaha Radian, after he finished college. He credits the open, freewheeling nature of motorcycling with firing a sense of wonderment about his surroundings that led to rediscovering his native region. He shares his best finds with you in this book.

For many of the tours in this volume, Dale relied on his trusty Honda Gold Wing. He's not sure if it was the size of the Wing, the pop-up camper he was pulling, or the bright-red Aerostitch suit that garnered the most friendly smiles in his travels, but he got a lot of them. His current ride is a Honda ST-1300, but the next time you see him, he may be aboard the all-electric bike he's building.

Read more about Dale's recent adventures and new projects at appalachianhighways.com. He welcomes your contact by e-mail at dale@coyner.com.